Comparing Economic Systems

Also by Andrea Boltho

FOREIGN TRADE CRITERIA IN SOCIALIST ECONOMIES

JAPAN — AN ECONOMIC SURVEY

THE EUROPEAN ECONOMY: Growth and Crisis (*editor*)

Also by Alessandro Vercelli

MACROECONOMICS: A Survey of Research Strategies (*co-editor with N. Dimitri*)

METHODOLOGICAL FOUNDATIONS OF MACROECONOMICS: Keynes and Lucas

SUSTAINABILITY: Dynamics and Uncertainty (*co-editor with G. Chichilnisky and G. Heal*)

Also by Hiroshi Yoshikawa

MACROECONOMICS AND THE JAPANESE ECONOMY

Comparing Economic Systems

Italy and Japan

Edited by

Andrea Boltho
Fellow
Magdalen College
Oxford

Alessandro Vercelli
Professor of Economics
University of Siena
Italy

and

Hiroshi Yoshikawa
Professor of Economics
University of Tokyo
Japan

Editorial matter, selection and Chapter 1 © Andrea Boltho,
Alessandro Vercelli and Hiroshi Yoshikawa 2001
Chapter 6 © Andrea Boltho 2001
Chapters 2–5, 7–11 © Palgrave Publishers Ltd 2001

Chapters 1, 2, 3, 9 and 10 were originally published (under different titles)
in *Economic Systems* Volume 23, 1999, published by Physica-Verlag.

First published 2001 by
PALGRAVE
Houndmills, Basingstoke, Hampshire RG21 6XS and
175 Fifth Avenue, New York, N. Y. 10010
Companies and representatives throughout the world

PALGRAVE is the new global academic imprint of
St. Martin's Press LLC Scholarly and Reference Division and
Palgrave Publishers Ltd (formerly Macmillan Press Ltd).

ISBN 0–333–92893–8

This book is printed on paper suitable for recycling and
made from fully managed and sustained forest sources.

A catalogue record for this book is available
from the British Library.

Library of Congress Cataloging-in-Publication Data
have been applied for.

10   9   8   7   6   5   4   3   2   1
10   09   08   07   06   05   04   03   02   01

Printed and bound in Great Britain by
Antony Rowe Ltd, Chippenham, Wiltshire

Contents

List of Figures

List of Tables

Preface

This volume is the outcome of a comparative venture by Italian and Japanese economists carried out by the Dipartimento di Economia Politica of the University of Siena and the Faculty of Economics of the University of Tokyo. The origins of the project go back to the autumn of 1993 when one of the editors, Alessandro Vercelli, first visited the Tokyo faculty and, together with the late Professor Tsuneo Ishikawa, laid the basis for a programme of exchanges and collaboration. Several conferences were held in both Siena and Tokyo between 1995 and 1997, and individual project members visited their respective partners in the other country. The Siena team was reinforced by a number of other Italian specialists (most with an erstwhile Siena connection), and Andrea Boltho joined the editorial team at the time of the final conference held in Tokyo in October 1997.

The project has benefited from help from many quarters, help without which it would not have been completed. In particular, generous financial aid was provided by Japan's Ministry of Education, by the Zengin Foundation for Studies on Economics and Finance, and by the Japan Foundation. The editors are also very grateful to Ms Tsukasa Atsuya and to Mr Roberto Veneziani for the devotion and efficiency they have shown to the project.

Finally, it is with great sadness that we record the loss, during the course of this venture, of two very good friends. Tsuneo Ishikawa passed away in June 1998 in Tokyo. Not only was he a distinguished scholar and a great teacher, but he also impressed everybody who ever met him with his warmth and enthusiasm. From the very beginning in 1993 to his untimely death, he was the project's clear leader. Only six months earlier, in December 1997, Bruno Miconi passed away in Siena. He had taken part in all the project's activities and had greatly added to the liveliness of our meetings both through his scholarship and his personal charm. Now that our collective work has come to fruition, we dedicate this volume, with our affection and gratitude, to these two friends.

A.V.
H.Y.
A.B.

Note Chapters 1, 2, 3, 9 and 10 were originally published (under different titles) in *Economic Systems*, vol. 23, 1999, published by Physica-Verlag.

Notes and List of Abbreviations

Unless otherwise stated, 'the pre- and postwar periods' refer to the years since the Second World War. Years are always calendar years. *Mezzogiorno* stands for Southern Italy. The signs $ and ¥ refer to United States dollars and Japanese yen respectively; bn stands for billion and equals one thousand millions.

Abbreviations used in more than one chapter are as follows:

EMS	European Monetary System
EMU	European Monetary Union
EPA	Economic Planning Agency, Tokyo
FDI	Foreign direct investment
IMF	International Monetary Fund, Washington, DC
INPS	Istituto nazionale per la previdenza sociale, Rome
IRI	Istituto per la ricostruzione industriale, Rome
ISER	Institute of Social and Economic Research, Osaka
ISTAT	Istituto centrale di statistica, Rome
MITI	Ministry of International Trade and Industry, Tokyo
NIESR	National Institute for Social and Economic Research, London
OECD	Organisation for Economic Co-operation and Development, Paris
PPP	Purchasing power parity
R&D	Research and Development

Notes on the Contributors

Fabrizio Barca graduated from Rome University and did research at Cambridge, MIT and Stanford. He has taught at Bocconi University as well as in Siena, Modena and Rome. He was Division Chief in the Bank of Italy's Research Department, Head of the Treasury's Development Policies Department, and is now Adviser to the Treasury Minister. He has published widely on the theory of the firm, on corporate governance and on Italy's economic history.

Andrea Boltho was educated in Italy and at the Universities of London (LSE), Paris and Oxford. From 1966 to 1977 he worked at the OECD's Economics Department. In 1973–74 he was at the Economic Planning Agency in Tokyo. Since 1977 he has been a Fellow of Magdalen College, Oxford. Among his works are: *Japan – an Economic Survey* (1975) and *The European Economy: Growth and Crisis* (ed., 1982).

Giorgio Brunello studied at the Universities of Venice, London (LSE) and Osaka, where he obtained his PhD. He has taught at Osaka, Venice and is currently Professor of Economics at Padua University. He is an Associate Editor of *Labour Economics* and *Research in Economics*. Among his works is *Japanese Internal Labour Markets in Transition* (co-editor, forthcoming).

Paolo Carnazza graduated in economics from the University of Siena and obtained a Master's degree at the University of York. He is presently Head of the Business and Consumer Surveys Unit at ISAE, an economic research institute. His main interests are in the area of business cycle analysis and industrial economics.

Marcello de Cecco graduated from Parma and Cambridge Universities and taught at Siena, the European University Institute and Rome's 'La Sapienza' University, where is he Professor of Monetary Economics. He has held the Giannini Chair at Berkeley, was a member of the Princeton Institute for Advanced Studies, and of the Harvard Center of International Affairs and was a Visiting Scholar at the IMF. Since 1997 he has been on the Prime Minister's Council of Economic Advisers.

Massimo Di Matteo studied at the Universities of Oxford and Siena, where he is Professor of Economics. His publications and research activities range from issues of economic dynamics to problems of international trade.

Giovanni Federico was taught at the University of Pisa and at the Scuola Normale Superiore of Pisa. Since 1981 he has been a Life Fellow at Pisa University. Among his works is *An Economic History of the Silk Industry, 1830–1930* (1997).

Giovanni Ferri graduated from Siena University, holds a PhD from New York University and is Associate Professor of Economics at Bari University. From 1984 to 1997 he was at the Bank of Italy's Research Department, *inter alia* as Deputy Director. In 1998–99 he was Principal Financial Economist at the World Bank. He has published extensively in the areas of monetary economics and policy.

Yuji Genda is a graduate of the University of Tokyo and has been working since 1992 at Gakushuin University. He was Visiting Scholar at Harvard in 1995 and Senior Associate at St Antony's College and the Nissan Institute, Oxford in 1996. He has contributed to T. Tachibanaki (ed.), *Wage Differentials: an International Comparison* (1998).

Akiyoshi Horiuchi studied at the University of Tokyo and has taught at Yokohama National University, at Hitotsubashi University and, since 1984, at Tokyo University. He was Visiting Professor at the LSE (1990) and at the Australian National University (1994). He has written extensively on monetary economics, including a forthcoming article in the *Journal of Banking and Finance*.

Alessandro Innocenti obtained his PhD from the University of Florence and is now Professor of Economics at the University of Siena where he teaches economic policy and microeconomics. His publications and research have been mainly in the areas of industrial organization and Italy's 'industrial districts'.

Kanji Ishii graduated from Tokyo University where he taught in the Faculty of Economics from 1968 to 1997. Since 1998 he has been Professor at Tokyo Keizai University. Among his works is 'Japan' in R.E. Cameron and V.I. Bovykin (eds), *International Banking, 1870–1914* (1991). Since 1998 he has been a Councillor in the Bank of Japan's Institute for Monetary and Economic Studies.

Tsuneo Ishikawa, after graduating from the University of Tokyo, obtained his PhD from Johns Hopkins University. He was Assistant Professor at Harvard in 1973–75 and then Professor at Tokyo until his untimely death in 1998. His main areas of research were income distribution, labour and macroeconomics and his book *Income and Wealth* (1991), is to be republished by Oxford University Press.

Katsuhito Iwai was educated at the University of Tokyo and at MIT. He taught at Yale from 1973 to 1981 and since then at Tokyo. He was Visiting Professor at the Universities of Princeton and Pennsylvania in 1988–89 and Visiting Fellow at Siena University in 1997. Among his works is *Disequilibrium Dynamics: a Theoretical Analysis of Inflation and Unemployment* (1981).

Kiyohiko G. Nishimura studied at Tokyo and Yale Universities and was Research Fellow at the Brookings Institution before joining Tokyo University in 1983. In 1998 he received the Japanese Economic Association Nakahara Prize for Young Economists. Since 1999 he is a member of the Government's Regulatory Reform Committee. Among his works is *Imperfect Competition, Differential Information, and Microfoundations of Macroeconomics* (1992).

Ugo Pagano obtained his PhD and taught at Cambridge, where he was Fellow of Pembroke College. Now Professor of Economic Policy at Siena, Recurrent Visiting Professor at Prague's Central European University and President of the Italian Association for the Study of Comparative Economic Systems. Has written *Work and Welfare in Economic Theory* (1985) and co-edited *Democracy and Efficiency in the Economic Enterprise* (1995) and *The Politics and Economics of Power* (1999).

Maria Grazia Pazienza studied at the Universities of Rome and Siena, has worked at the Centro Europa Ricerche and is now Lecturer in Public Finance at the University of Florence.

Lionello F. Punzo was educated at the University of Siena and LSE, has taught at UCLA, Mexico, and IAS (Vienna), visited ISER, Osaka University in 1996, and is now Professor of Economics at Siena. Among his works are *The Dynamics of a Capitalist Economy* (with R. Goodwin) (1987), *Economic Performance* (ed. with B. Boehm, 1994), and *European Economies in Transition* (with O. Fabel and F. Farina, 2000).

Marcello Signorelli studied at the Universities of Siena, Florence and Warwick and was Research Fellow at Columbia. He has taught Economic Policy at Sassari and Perugia Universities and has been a post-doctoral researcher at Siena since 1995. His main research interests cover the labour market and Italy's macroeconomic performance.

Sandro Trento studied at the Universities of Rome and Northwestern and was exchange visitor at Stanford. Since 1990 he works in the Bank of Italy's Research Department where he is responsible for sectoral and regional analysis. In 1997 he was one of the Prime Minister's Economic Advisers. Among his works is a textbook on anti-trust economics: *Economia e politica della concorrenza* (1995).

Alessandro Vercelli graduated from Turin University and was Research Fellow at St Antony's College, Oxford. Since 1976 he is Professor of Economics at the University of Siena where he is also Editor of *Economic Notes*. Among his works are *Methodological Foundations of Macroeconomics: Keynes and Lucas* (1991), *Macroeconomics: a Survey of Research Strategies* (ed. with N. Dimitri, 1992) and *Sustainability: Dynamics and Uncertainty* (with G. Chichilnisky and G. Heal, 1998).

Hiroshi Yoshikawa studied at the Universities of Tokyo and Yale and has taught at the State University of New York, at Osaka University and, since 1982, at Tokyo University. In 1991 he was Nissan Fellow at St Antony's College, Oxford. Throughout his career he has advised Japan's major official policy-making institutions. Among his works is *Macroeconomics and the Japanese Economy* (1995).

1
Introduction*

Andrea Boltho, Alessandro Vercelli and Hiroshi Yoshikawa

1 Introduction

The idea that modern economies should gradually converge on a single model gathered strength in the last decade of the twentieth century. The 1990s witnessed a prolonged and unexpected expansion in the American economy, which raised the possibility of the emergence of a 'new paradigm' associating rapid growth and low inflation. As America boomed, socialism collapsed in Eastern Europe, while the varieties of capitalism that had been tried in Western Europe and in East Asia encountered serious problems: high unemployment in many European Union (EU) countries, prolonged stagnation in Japan, severe financial crises in several smaller East Asian economies. At the beginning of the twenty-first century, there is a growing conviction in many circles that the American model (the so-called 'Washington consensus') has become a 'global' standard, providing the ultimate blueprint for the optimal economic organization of all societies.

The present volume is sceptical about this view. The mere copying of foreign practices and institutions is far from being a sufficient recipe for success. What may work in one set of circumstances, may well be much less effective in a different environment. The wealth of nations is a function of numerous factors, many of which stem from, or are conditioned by, past history. To understand such factors, one of the most fruitful methods of enquiry is the detailed comparative analysis of the economic histories, policies and institutions of various countries. The present book attempts this, by looking at Japan and Italy (the world's second and fifth largest economies respectively).[1]

* This is a modified version of a paper originally published by Physica-Verlag in *Economic Systems* (Andrea Boltho, 'Italy and Japan – Convergence or Continuing Diversity?', 23, 1, 1–10, 1999).

The two countries have seldom been compared, be this in economics or, for that matter, in politics (an area in which postwar similarities would seem to abound). Comparative work on the Italian economy has concentrated on the differences and similarities with the other major European countries. The stress has been on, for instance, divergences in policy-making (because of Italy's poor inflation and public finance record), trends in foreign trade specialization (in view of Italy's concentration on consumer goods), issues of regional development (given the country's *Mezzogiorno* problem), and so on. In Japan, on the other hand, most comparative work on the economy has concentrated on similarities and differences with the US economy. Thus, popular topics have been the Japanese custom of 'lifetime employment' in large-scale firms (little practiced in the United States), the efficiency (or inefficiency) of Japan's industrial policies (often invoked by US proponents of trade intervention against Japanese exports), the presence of detailed government interference in the private sector (so-called 'administrative guidance'), and the very un-American forms of corporate governance.

Yet, while Japan is, indeed, very different from the United States in these and other aspects, it is less different from Europe and especially from Continental European countries such as France, Germany or Italy. Bar, however, some Anglo-Japanese studies,[2] comparisons with the rest of Europe have been very few and far between.[3] Italy, because of a number of both historical and economic similarities, would seem to be an obvious candidate for a comparison with Japan, just as much as, if not more so than, France or Germany. Hence, the aim of this book is to provide a comparative perspective on a number of aspects of the Italian and Japanese economies, through a set of essays written in co-operation by specialists coming from both countries. The present introductory chapter sets the scene by briefly looking at a few major themes – growth, cycles, the labour market, foreign trade, corporate governance and economic policies.

2   Growth, cycles and employment

Italy and Japan began their modernization at roughly the same time: Italy soon after its 1861 unification, Japan soon after the 1860s Meiji restoration. At the time, both countries were still largely agricultural, with 62 per cent of the labour force in Italy and 70 per cent in Japan working on the land in 1870, as against 50 per cent in France, Germany or the United States and less than 25 per cent in Britain (Maddison, 1991). The abundance of 'cheap labour' was one of the 'advantages of

Table 1.1 Longer-run growth trends (average annual trend growth rates in GDP)

	Italy	Western Europe[a]	Japan	East Asia[b]
1870–1938	2.0	1.7	2.8[c]	1.5[d]
1950–73	5.5	4.5	8.9	4.2
1973–90	2.7	2.1	3.9	6.6

a. Excluding Italy; sum of 12 countries; PPP weights.
b. Excluding Japan; sum of 7 countries; PPP weights.
c. Average annual percentage change.
d. 1900–38; average annual percentage change.
Source: Maddison (1995).

backwardness' and helped the two economies in recording a relatively rapid if turbulent, industrial transformation (Table 1.1). By the late 1930s, the incomes per capita in both countries (measured in PPP) had closed part of the gap with more affluent nations. Italy, at the time, was still a good deal richer than Japan. Its relative income per capita lead had, however, declined from roughly 2 in 1870 to 1.4.

The Second World War was much more destructive in Japan and, by 1950, the gap in living standards between the two economies had climbed back to 1.8. Some of the earlier similarities, however, were still present and, in particular, very similar shares of the agricultural labour force (45 per cent in Italy, 48 in Japan), a huge backlog vis-à-vis US technology levels,[4] and a 'dual' industrial structure, with nearly 60 per cent of manufacturing workers employed in establishments with less than 100 employees (a much greater share than that seen in other major economies at the time).

Both countries grew very rapidly in the 'Golden Age' of the 1950s and 1960s not only by their own historical standards but also in comparison to the regions surrounding them. As is well known, Japan performed more strongly and by 1972 it had overtaken Italy in per capita GDP. Common supply factors, such as relatively cheap labour and the technological backlog, play an important role in explaining these exceptional developments. In their contribution to this book, however, Massimo Di Matteo and Hiroshi Yoshikawa put forward the intriguing (and largely convincing) thesis that growth in the 1950s and 1960 was led by demand rather than by supply. Their stress is on rapid internal migration from rural to urban areas and the ensuing consumption and/or construction booms. They also emphasize the role of business investment, galvanized by high demand and high profit expectations, themselves a function of a buoyant world economic climate, the opening up of the economy to international trade (in the case of Italy), and the government's commitment to growth (in the case of Japan). These various arguments make an unorthodox explanation of rapid growth quite compelling.

The post-1970 (or post-1973) deceleration owed a good deal to the waning of these various favourable factors. Internal migration slowed down, as did trade liberalization; more importantly, the growth of the OECD economies, hit by various supply and demand shocks, decelerated sharply and government commitments to growth and full employment were sacrificed for the sake of price and financial stability. More recently, both countries have slowed down further. For virtually the first time since the war, economic growth, at less than $1\frac{1}{2}$ per cent per annum in the decade from the 1989 peak, has been below the OECD average.

Italy's economic deceleration came as a consequence of its successful attempt to meet the budget deficit and inflation criteria of the Maastricht Treaty. Japan, on the other hand, entered a prolonged period of virtual stagnation in the wake of its stock exchange collapse in the early 1990s. These events are, as yet, too recent for any fully fledged explanation to be forthcoming, but for both Italy and Japan, for all their exceptional nature, they seem to presage the maturity that usually comes from affluence and leads to much lower rates of expansion.

While the growth experiences of the two countries were broadly similar, their cyclical experiences have differed. In the 1950s and 1960s, in particular, Japan's buoyant expansion was accompanied by a somewhat greater cyclical variability in output than was the case in Italy (Table 1.2). Prima facie, this suggests that Japan's growth successes of these years must be qualified to the extent that cyclical fluctuations have welfare costs. Yet,

Table 1.2   Cyclical developments

		Italy	*Japan*
Standard deviations			
GDP growth	1950–73	2.0	2.6
	1973–90	2.3	1.7
Inflation	1950–73	2.6	3.7
	1973–90	5.6	6.0
Unemployment	1950–73	2.1	0.4
	1973–90	2.7	0.7
Deviations from 'potential' [a]			
Non-agricultural GDP	1950–79	1.8	3.9 [b]

a. Average percentage shortfall of GDP from potential level, proxied by a 'trend through peaks' line.
b. 1953–79.
Sources: Boltho (1989) and Maddison (1991 and 1995).

as Table 1.2 shows, Japan's output fluctuations have had very little effect on unemployment, whose variability was a good deal less pronounced than it was in Italy.

In other words, Japan was able to spread the costs of recessions across the whole labour force – in the form, for instance, of reduced working hours, lower hourly wages, smaller bonus payments and falling participation rates for secondary members of the work force. By so doing, it avoided increases in open unemployment for primary male employees. Most observers would consider this a clear success. In Italy, by contrast, the negative effects of somewhat less severe recessions were borne much more than in Japan by a smaller segment of the workforce – those who were made redundant.

Not only was Japanese unemployment less cyclical than Italy's – it was also much lower. In the 1950–73 period, for instance, the unemployment rate averaged barely $1\frac{1}{2}$ per cent as against $4\frac{1}{2}$ per cent in Italy. This differential unemployment performance has continued in the post-1973 world, as detailed in the contribution on labour market developments written by Yuji Genda, Maria Grazia Pazienza and Marcello Signorelli (Chapter 7). Even in late 1999, after a decade of near stagnation, Japan's unemployment rate (at some $4\frac{1}{2}$ per cent of the labour force) remained relatively low. Italy, on the other hand, saw its unemployment rate more than double after 1973 to a level of 12 per cent. Nor does Japan suffer from the pronounced regional divisions that afflict Italy. The gap in the rate of joblessness between the highest and lowest unemployment regions in Japan is a few percentage points at most, whereas that between Italy's South and Centre-North stood, in the mid-1990s, at almost 14 percentage points. In addition, the differences in labour market performance go beyond open unemployment. Thus, participation rates are much higher in Japan. The share of the working age population active in the labour force has been well above 70 per cent virtually throughout the postwar period, as against a rate barely above 60 per cent in Italy, with the differences particularly marked for the female population.

The reasons for Japan's higher and more stable employment levels are, of course, numerous. The country's practice of 'lifetime employment' has often been put forward as one of them. Yet, this practice is not as widespread in Japan as often thought, nor has it been absent in Italy. Employment guarantees have, on the whole, been provided to most workers in both Japan's large-scale firms and in Italy's large state-owned sector (as well as in both countries' public administrations), but not in the rest of the economy. The 70 per cent of the labour force working in smaller firms hardly benefit from formal or informal employment commitments.

What differentiates Japan from Italy (as well as from other countries), as argued by Genda et al., is the greater importance given to on-the-job training (OJT). The much higher sunk costs that Japanese firms incur in training their workers have thus been one important reason for Japan's much greater job stability.

Other institutional differences may also be significant. The nature of trade unionism, for instance, is likely to have played a role in limiting Japanese unemployment, given the more decentralized structure of Japanese unions compared to Italian ones (Calmfors and Driffill, 1988). Thus, the threat to firm survival has frequently moderated workers' claims in Japan. In Italy this probably happens in the 'underground' economy, but much less so in the official one. Equally, or even more, important may have been trade union ideology. Japanese unions (as opposed to Japanese economists) have largely eschewed Marxism and adopted very pragmatic attitudes and policies. Italian unions, by contrast, have, especially in the 1960s and 1970s, embraced a very confrontational attitude to their dealings with the corporate sector. This led to virulent strike activity[5] and, in 1970, to the adoption on the part of the government of legislation (the *Statuto dei Lavoratori*, or Workers' Statute). This legislation defused some of the tensions that had been accumulated in the 1960s, but severely limited firms' freedom to manage their workforce and introduced unprecedented rigidity into the country's labour market.

3 External economic relations

Both Italy and Japan made major inroads on foreign markets after the Second World War, as illustrated in Andrea Boltho's contribution to this volume (Chapter 6). Interestingly, the postwar successes were not unprecedented. In their early history of industrialization, the two countries experienced a strikingly similar expansion of one of their major exports – silk. The contribution by Giovanni Federico and Kanji Ishii (Chapter 11) traces the story of Italy's domination of world trade in silk in the late nineteenth century and of Japan's domination of the same market in the earlier part of the twentieth century. At the time, it was Italy that produced the highest quality products, with Japan (and China) at a lower development stage.

Since the war, however, foreign trade developments have differed. Though both countries began with relatively similar comparative advantage patterns, it was Japan that increasingly upgraded its sales abroad. High-tech products now dominate Japanese exports; in contrast, Italy mostly exports more traditional consumer goods. In addition, thanks to the strength of its manufacturing sector, Japan has established a widespread network of foreign subsidiaries. The stock of FDI by Japanese firms (at over $300 bn in the late 1990s), was nearly twice as large as that of Italy (United Nations, 1999). Moreover, most of this capital reflected the building of new capacity on greenfield sites rather than acquisitions of existing establishments or equity participations.

Specialization in high-tech products, a relatively low penetration of foreign manufactures in the domestic market, continuing large current account surpluses, or massive stocks of FDI abroad, might all point to a clear 'superiority' of Japan's external performance over that of Italy. Yet, such a 'mercantilist' view needs to be qualified. While Boltho argues that protectionism may have helped Japanese industry in achieving scale economies in the 1950s and 1960s, recent research has suggested that the lack of import penetration may have slowed down productivity growth relative to what it could otherwise have been (Lawrence and Weinstein, 1999).

Turning to Italy, the trends in the country's comparative advantage suggest that a specialization relying on small firms producing consumer goods need not be a growth-retarding factor relative to one relying on large firms producing capital goods. Italy's ostensible concentration on 'traditional' exports conceals a continuous upgrading in terms of style, design and quality that is powerfully helped by the country's so-called 'industrial districts'. As argued by Paolo Carnazza, Alessandro Innocenti and Alessandro Vercelli in their work on smaller firms in the two economies (Chapter 8), innovation is, in fact, extremely rapid in these industrial clusters, helped in no small measure by a subcontracting system that involves large numbers of highly specialized small enterprises trading with each other. This is in stark contrast to much of Japan's subcontracting activity which has traditionally relied on a vertical division of labour, with smaller firms supplying large quantities of standardized parts for the use of the bigger companies.

Comparative advantage is largely determined by factor endowment. In modern economies one of the most important factors of production is human capital. The accumulation of this factor is studied in Chapter 10 by Giorgio Brunello and the late Tsuneo Ishikawa. They look at differences in education and training in the two countries. Interestingly, they argue that, though the Japanese formal schooling and less formal vocational training system may seem superior to the Italian one in terms of standard indicators of performance, there is no a priori reason as to why such a system should, in fact, deliver a more welfare-enhancing outcome. Much depends on the nature of the technology that firms face. If the production system requires the mastering of complex technologies (as it probably has done, at least until recently), this would put a premium on the acquisition of academic skills, similar to those fostered in Japanese schools. If, instead, demand and technology were to favour the production by small firms of highly differentiated goods in small runs (as, arguably, may be increasingly occurring), then the development of more individual skills, such as those broadly encouraged by the less structured Italian educational system, would be preferable.

4   Governance and government

A further area in which the two countries differ profoundly is that of corporate governance, an issue addressed in Chapter 2 by Fabrizio Barca, Katsuhito Iwai, Ugo Pagano and Sandro Trento. However, this was not always so. Prewar Italy and Japan were characterized by the presence of rather similar, family-dominated, corporate empires, but these gave way in the postwar period to new institutional set-ups which emerged as a result of two shocks – the early 1930s crisis in Italy and the late 1940s American occupation of Japan. The virtual bankruptcy of large segments of Italian industry during the Great Depression led at the time to the de facto nationalization of nearly one-quarter of the Italian economy. After the war, these public enterprises coexisted with some of the large family firms that had dominated Italy's corporate sector from the beginning of the century and had survived the difficulties of the 1930s. In Japan, by contrast, the occupation authorities dismantled the prewar family empires (or *zaibatsu*); new *keiretsu* groups took their place and developed a structure in which important stakeholders, such as managers and employees, saw their power greatly enhanced. The discussion by Barca et al. makes it clear that history conditions corporate governance systems and that historical approaches are necessary to understand their evolution.

Similarly embedded in history are the institutional differences that characterize the two countries' financial structures. The nature and behaviour of Italian and Japanese banks are in stark contrast to each other, as illustrated by the chapters written by Marcello de Cecco and Giovanni Ferri on Italy (Chapter 4) and by Akiyoshi Horiuchi on Japan (Chapter 5). In Japan, the major banks took it upon themselves after the war to monitor the behaviour of the major *keiretsu*. There may not be total agreement on whether this monitoring role was performed satisfactorily, particularly in the more recent period, but at least a mechanism was in place that put some limits on the discretionary powers of corporate managers. This mechanism was absent in Italy. With the single exception of an ubiquitous merchant bank called Mediobanca, Italy's financial institutions were detached from the corporate governance of the country's private sector. Small firms may have received some inputs from their local banks, but large private firms were left in the hands of private family groups which, with the help of Mediobanca, often extended their dominance over the country's industry. As for state-owned corporations, these moved from (relatively efficient) managerial control in the 1950s to (extremely inefficient) political control from the 1960s onwards.

Clearly, neither Italy nor Japan experienced Anglo-American forms of corporate governance. Cross-shareholdings in Japan, family (or political) control in Italy, made for a much less transparent governance system. The stock market played virtually no role and the interests of minority shareholders were seldom, if ever, taken into consideration. Yet, given the relatively good economic performances of the two countries over the last half-century, it would be difficult to argue that an alternative institutional set-up would necessarily have produced better outcomes. Indeed, only a few years ago Japanese managerial practices were seen as 'the model' that modern capitalism was bound to follow, just as today it is the Anglo-American variety that is being preached as the only secure road to prosperity. What the Italian and Japanese experiences probably teach us is that there is no single recipe in this area and that the varieties of capitalism that exist have produced, and will continue to produce, a variety of outcomes (Dore et al., 1999).

A further difference, not much explored in the pages that follow, concerns the general issue of public sector intervention in the two economies since the war. In both countries intervention was pervasive – governments continuously pursued fiscal and monetary policies in an attempt to manage the economy, dabbled for a time in long-run indicative planning, increasingly provided welfare services, frequently promoted certain industries, often interfered with the forces of competition, and so on. Regulation was widespread in both economies. Retail service activities, for instance, were subject to severe restrictions, as pointed out in Chapter 9 of this book by Kiyohiko Nishimura and Lionello Punzo. Interestingly, however, these two authors suggest that the Italian and Japanese small shop-centred retail trade system, with its apparently low levels of productivity, is not solely the result of legislation which restricts the opening of large-scale stores. In their interpretation, some of the alleged 'inefficiencies' of the two countries' distribution sectors arise, in fact, from the way manufacturing firms have rationally organized their sales operations, while others represent a relatively efficient response to diversified consumer preferences.

Taking a broader view of this continuous government involvement in the economy leads one to the, admittedly tentative, judgement that Japanese policies were, on the whole, better run and more effective than their Italian counterparts. The recognition of problems was, until recently at least, more rapid; the implementation of new measures prompter; the co-ordination between various government agencies more coherent; the hijacking of public funds for purely private gain less frequent, and so on.[6] Most importantly, perhaps, Japanese policy-makers were, more than their Italian counterparts, aware of the virtues of competition and readier to let domestic market forces run their course. While policies are never faultless, of course, those that Japan followed between the 1950s and the 1980s strike the observer as being less error-prone than those of Italy.

This is unlikely to have been due to the presence in Japan of a more appropriate political or institutional structure. On the contrary, Italy and Japan appear to share some similar features in this area. Until the early 1990s, both countries enjoyed a long period of enviable political stability based on the continuous presence in power of a single dominant party (Pempel, 1990). In Japan, the Liberal Democrats were able to run the country alone, without the need for political partners, until the early 1990s. In Italy, despite a countless number of governments, stability was assured by the hegemony wielded in these various administrations by the Christian Democrats. Yet, for all this hegemony, governments in both countries basically represented broad coalitions. In Italy these coalitions were made up by different parties, in Japan by different factions within a single party.

Coalitions are seldom the form of government best suited to tackle economic priorities. First best solutions are, almost inevitably, foregone, particularly so in the area of fiscal policy. Coalitions tend to have a greater propensity to spend (and a lesser propensity to tax) than single-party administrations, since each coalition member has distinct objectives, usually enjoys veto powers, and is seldom able to enter into binding commitments with his partners (Roubini and Sachs, 1989). Yet, despite Italy and Japan sharing this unfortunate institutional similarity, Italy presided over a public finance disaster between the mid-1960s and the mid-1990s, while Japanese fiscal policies (at least until recently) have been a good deal more prudent.

Turning to inflation, Italy's rate of price increases since 1973 has been three times as high as Japan's. This can hardly be ascribed to the lesser independence from the government of the Bank of Italy. Comparative research on this topic has suggested that both the Bank of Italy and the Bank of Japan have, until the mid-1990s, been subject to the control of their Treasuries or Ministries of Finance (Alesina and Summers, 1993). In fact, if anything, from the late 1970s the Bank of Italy managed to acquire an increasing degree of independence from the politicians, yet this was insufficient to prevent a much higher rate of inflation than that which prevailed in Japan.

The major reason for these very different outcomes in the two countries almost certainly lies in the different actors who were in charge of policy. In Italy, the politicians played an increasing role in decision-making from the 1960s onwards, and all the drawbacks of coalition governments mentioned above manifested themselves in full. In Japan, on the other hand, economic policy-making was very largely in the hands of a prestigious and capable bureaucracy, largely untainted by the corruption of the political class. This bureaucracy was usually able to ward off the myopic interests of the politicians and to preserve a longer-term perspective in the framing of policies. Its regulatory zeal may, at times, have had negative side-effects in dampening competition, yet that same regulatory zeal seems a model of efficiency when compared to the incoherent interference and meddling of Italian politicians and civil servants, particularly in the 1970s and 1980s (Arcelli and Micossi, 1997).

Interestingly, both models seem to be changing. Japan's bureaucrats appear to have lost their grip on power, while the politicians have become much more activist. The policy stalemate in which the country has found itself since the beginning of the 1990s probably owes a good deal to this switch in the location of power. Italy, on the other hand, has relinquished some of its erstwhile policy discretion. Responsibility for monetary policy has been largely devolved to the European Central Bank; fiscal activism has been severely limited by the signing of the EU's 'Stability Pact'; and government interference with industry has been constrained by the creation of a number of independent regulatory authorities. These changes have already led to different economic outcomes in the last few years, outcomes that have broadly been more favourable to Italy than to Japan. Over the 1990s, for instance, the two countries' growth rates have been almost identical, for the first time since the war. Much in the future will depend on the extent to which Japan's policy-makers are able to re-establish their erstwhile efficiency and on whether Western Europe, and hence Italy, will be able to cope with the inevitable stresses and strains of monetary union. In neither case is success ensured.

5   Concluding remarks

If a general conclusion emerges both from this very brief survey of some selected features of the Italian and Japanese economies and from the more detailed chapters that follow, it is that behind numerous apparent similarities are hidden equally numerous, but perhaps less apparent, differences. Both countries, it has been argued, have had successful growth and foreign trade experiences through most of the post-war period. Yet, Japan's growth was spearheaded by large-scale conglomerates, Italy's, to a much greater extent, by small and medium-sized firms. Japanese exports switched from relatively labour-intensive products to high-tech capital goods; Italy remained committed to its original comparative advantage pattern, largely based on consumer goods. These are, no doubt, increasingly sophisticated but in no way require the same amount and the same kind of R&D inputs that enter Japanese export production.

In both countries small firms account for a much larger share of the workforce than in any other major economy. Yet, small firms in Japan, much more than in Italy, have lower productivity levels, pay well below average wages and rely less on a qualified workforce than larger establishments. They are also often part of vertical subcontracting arrangements that put them into very dependent positions vis-à-vis the major firms. More generally, they are considered as the least developed and least modern segment of the economy. Similar features exist, of course, also in Italy, particularly in the Southern part of the country. However, many small firms, especially those operating in the industrial districts of the Centre and the North, are highly innovative, highly profitable and often pay above average wages. Their successes are in some ways more reminiscent of Silicon Valley (if in a very different area of activity) than of the dualism often associated with small firms in Japan.

Both Italy and Japan have corporate governance models that are far away from those of the Anglo-American model.[7] Thus, in neither country have shareholders ever mattered much. Yet, other differences between the two countries overshadow that initial similarity. Thus, family owners have traditionally dominated Italian private firms, while managers have, since the Second World War, done the same in Japanese ones. This list could be extended to embrace, for instance, industrial relations and other political or even social features. Suffice it to say that the experience of the last 50 years has shown not only how many of these differences have tenaciously persisted, but also that there has been little movement towards convergence between the two economic systems. Ongoing changes may alter this in the future, but the analysis contained in this volume suggests that this process is likely to be both slow and hesitant.

Notes

1. At least when measured in dollar terms. If GDP is measured in PPPs, they become the third and seventh largest economies respectively.
2. By far the most interesting of these is Dore (1973), even if the subject matter of the work is not purely economic.
3. A number of papers comparing Italy and Japan can be found in Fodella (1983); a relatively old comparison with France, limited to aspects of economic planning, appears in Sautter and Baba (1978), while a more recent and rather complete comparison with Germany can be found in Ifo Institute for Economic Research and Sakura Institute of Research (1997).
4. In 1950 the ratio between hourly productivity in the whole economy and the US level (taken as a rough proxy for the technological gap) stood at 31 per cent in Italy and at only 15 per cent in Japan (Maddison, 1991).
5. To take just one, but vivid, example, in the period 1969–97, Italy lost an annual average of some 1000 working days per 1000 employees because of strike activity, as against a figure of only 80 in Japan (sources: NIESR, *National Institute Economic Review*, September 1997, and UK Department of Employment, *Gazette* [various issues]).
6. The earlier evidence showing larger cyclical fluctuations in Japan than in Italy might seem to contradict this conclusion. Yet, while Italian governments since the 1960s have tried, without much success, to dampen cycles, Japanese governments, in the 'high growth period' at least, seem to have almost willingly engineered them (Ackley and Ishi, 1976) – policies were geared to high growth, but this had to be sharply interrupted whenever problems arose on the external front. Once Japan began to float in the early 1970s and felt that it no longer faced a balance of payments constraint, its cyclical performance improved, as indirectly suggested by the data in Table 1.2.
7. It is true, however, that at the very end of the 1990s cautious movements towards the adoption of some features of this model could be spotted in both countries, albeit in different areas (such as widespread privatizations and the appearance of hostile take-over bids in Italy; declines in cross-shareholdings and diminishing job tenures in Japan).

References

Ackley, G. and H. Ishi (1976) 'Fiscal, Monetary and Related Policies', in H. Patrick and H. Rosovsky (eds), *Asia's New Giant – How the Japanese Economy Works*, Washington, DC: Brookings Institution.

Alesina, A. and L.H. Summers (1993) 'Central Bank Independence and Macroeconomic Performance: Some Comparative Evidence', *Journal of Money, Credit and Banking*, 25, 2, 151–62.

Arcelli, M. and S. Micossi (1997) 'La politica economica negli anni Ottanta (e nei primi anni Novanta)', in M. Arcelli (ed.), *Storia, economia e società in Italia, 1947–1997*, Bari: Laterza.

Boltho, A. (1989) 'Did Policy Activism Work?', *European Economic Review*, 33, 9, 1709–26.

Calmfors, L. and J. Driffill (1988) 'Bargaining Structure, Corporatism and Macroeconomic Performance', *Economic Policy*, 6, 13–61.

Dore, R. (1973) *British Factory – Japanese Factory: the Origins of National Diversity in Industrial Relations*, London: George Allen & Unwin.

Dore, R., W. Lazonick and M. O'Sullivan (1999) 'Varieties of Capitalism in the Twentieth Century', *Oxford Review of Economic Policy*, 15, 4, 102–20.

Fodella, G. (ed.) (1983), *Japan's Economy in a Comparative Perspective*, Tenterden, Kent: Paul Norbury.

Ifo Institute for Economic Research and Sakura Institute of Research (1997) *A Comparative Analysis of Japanese and German Economic Success*, Tokyo: Springer-Verlag.

Lawrence, R.Z. and D.E. Weinstein (1999) 'Trade and Growth: Import-led or Export-led? Evidence from Japan and Korea', NBER Working Paper, No. 7264.

Maddison, A. (1991) *Dynamic Forces in Capitalist Development: a Long-run Comparative View*, Oxford: Oxford University Press.

Maddison, A. (1995) *Monitoring the World Economy, 1820–1992*, Paris: OECD.

Pempel, T.J. (1990) 'Introduction', in T.J. Pempel (ed.), *Uncommon Democracies: The One-Party Dominant Regime*, Ithaca, NY: Cornell University Press.

Roubini, N. and J. Sachs (1989) 'Political and Economic Determinants of Budget Deficits in the Industrial Democracies', *European Economic Review*, 33, 5, 903–38.

Sautter, C. and M. Baba (1978) *La planification en France et au Japon*, Collections de l'INSEE, Série C, No. 1961.

United Nations (1999) *World Investment Report, 1999*, Geneva.

2
Divergences in Corporate Governance Models: The Role of Institutional Shocks*

Fabrizio Barca, Katsuhito Iwai, Ugo Pagano and Sandro Trento

1 Introduction

This chapter looks at the evolution of the Italian and Japanese corporate governance systems and, in particular, at how a form of capitalism that was rather similar before the Second World War has sharply diverged in the postwar period. In our opinion, this divergence can be traced to the very different consequences that defeat in war and the policies of the winning powers had on the two countries' economic institutions. In prewar times both Italy and Japan had shared a system of family control in their large private firms. In the immediate postwar years, American (and British) policies reinforced the ownership structures that had emerged during the fascist period in Italy. By contrast, in Japan, the American occupation ended the power of the *zaibatsu* families that had dominated the Japanese economy since the Meiji restoration. These policies appear to have had lasting results – Italy's large firm sector is still stuck with the contradictions of family capitalism, while Japan has produced a new

* This is a modified version of a paper originally published by Physica-Verlag in *Economic Systems* (Fabrizio Barca, Katsuhito Iwai, Ugo Pagano, Sandro Trento, 'The Divergence of the Italian and Japanese Corporate Governance Models: the Role of Institutional Shocks', 23, 1, 35–59, 1999). Part of this chapter was written while the second author visited the Dipartimento di Economia Politica of the University of Siena under a Japan Society for the Promotion of Science (JSPS) scholarship. He is grateful to the first institution for its hospitality and to the second for its financial support. The usual disclaimers apply. The authors would like to thank Andrea Boltho for many valuable comments and suggestions.

organizational form, the 'Japanese company', that has occupied a rising share of world markets and, after some time, an increasing share of economic books trying to explain its success.

This chapter's main purpose is thus to compare the patterns of development induced by institutional changes. The next section puts forward a theoretical framework for analysing these issues – in particular, we try to explain why institutional shocks can produce such lasting systemic divergence in corporate governance in economies that are organized according to a very similar legal framework. Sections 3 to 6 provide a comparative account of recent Italian and Japanese histories. We argue, in particular, that American (and, in the case of Italy, also British) policies had a decisive role in determining the different destinies of Italian and Japanese family capitalism. We also discuss the view that inter-firm share holding can either promote (Japan) or inhibit (Italy) the expansion of large corporations and we try to spell out other mechanisms that have made each model self-sustaining after the initial institutional shock.

2 The diversity of business organizations: a theory of the relevance of institutional shocks

Among the many institutions of today's capitalism nothing has contributed more to its history of colossal expansion than the public corporation or joint-stock company. Yet, its ownership structures and control mechanisms vary widely both over time and across countries. As was reported in Berle and Means' (1933) classic work on corporate governance, America's typical large corporation had (at least until recently) fragmented shareholders with small holdings and little voice in management. Italy's family empires, on the other hand, have developed a pyramidal ownership structure that enables a family, or a tight-knit group of people at the top, to exercise monolithic control over a large number of firms through a hierarchical chain of corporate shareholdings. *Zaibatsu* groups in prewar Japan had a similar pyramidal ownership structure. Their postwar successors, *keiretsu* groups, give us yet another model of ownership and control – a set of corporations is connected through an intricate network of cross-shareholdings which effectively shields it from outside take-overs. Further varieties of ownership structures and control mechanisms can, no doubt, be found elsewhere.

This leads us to pose the following questions as to the diversity of the corporation's ownership and control systems. Why is such diversity possible? How does it emerge? Why does it persist? Why does it matter?

How is it then possible that the public corporation, the most capitalist among the supposedly universal capitalist institutions, has developed such a wide variety of ownership and control systems? Our answer to this question is straightforward.[1] We claim that it is the very legal nature of the 'corporation' that is responsible for this diversity. The law speaks of the corporation as a 'legal person' – a subject of rights and duties, capable of owning property, entering into contracts, and suing and being sued in its own name, separate and distinct from its constituent shareholders. For many centuries, philosophers, political scientists, sociologists, economists, and above all lawyers have conducted a heated debate as to what constitutes the 'essence' of this bodiless 'person'. It is not our purpose to review this 'corporate personality controversy'. All we would like to do here is to work out the implications of the fact that a corporation, which is not naturally a person, is nevertheless legally treated as one.

Our starting point is one of the most elementary facts in corporate law. If you take away a gadget from the company of which you are a shareholder, you will be considered a thief. Why? Because a corporate shareholder is not, in fact, the legal owner of the corporate assets. It is the corporation itself, as a 'legal person', that owns these. A shareholder only owns a share of the corporation – a fraction of the company as a 'thing', separate and distinct from the underlying assets. This observation leads us immediately to the most crucial characterization of a corporation. In contrast to sole ownership or partnership firms, an incorporated firm is composed of not one but of *two* ownership relations – the shareholders own the corporation and the corporation, in turn, owns the corporate assets. In this two-tier structure the corporation is playing a *dual* role, being both a 'person' and a 'thing'. In regard to corporate assets it acts legally as a person, as a subject of property rights; in regard to the shareholders it is acted on legally as a thing, as an object of property rights. Though it is neither a person nor a thing, legally it is endowed with both personality and 'thingness'. It is this duality that lies at the root of the diversity in ownership structures and control mechanisms.

As we have seen, a corporation as a legal person can own things and a corporation as a legal thing can be owned by persons. This, in turn, allows a corporation as a person to own other corporations as things, in other words to become a 'holding company', opening the way to an important organizational innovation – the pyramidal system of ownership and control. At the top is a natural person who owns a corporation as a thing. But, being also a legal person, that corporation can own another corporation as a thing, which again, as a legal person, can own another corporation as a thing, and so on. This is, however, not the whole picture given that a public company can be controlled without the need to own all its shares. As long as there is a sufficiently large number of small passive investors, share ownership just slightly above 50 per cent is sufficient for control. This implies that one unit of capital can in principle control almost two units of capital, if each half buys a bare majority of the shares of a corporation with a capital close to one unit. It then follows that, as more and more layers are added to the ownership hierarchy, a capitalist at the top can multiply the controlling power of his capital by an order close to 2^n, where n is the number of lower hierarchical layers.[2] Moreover, as note 2 indicates, if this hierarchical structure is combined with cross-shareholdings at each hierarchical layer, the capitalist at the top can further enhance the leverage of his own capital.[3] The pyramidal system of ownership and control of present-day Italian family empires and of prewar Japanese *zaibatsu* fits in with this picture.

Let us now look at another system of ownership and control. To this end we push the logic behind the holding company further and let it 'loop the loop'. If a corporation as a person can own other corporations as things, the same corporation as a person should be able to own *itself* as a thing by holding a majority of its own shares under its own name. That corporation will then be free from any control by real human beings and will become a kind of self-determining subject, at least in the realm of law. It would thus be able to grant de facto control rights to its managers and core employees. In reality, many countries forbid firms from repurchasing their own outstanding shares. Japan, for instance, used to prohibit share buybacks, though the ban was partially lifted in 1995. And even in countries (like the United States) which allow the practice, the repurchased shares generally lose their voting rights.

There is, however, an important loophole. Suppose that two corporations, A and B, hold a majority of each other's shares. Corporation A as a person owns corporation B as a thing, and corporation B as a person simultaneously owns corporation A as a thing. Then, even though each corporation does not own itself directly, it does so indirectly. One might object to the practical relevancy of this by pointing to the fact that some countries impose legal limits on the extent of such cross-shareholdings. Japanese law, for instance, forbids banks and other financial institutions from owning more than 5 per cent of the shares of any domestic firm. Yet, even these limits can be circumvented. If, for instance, 12 corporations get together and hold 5 per cent of each others' shares (but their own), simple arithmetic $[(12 - 1) \times 0.05 = 55$ per cent$]$ tells us that a majority block of each corporation's shares can be effectively insulated. These 12 corporations would indeed become their own owners, at least as a group, and be immune from any take-over attempts. If the group increased its members, the necessary ratio of mutual shareholdings would be further reduced.[4] The ownership structure of Japanese *keiretsu* groups fits in with this picture.

We have tried to show so far that the supposedly universal law of corporations is capable of generating (at least) two totally different systems of ownership and control. One of these allows a capitalist at the top of a pyramid to exercise control over a large amount of assets with a minimum of own capital; the other effectively shields a group of corporations from the control of any outside capitalist, thereby granting de facto control rights to its managers and core employees. What we have not shown yet is how such divergent organizational arrangements actually take form and, in particular, why institutional shocks can suddenly alter them.

Standard economic theory is of very little use in explaining both the birth of, and changes in, ownership or control systems. In the neo-classical framework this issue is ignored. In a world of perfect competition and zero transaction costs, complete contracts can be written which specify the conditions under which a coalition of agents will participate in the production of a certain good. In this framework, the assignment of control rights does not matter since the ex-ante contract leaves no room for ex-post decisions on the part of those who control the organization.

In the 'New Institutional' (or 'New Property Rights') framework the assumption of costly and/or incomplete contracts implies that important ex-post decisions may be left to the holders of control rights. The assignment of such rights thus matters. It can be shown that the 'second best' solution is to assign them to those individual(s) whom it would be most expensive to monitor since this minimizes agency costs (Hart, 1995). In a market characterized by zero transaction costs, this second best solution should always be attained. In this framework the reassignment of ownership and control rights which occurred in Japan under the American occupation should not have mattered. If the new rights implied lower agency costs they would have occurred independently of US policies, whereas if they implied higher costs they would have been undone by the market. In this instance too institutional shocks are irrelevant.

The relevance of institutional shocks becomes evident, however, if we move beyond these frameworks and acknowledge that, in a world in which the control of firms matters, it is inconsistent to assume the existence of a costless perfect market for control itself. Three distinct problems arise. While the first of these is relatively well known, the latter two merit a more detailed discussion.

(i)   *Information problems.* Due to asymmetric and imperfect information on who are the highest-agency-costs individuals, efficiency-enhancing transfers of control may not take place. Indeed, the opposite could occur. Because of this market failure, institutional shocks that result in a forceful reallocation of control can make a difference;

(ii) *Multiplicity of organizational equilibria.* The choice of 'technology' (that is, the choice of the least-cost combination of specific physical and human capital, which it is difficult and expensive to monitor) cannot be taken exogenously, but is influenced by the initial allocation of control rights. Institutional shocks, by transferring such control rights, can permanently shift the economy from one equilibrium to another;

(iii) *Separation between ownership and control.* Since the allocation of wealth among members of a society does not necessarily coincide with that of the 'skills' needed to run an organization, control must be separated from ownership and institutions are needed to sustain this separation. Alternative institutional arrangements (or corporate governance systems) are possible and these can achieve separation in different ways and with different effects on the allocation of rights and on the efficiency of the ultimate outcome.

2.1   Multiplicity of organizational equilibria

An 'organizational equilibrium' can be defined as any combination of property rights and 'technology' (in the sense given above) which has the following characteristics: with given property rights, the current technology is the most efficient available; conversely, with this technology, the current property rights are the most efficient. Causation can flow from technology to property rights and vice versa, raising the possibility of multiple equilibria.[5] Thus, initial ownership conditions can matter for the selection of a particular equilibrium. Owners will tend to choose the technology that is most likely to maintain and strengthen their control. Property rights and technology thus have a self-reinforcing character since changing one component at a time damages efficiency thereby reducing the total income available for distribution between the various parties.

Institutional shocks which change property rights, such as the one that occurred in Japan after the war, can, however, move the economy from one 'organizational equilibrium' to another because the new 'ownership system' will alter the mix of agency costs. Substitution will occur towards the more intensive use of those inputs that have invested in firm-specific assets and will require little monitoring (such as, for instance, 'lifetime employees'). Conversely, less intensive use will be made of inputs (such as, for instance, 'temporary workers or temporary managers') which hold no rights to the enterprise, have made little firm-specific investment, and whose efforts need to be constantly controlled. This complementarity between property rights and technology inhibits the possibility of a gradual evolution from one equilibrium to another. This, in turn, suggests that transitions can be abrupt (Pagano and Rowthorn, 1995, Sect. 7).

A further crucial component of an 'organizational equilibrium' is the presence of what have been called 'network externalities'. These can be both technological and institutional. Technological network externalities (Arthur, 1989) arise from the standardization of production processes – the more firms there are which use a particular production technique (for example, the assembly-belt, 'just-in-time' manufacturing, or information technology) the more likely it is that the particular technique will become the dominant standard as supplying industries will concentrate their production and innovation efforts in that area. This homogenization of technology can be paralleled by a homogenization of institutional standards (David, 1994). Once a given property rights system exists, legislation, legal expertise, contract enforcement by courts, even customary rules of behaviour, can all be used repeatedly with little extra cost, thereby reinforcing the existing system. And it is the presence of such network externalities that explains why not all the potentially efficient organizational models adopted by different firms survive – it is only those that at any time exist in sufficiently large numbers, and therefore benefit from the scale economies provided by network externalities, that will generate a coherent organizational equilibrium.

In summary, the equilibrium arises from the combination of various forces – a set of property rights (usually inherited from history), a combination of inputs with different agency costs (themselves often a function of existing property rights), and a technological and institutional framework, cemented by network externalities, that reinforces any existing set of property and production relations. Such equilibria tend to change only seldom, and then in discrete rather than continuous fashion, either because of institutional shocks that alter the legal framework or the system of property rights, or as a result of major changes in production technology (such as, for instance, the on-going switch from large-to small-scale production made possible by the application of numerically controlled machine tools). The multiple causation channels running between these different determinants imply that once some shock occurs, it may have lasting consequences.

2.2   Separation of ownership and control

Arguably, it is the separation of enterprise ownership from control that has allowed the extraordinary economic development of this century. For this separation to work in practice, a solution must be found to the fundamental conflict of interest that arises between the investors who own the assets and the managers who control them. Mechanisms must exist that protect investors from failures on the part of managers such as the enhancement of the latters' own non-monetary benefits, their acting in the interest of their own assets, their embezzling funds, and so on. In a world of uncertainty, these problems cannot be addressed by writing contracts where all wrongful doing is ruled out. Nor are mechanisms linking managerial income to the market value of the firm likely to be very effective (Hart, 1995). Investors must therefore be granted monitoring powers. Since information, however, is inevitably incomplete, managers can be punished when no mistakes or abuses have been committed, or may, alternatively, go free when interference would have been justified.

A trade-off thus arises between certainty of control and the protection of investors. The harder it is for investors to monitor control, the more deterred they will be from providing finance. Conversely, the easier it is to interfere with control, the less effective control will be as a means to encourage profit-maximizing behaviour by managers. Numerous alternative institutions have been developed to address this trade-off – some rely on inside monitoring, some on ex-post outside monitoring, some on market pressures and some on political monitoring, some even on pure trust.

From the point of view of this chapter, an interesting variant is provided by inter-firm shareholdings, widespread in both Italy and Japan. In the case of pyramidal groups, controlling shareholders, by dispersing the voting rights of other shareholders, can expand their control well beyond their personal means. In Italy, where this system has been exploited furthest, for the average of existing pyramidal groups with at least one listed company and controlled by one set of family shareholders, controllers hold about 12 or 13 per cent of total group capital (about 5 per cent for Fiat). Alternatively, inter-firm shareholding, when it does not amount to the simple control of one firm by another, may help to consolidate managerial power – mutual corporate cross-shareholding as practised in Japan, can allow managers with few or no shares of their own to support each other against stockholder interference.

Clearly, neither of these two systems is necessarily ideal. In the first (or 'Italian' system), managers may benefit from an internal promotion market, but their career prospects will be uncertain given the dominant role of the corporation's owners – the accumulation of firm-specific capital remains a risky undertaking. In the second (or 'Japanese' system), on the other hand, both managers and employees will invest in such firm-specific capital, but the provision of outside finance may be limited should it be felt, by banks for instance, that monitoring is insufficient. In the event, Japan was for a long time able to avoid problems of this nature and finance was forthcoming through the so-called 'main bank' system (discussed below).

3 Continuity and discontinuity in Japan's corporate system

In Japan today there are six large corporate groups, called *keiretsu* – Mitsubishi, Mitsui, Sumitomo, Fuyo, Sanwa and Daiichi-Kangin. Though their weight has been declining in recent years, their core members still account for about 15 per cent of the assets, sales and profits of the economy's non-financial sector. Each *keiretsu* consists of a number of corporations, clustered around a main bank and connected through intricate cross-shareholdings. Table 2.1 shows the matrix of shareholdings among 20 core-member corporations of Sumitomo in 1995. The tightly knit nature of the group is shown by the presence of very few vacant cells.

The three largest *keiretsu*, Mitsubishi, Mitsui and Sumitomo, are the descendants of the three largest *zaibatsu* of the prewar period, and at least a part of the Fuyo group can also be traced back to the fourth largest *zaibatsu*, Yasuda. These four *zaibatsu* held 25 per cent of total paid-in capital of the entire corporate sector in 1946, just before their dissolution; if we include lesser ones, the *zaibatsu*'s share was as high as 35 per cent (Hadley, 1970). In stark contrast to their postwar descendants, each *zaibatsu* had a pyramidal ownership structure, with the founder family group at its top and a holding company functioning as its organizational centre. The family members were in general the exclusive owners of the holding company, which in turn owned a large proportion of each of the dozen or so core corporations, distributed over a wide range of both financial and industrial sectors. The extent of

Table 2.1 Cross-shareholdings among 20 core corporations of the Sumitomo group, 1993 (percentages)

Issuer	Sum. Bank	Sum. TrBnk	Sum. Life	Sum. Mrin.	Sum. Corp.	Sum. ClMn	Sum. Cons.	Sum. For.	Sum. Chm.	Sum. Bakl.	Japan Glass	Sum. Cem.	Sum. Met.	Sum. MtMn	Sum. LgMt	Sum. Elec.	Sum. Hv In.	NEC	Sum. REst.	Sum. Stor.	Total[a]
S. Bank	—	2.8	—	1.8	1.7	0.0	0.0	0.1	1.1	0.2	1.1	0.2	1.3	0.4	—	0.9	0.2	1.1	0.1	0.2	19.3
S. Trust Bank	3.3	—	—	1.5	2.5	0.0	0.0	0.2	1.2	0.5	1.4	0.5	2.3	1.2	0.0	1.7	0.4	2.8	—	1.5	25.3
S. Life	—	—	—	—	—	—	—	—	—	—	—	—	—	—	—	—	—	—	—	—	—
S. Marine Insur.	4.4	6.3	4.6	—	2.3	0.1	0.1	0.1	1.2	0.3	1.2	0.3	1.0	1.0	—	0.9	0.6	1.8	0.1	0.8	27.1
S. Corporation	4.8	5.8	5.1	2.9	—	0.1	0.0	0.3	1.6	0.3	1.0	0.4	2.7	1.7	—	1.0	0.8	3.7	0.1	0.4	32.8
S. Coal Mining	4.8	4.0	2.5	2.4	3.4	—	0.8	—	2.5	—	0.4	1.0	4.9	2.1	—	—	1.7	4.2	—	0.2	34.8
S. Construction	4.4	2.9	5.8	1.4	—	3.1	—	0.6	1.1	—	0.6	2.3	—	3.3	—	1.0	—	—	0.4	0.2	27.0
S. Forestry	4.3	7.0	7.2	—	2.6	0.1	0.4	—	—	0.4	—	0.3	—	7.3	—	—	0.2	1.4	—	—	31.1
S. Chemical	4.7	5.3	8.9	1.4	1.3	0.0	0.1	0.1	—	0.1	0.4	0.3	—	0.2	—	0.3	0.2	0.5	0.0	0.2	23.9
S. Bakelite	4.8	7.1	5.9	1.3	2.1	—	0.3	0.4	21.6	—	0.3	0.5	0.9	—	—	0.3	—	1.3	0.4	0.1	48.2
Japan Glass	5.0	6.8	5.5	2.3	1.6	—	0.1	0.1	1.2	0.5	—	0.8	—	0.3	—	0.3	0.6	—	0.5	0.2	25.6
S. Cement	4.6	5.4	8.5	1.0	2.3	1.9	0.6	0.4	1.1	0.4	0.8	—	1.0	1.1	—	0.3	2.2	0.8	0.2	—	32.8
S. Metals	4.0	6.2	5.5	—	1.6	0.1	0.0	—	—	0.1	0.1	0.1	—	0.5	—	0.3	0.2	0.6	0.0	0.1	19.2
S. Metal Mining	4.6	10.0	4.8	1.5	2.5	0.1	0.2	0.3	—	—	0.3	0.7	0.8	—	—	1.0	0.3	2.4	0.1	0.1	29.6
S. Light Metals	4.7	5.8	4.0	1.4	4.0	—	—	—	1.3	—	—	0.4	23.3	0.9	—	0.8	0.6	0.8	—	0.2	48.2
S. Electric	3.8	5.4	7.0	—	0.8	0.0	0.0	0.1	—	—	—	0.1	—	0.8	—	—	0.1	2.4	—	0.1	20.6
S. Heavy Industry	4.6	6.4	7.8	2.5	3.0	0.1	0.1	0.1	—	—	0.5	1.3	—	0.7	—	0.7	—	—	—	0.3	27.9
NEC	5.0	4.8	6.8	2.6	2.2	0.0	0.0	0.1	0.4	0.1	0.2	0.1	0.7	1.0	—	2.2	0.1	—	0.0	0.2	26.4
S. Real Estate	3.4	5.1	2.3	1.6	0.5	0.0	0.2	—	0.4	0.2	0.7	0.1	0.5	0.3	—	0.5	—	0.7	—	0.5	17.2
S. Storage	4.7	6.7	8.4	5.4	2.4	—	0.3	—	1.5	0.1	0.8	—	2.2	—	—	0.9	0.9	3.9	0.3	—	38.5

Note: 0.0 = very small percentage, and — = no holding or not available. a. Totals do not add because of rounding. Source: Toyo Keizai (1995).

Table 2.2 Composition of insider ownership for five key corporations of the Sumitomo *zaibatsu*, 1937 (percentages)

Owner:	Sumitomo family	Sumitomo Holding Co.	Directors of Holding Co.	Group companies	Total insiders
Owned company					
Sumitomo Bank	20	35	—	—	55
Sumitomo Trust Bank	2	—	—	37	39
Sumitomo Life Insur.	70	26	4	—	100
Sumitomo Chem. Eng.	10	23	—	5	38
Sumitomo Metal Eng.	12	27	—	9	49

Source: Sakudo (1979).

ownership by Sumitomo insiders (that is, the family, the holding company, its directors and the core corporations) is illustrated for five key companies in Table 2.2.

The *zaibatsu* and *keiretsu* are two organizational species separated by a deep structural discontinuity. The next section will provide an account of the 'institutional shock' which destroyed the prewar ownership structure in one stroke. What is interesting about this revolution imposed by the American occupation forces is the divergence between intentions and consequences. It is true that the prewar *zaibatsu* system was destroyed. But in spite of the attempt to 'Americanize' the economy, what emerged was not a Japanese copy of the American corporate system but a distinctively 'Japanese' organization. The purpose of this section is to locate the underlying tendency in prewar Japan that quietly swayed the course of this postwar revolution. We will see that the prewar *zaibatsu* contained the germs of the postwar system.

The *zaibatsu* were formed and developed in Japan's early period of industrialization. Their origins were diverse, but they all involved finance, shipping and mining. Their diversification from merchants to industrialists began in the 1870s and 1880s. Their most notable feature around this period is their 'self-financing' nature thanks to the very lucrative activities of their core firms (usually those in banking, mining or foreign trade) (Morikawa, 1992). This self-financing mechanism played a pivotal role in overcoming the insufficiency of primitive capital accumulation in Meiji Japan. But the transformation into real *zaibatsu* had to wait for the procurement boom of the First World War during which Japan promoted its heavy industries. At that time, the *zaibatsu* relinquished a part of their self-financing mechanism and erected a pyramidal structure of ownership. Such a structure allowed them to control a large amount of assets with a minimum of own capital and facilitated their entry into capital-intensive industry. Of course, the *zaibatsu*'s pyramidal structure was hardly unusual – it is a structure observed among family-owned conglomerates all over the world. Yet, the *zaibatsu* were *zaibatsu* because of a number of characteristics unique to them.[6]

The first and probably most important feature was the restricted nature of their family ownership. For instance, eleven Mitsui families formed a system called *Oomotokata* (meaning approximately 'the foundation') which pooled all their capital and placed it under their joint management. All investments were paid out from *Oomotokata* and all accrued profits were returned to it. In fact, the eleven families were bound by a constitution that stipulated that they should never divide the pooled capital among themselves and would only receive dividends in proportion to their fixed shares for their family expenses (Yasuda, 1970, 1982).

It was natural that under such restricted ownership the owner families were apt to dissociate themselves from active management. Indeed, this was the second distinctive feature of the *zaibatsu* – they allowed a certain autonomy to professional managers. Of course, this was limited in the sense that major decisions were strictly screened and performance was closely scrutinized. Yet, in comparison with the owners of non-*zaibatsu* corporations in the same period, *zaibatsu* headquarters seem to have had much longer time-horizons in the control of their managers,[7] and this resulted in an internal promotion system.[8] An increasingly large number of managers and workers were hired fresh out of colleges and schools, trained on the job and promoted internally. This prepared the *zaibatsu* for entry into the heavy and chemical industries that demanded skilled workers and professional managers. And as these managers and workers accumulated firm-specific skills and know-how, they began to identify themselves as 'insiders' of the corporation and take interest in its survival and growth.

This leads to the third and last *zaibatsu* feature: their constant diversification drive. In general, family-owned conglomerates are conservative in their business outlook. Yet, despite their traditional origins, Mitsui, Mitsubishi and Sumitomo all tried to set foot in almost every heavy industrial sector (Yasuda, however, remained more traditional). It is not an exaggeration to say that the *zaibatsu* took the lead in the heavy and chemical industrialization of Japan in the 1920s and greatly benefited from the second boom in these sectors that followed the depression of the early 1930s.

Such success was not, however, without costs. First, it incited fierce anti-*zaibatsu* campaigns both from the right and the left. Second, the advance of heavy industry required ever larger fixed investments. Partly to appease public opinion and partly to finance this increasing demand for capital, the *zaibatsu* began selling shares of their key corporations to outsiders. The lack of funds became so acute in the early 1940s that most *zaibatsu* (with the exception of Yasuda) had to open up even their holding companies to the public. In spite of these difficulties, however, the 1930s did not mark any structural divide for the Japanese economy, unlike what happened in Italy.

The Second World War brought much greater government interference and, in particular, forced a separation between ownership and management. The wartime government also reorganized the financial market. It divided war-related corporations into a dozen or so groups and assigned to each a single bank as the main supplier of their loan demands. Such forced clustering of corporations around a government-designated bank is said to have paved the way for the postwar formation of non-*zaibatsu keiretsu*, such as Fuyo, Sanwa and Daiichi-Kangin.

By the time defeat came, a trend towards the separation of management from ownership had clearly set in and it was this undercurrent that would be tapped by the postwar economy. Yet, too much emphasis should not be put on the continuity between pre- and postwar Japan. The *zaibatsu* were still family-owned conglomerates par excellence and the families fought hard to preserve their closed ownership. The birth of the truly 'Japanese' corporate system needed a sudden and significant institutional shock that would destroy the old structure.

4 The United States' 'anti-capitalist' revolution in Japan

The impact of the policies implemented by the US authorities in the first two years of postwar occupation was truly revolutionary, especially when compared to the conservative approach followed in Italy in the same period.[9] These policies were inspired by the idea that only a 'democratic' economy was compatible with the development of a peaceful and democratic society. The hierarchical *zaibatsu* structure was considered to have been the ultimate cause of Japanese militarism – an analysis that had no counterpart in the explanation of the causes of the rise (or, indeed, the 'invention') of fascism in Italy. The fear of a possible revival of this militarism was a major motivation behind the American reformist approach. This involved the dissolution of the *zaibatsu* and the dispersion of their stock so as to prevent any undesirable concentration of economic power.

The elimination of the *zaibatsu*, and the personnel purge that went with it, created the conditions for a managerial revolution, with most new managers emerging from within their companies (often with the agreement of the labour unions). In one stroke, a promotion mechanism was created that was isolated not only from the succession problems typical of 'family capitalism', but also from the interference of 'outside directors' who in the Anglo-American world represent the interests of large shareholders. What was missing in the new arrangements was a system by which internal promotions could be monitored, given the great dispersion of individual shareholding. According to the American authorities, this standard agency problem was to be solved by the 'classic' means of equity finance and the creation of a market for corporate control. Yet, in the event, a drastically different system of corporate governance emerged, made up of cross-shareholding, debt financing, and a main-bank-delegated monitoring system.

Much of this happened more by accident than by design. Cross-shareholding had been explicitly outlawed in 1947 and banks, along the lines of the US's Glass–Steagall Act, had been prohibited from underwriting, holding and dealing in corporate securities. And the stock market collapse of 1949 clearly threatened insider control by making take-over bids both easier and cheaper. Yet, by then, rebuilding a stable anti-communist Japan had become far more important for the occupation authorities than the implementation of an ideal 'democratic economy'. Given that the Americans were at that time engaged in a 'macro confrontation' with the central trade unions, seen to be sympathetic to the Soviet Union, they were reluctant to also upset the stability of micro relations at the firm level. Here, 'insider' managers and workers could have faced large losses of much irreversible human capital had outsiders, not bound by any forms of 'implicit' contracts, been allowed to bid for take-overs.

America's turnaround meant that much of the legal framework introduced at the outset was made ineffective. Take-overs were resisted by share price manipulations not dissimilar to 'company buyouts', even though these were not allowed under Japanese law. The sale of the remaining *zaibatsu* assets was postponed and, in the process of maintaining stock prices, shareholding by institutions such as insurance companies and even banks was not only permitted but also encouraged. Cross-shareholding became possible and helped stabilize the power of top management against the risk of take-overs. While in Italy cross-shareholding had marked the extension of the hierarchical control on managers by family capitalism, in Japan it was to guarantee their autonomy from shareholders. In addition to cross-shareholding, banks also played a crucial role in this reconstruction of a managerial version of the *zaibatsu*. The system that emerged, known as the 'main bank system', involved the delegation of monitoring to a single bank.

This provided a way of solving the problems arising from the separation between ownership and control – it safeguarded the interests of the individuals providing finance, yet did not upset the internal promotion system and its great potential for accumulating firm-specific human capital.

The implicit contracts, so prevalent at least in large Japanese firms, imply, however, a 'truncation' of shareholder rights. Job security means that owners cannot employ a firm's assets without at the same time employing the firm's managers and workers. In other words, the Japanese blend of capitalism has involved the 'unbundling' and redistribution of the right to dispose of physical assets that belong exclusively to shareholders in family or securities based governance systems. The interaction between employee rights and the accumulation of their human capital has produced one of those multiple self-reinforcing organizational equilibria discussed in Section 2 above. Banks have been an essential ingredient in this mechanism – they provided the ex-ante, interim and ex-post monitoring that are performed by different agents in securities based markets, they did not in general interfere with the internal promotion system and they intervened directly only in cases of financial distress.

Of late, the system has come under attack as initiative has passed from the providers of funds (the banks) to borrowers (the firms) who have taken the formers' willingness to lend for granted. As most dramatically shown in the bubble of the late 1980s and its aftermath 'the main bank system as a social device for corporate monitoring appears to be under severe test' (Aoki, 1994, p. 137). Despite these difficulties, however, any reversal to a more Anglo-American system of governance seems very unlikely because 'a quantum leap to the securities-based decentralized financial system, particularly the establishment of an active market for control, may be incompatible with other institutional features of the Japanese economy' (ibid., p. 138), in particular the implicit contracts between workers and managers that involve job security and internal promotion in exchange for investment in highly specific human capital and for effort that is difficult to monitor.

5 Changes in Italian corporate governance between the wars

Italy industrialized only at the end of the nineteenth century. The country was traditionally marked by shortages of capital and raw materials and by the lack of a large market (due to its earlier division into small, independent states).[10] The model of development that emerged after unification was centred on heavy industry, sustained by public procurements, protected by high tariffs,[11] and financed by so-called 'mixed banks' (which operated through a *mix* of short-term credit and equity subscription). According to Gerschenkron (1962), Italy's mixed banks acted, at first, as a *substitute agent* to overcome the scanty primitive accumulation of capital, and later as the channel by which diffuse, fragmented savings that the holders had no intention of putting into illiquid form could be funnelled into equity for which there would otherwise have been few buyers.

The natural corollary to the prevalence of debt capital was the failure of the stock market to take off. Following the turn of the century it was the mixed banks themselves that sponsored its development, with a view to making their equity shares more liquid and more easily disposable. With an inadequate stock market and stable, non-competitive relations between banks and industry, the groundwork was laid, between 1900 and 1913, for an intensive concentration of control and the formation of corporate family-based pyramidal groups. Two major changes intervened as a consequence of the large profits made from military procurements during the First World War. First, the main banks acquired significant equity stakes in many industrial sectors and so from a 'German style' moved toward a 'Japanese-style' of banking. Second, healthier corporate finances powerfully spurred further concentration, especially by mergers and buyouts. In these years, the power relations between banks and industrial corporations were inverted, and pyramidal groups now made take-over bids for the leading banks, although unsuccessfully.

The 1929 stock market crash thus hit the economy at a time of pronounced industrial and financial concentration. The intermingling of credit and industrial capital, the underdevelopment of the stock market, but above all the creation of corporate groups based on cross-shareholdings, made the crisis particularly acute, hindering adjustment and fostering domino effects. A tight monetary policy and the decision to defend the lira's external value amplified the destructive nature of the shock. The leading banks found it simply impossible to liquidate their assets, which consisted primarily of equity holdings in the crisis-torn industrial groups. This paved the way for the most sweeping reallocation of ownership in the history of Italy as the government simply took over large segments of the private sector.

The refinancing of the troubled banks was accomplished by a buy-out of their industrial holdings which were transferred to a new agency created especially for this purpose in 1933 – IRI, which took over the entire equity capital of the mixed banks (or more than 21 per cent of all the equity capital of limited companies at the time).[12] The decision not to reprivatize reflected in part the fascist regime's desire to use public corporations as an instrument of industrial policy, but was primarily due to difficulties in finding buyers for so many firms (Cianci, 1977). Meanwhile, industrial concentration in the rest of the private sector had increased notably – by 1936 fewer than one per cent of all Italian companies accounted for half the total share capital (Aleotti, 1990).

The creation of IRI was accompanied in 1936 by a reform which prohibited banks from holding equity in industrial companies and required maturity specialization in their lending activities, assigning short-term credit to ordinary banks and longer-term credit to special institutions. Thus, the German-style mixed bank vanished from the scene. But the Italian solution was not intended to re-launch the stock market as a means for attaining a broader ownership base; the dominant logic continued to see the banks as the linchpin of industrial finance.

For Italy, the crisis of the 1930s thus represents a truly structural divide, with an outright transformation of the previous model of corporate governance. With the massive intervention of the state, Italy moved from an ownership pattern based on the corporate family group and mixed banks (similar in some ways to the German model) to one centred on the corporate group but subdivided into state-owned and private groups controlled by families. A characteristic feature of the Anglo-American model of corporate control was introduced, namely the separation of the banking and industrial sectors. The bank as a controller, mandated to oversee the rehabilitation and restructuring of firms in crisis, disappeared. The resulting vacuum was partly filled by the state holding company, which was repeatedly required to take over firms in financial distress. Japan's experience was very different. The negative impact of the Great Depression was reduced by a devaluation of the exchange rate and the Japanese *zaibatsu* were powerful enough to prevent any major state encroachment on their power.

6   Continuity and change in Italian corporate governance in the postwar period

The Italian model of corporate governance that followed the restructuring of 1933–36 was based on two major actors – family-controlled pyramidal groups and state-owned pyramidal groups. The end of the war and of fascism, the institution of a republic, and the drafting of a democratic Constitution did little to alter that institutional structure. Most of its negative aspects were perceived by the Economic Committee of the Constitutional Assembly, but no reforms were implemented (Barca, 1994, ch. VIII).

Between 1943 and 1947 the Allied powers were a powerful actor on the Italian political scene. Churchill wanted to preserve the traditional ownership relationships in Italy. He was not interested in purging the country from fascist influences, and considered the monarchy as the preferred institutional solution for the future Italian state. The American point of view was initially quite different. The need to accelerate the process of reconstruction and the emergence of the Cold War induced, however, the Allies to support a quick return to the traditional system. Two other factors on the Italian side militated in the same direction – the Communist Party felt that existing institutions should at first be retained in order to allow rapid reconstruction; and a similar position was held by a small group of managers who emerged into positions of power in state-owned companies and enjoyed preferential links with the Americans (Barca, 1997).

As was shown in Section 4, the American attitude in Japan had clearly been one of *zaibatsu*-busting. The different approach followed by the Americans in Italy can be explained by taking into account two major factors – the much lower perceived risk of a future militarist revival in Italy (a risk that was reckoned to be relatively high in Japan and Germany), and the need to put in place a robust economic recovery in order to avoid a possible coming to power of the communists (a threat strongly feared in Europe but absent in Japan).

As a result of these various factors, state-owned companies were not dismantled, the structure of family corporate groups was not changed and no major reform was devised by the series of Christian-Democrat-led governments that ran Italy from 1947 to 1962. During this 'liberal' phase, Italy signed the Bretton Woods agreements, received financial transfers under the Marshall Plan,[13] and joined the NATO alliance, but little was done in terms of traditionally liberal reforms – no antitrust laws, no reform of the commercial code, no steps toward a more developed financial market. On the other hand, the clear choice in favour of European integration and free trade permitted the full unfolding of the development potential inherent in the model of corporate governance installed between 1933 and 1936.

That governance framework suited rapid development in the first 10–15 years after the war. State control gave a new generation of managers, broadly untainted by involvement with the fascist regime (and, in some cases, known opponents of it), the chance to acquire control of large enterprises; a sense of mission, linked to the postwar reconstruction climate, helped to make up for the monitoring failures of the model; while many of the strategic choices were clear-cut (providing the country with an adequate and stable supply of energy, developing and modernizing the steel industry, building a highway system, and so on). Though there had been a debate over whether or not to maintain state-owned enterprises in the late 1940s, the position that won the day considered them as an effective tool for speeding up reconstruction (Bottiglieri, 1984). They were also seen as a means to ensure a proper separation between ownership and control, probably one of the few available in a fast developing country without a real financial market. The structure of corporate governance in this sector became one in which management had effective control, while the oversight exercised by the political power structure was lax. It was management, not the political tutors, who took the decision to rebuild and renovate industry and to create a modern infrastructure.

Two major factors explain the satisfactory performance of the state-owned groups in the years going from 1945 to the late 1950s – the public managers' targets were relatively simple (to reconstruct the economy and foster growth, to build the basic transport and energy infrastructure, and to establish an engineering sector based on home steel production), and the ruling centre-right parties were strongly competing with the left to prove that capitalism was capable of bringing about rapid development (Barca and Trento, 1997). Both these conditions disappeared at the end of the 1950s. An attempt to introduce some tighter monitoring led to the creation of a Ministry for State Shareholding. This imposed multiple targets (to contest monopolies, to promote new industrial relations, to sustain employment, and to foster Southern economic development) many of which could not be fulfilled simultaneously. And the market for political control failed, as the politicians increasingly saw state-owned firms as a source of funds for their parties and of jobs for themselves or their acolytes.

Despite these later problems, state ownership had enabled some separation between ownership and control unlike what happened in private large firms. Fluidity in the former sector contrasted with immobility in the latter. Extraordinarily high profits (made possible by real wages rising more slowly than productivity, by the weak state of unions and by relatively high unemployment) provided the finance for very rapid growth. But this anomalous state of affairs came slowly to an end at the turn of the 1950s. Tensions arose in the labour market, wages rose very quickly and, by 1962–63, the share of self-financing had sharply declined; after a brief period of truce, labour market conflict resurfaced from the late 1960s onwards and profits were kept relatively low until the early 1980s. The resulting need for external capital strengthened, in turn, the pressures for a much more intense use of pyramidal groups. A growing role came to be played by Mediobanca, a merchant bank founded in 1946.[14] By holding strategic shares in private companies, Mediobanca had, on many occasions, allowed founding families to maintain their control. It could be argued that it had come to play a role not dissimilar to that of Japan's main banks, though it mostly specialized in ex-post

Table 2.3   Control–ownership leverage in three major Italian groups[a]

	Fiat	Pirelli	Falck
1947	1.9	8.9	2.5
1993	17.9	52.6	4.4

a. Ratio between group's net share capital and share capital held by founding family.
Source: Barca et al. (1997).

monitoring – that is, in devising rescue and restructuring plans once incumbent entrepreneurs had failed to deliver satisfactory results.

How intensely pyramidal groups have been used as a means to separate ownership from control comes out clearly from Table 2.3 which reports data for three major corporations – Fiat, Pirelli and Falck – in 1993 (and 1947). At a more aggregate level, recent research on the current ownership structure of Italian industry shows that in 1993 the average degree of leverage was about 8 for private non-banking holders of control (Barca, 1995; Barca et al., 1994).

This substantial increase in leverage has been achieved by expanding the group structure and by diluting the capital held by the family or by companies in the higher ranks of the group. Dilution has undoubtedly led to some weakening of family control, especially in those group companies which, by being closer to the core business, are clearly preferred by external shareholders. Table 2.4 illustrates this weakening. In 1947 the Agnelli and Falck families held a very high proportion of the group's shares; only the Pirelli family had no majority of votes in the key company Pirelli Spa, but control was then exerted through the support of a set of well-established households, mostly from the same town (Milan) and cultural roots. In 1993 the founding families still held large blocks of shares but these were certainly not sufficient to exert stable control, nor was financial support any longer provided by wealthy rentier-households.

A new ownership structure has thus arisen, at least in these companies, made up of founding families, financial and industrial firms. The latter play a role in Pirelli and Falck through cross-shareholdings, in a manner reminiscent of the Japanese practice. In Fiat the supporting role is played only by banks and insurance companies via shareholding and through the threat of 'white knight' action in case of take-overs. This suggests the presence of a tripolar equilibrium in which control is exerted through some agreement or compromise between the founding family, the top manager and the leading financial institution (Mediobanca). The

Table 2.4   Main shareholders of 'key companies' of three major Italian groups, 1947 and 1993 (percentage of total, ordinary and preferred voting capital)

Fiat group		Pirelli group		Falck group	
Shareholders	*Shares*	*Shareholders*	*Shares*	*Shareholders*	*Shares*
FIAT SPA (1947)		PIRELLI SPA (1947)		A.F.L. FALCK (1947)	
Agnelli family	70.2	Pirelli family	12.9	Falck family	73.1
Persons (37)	10.5	Persons (75)	23.2	Persons (40)	11.8
Vatican	0.4			Vatican	0.7
Banks (10)	2.8	Banks (4)	2.6		
Non-banking firms	2.5	Non-banking firms (11)	2.9	Non-banking firms (3)	14.4
'Others' (2207)	13.6	'Others'	58.4		
FIAT SPA (1993)		PIRELLI & CO. (1993)		A.F.L. FALCK (1993)	
Agnelli family	24.8	Pirelli family	8.7	Falck family	32.3
via IFI*	18.1				
via IFIL*	1.9				
via FIMEPAR*	4.8				
Banks	11.0	Banks	16.4	Banks	4.8
Mediobanca*	3.2	Mediobanca*	10.0	IMI	4.8
Istituto S.Paolo	3.4	Banque Indosuez	6.4		
Deutsche Bank	2.4*				
Banco di Roma	2.0				
Non-banking firms	4.8	Non-banking firms	32.9	Non-banking firms	28.3
Assicuraz.General.*	2.4	GIM* (Orlando)	6.7	Italmobil.* (Pesenti)	11.8
Alcatel*	2.0	SMI* (Orlando)	3.6	SidercaTechint*	5.9
Others	0.4	Gemina*	5.3	Ilva* (IRI)	4.9
		Sai* (Ligresti)	5.0	Finarvedi* (Arvedi)	4.7
		Camfin* (Tronch. Prov.)	5.0	Sofinda* (Danieli)	2.9
		CIR* (De Benedetti)	4.4	Pirelli & C.*	2.0
		SOPAF* (Vender)	2.9	Ras*	1.0
'Others'	59.4	'Others'	42.0	'Others'	29.7

Notes: Numbers in brackets show the number of shareholders when known. Asterisks indicate that among these shareholders there is an agreement on voting co-ordination and a mutual pact not to transfer shares to third parties (both these are legal under Italian commercial law).
Source: Barca *et al.* (1997).

instability of such arrangements might well explain the strong pressures arising today for a reform of Italian corporate governance.

A further, and very important, feature of Italy's industrial structure is the presence of a vast network of small-scale firms whose growth was powerfully reinforced by the crisis that hit the larger corporations from the 1960s onwards. In many areas of Central and Northern Italy so-called 'potential industrial districts' were slowly emerging in the 1950s and 1960s (Brusco and Paba, 1997) sustained by informal financing channels (especially family savings) and by technology and human capital accumulation. In addition, Central and Northern Italy also enjoyed a tradition of civic culture conducive to micro-industry development. However, it was only with the 1960s crisis of governance in large firms, that these 'potential districts' developed into fully-fledged ones. The 'institutional shock' provided, in particular, by the labour conflicts of the decade and by the adoption, in 1970, of a binding Workers' Statute, led large companies to decentralize some of their activities. Skilled workers were encouraged to set up their own firms since these, because of their small size, could be isolated from the conflicts impairing productivity in the larger corporations.

It was fortunate for the Italian economy that these developments occurred at a time when the world was beginning to face the consequences of the advent of information technology and programmable machines. These 'technological shocks' made small firms based on 'flexible specialization' competitive in world markets. The rapid growth of this small firm sector created conditions under which individuals could enjoy the rights related to ownership of their firms, had the incentives to develop the specific skills that were necessary for their development and, having developed these skills, often became very efficient owners. The institutional shock of the 1960s had an important role in bringing about the virtuous circle characterizing this self-reinforcing organizational equilibrium. Technological changes were allowing large sectors of industry to produce economically on a small scale and Italy was one of the few countries that fully exploited this opportunity. While (or, perhaps, because) the organization of governance in the larger firms was stuck in a form of family capitalism characterized by social immobility and class conflict, the governance system of small firms became a 'model' to be studied and imitated in other parts of the world.

7 Conclusions

The crucial years after the Second World War led to a parting of the way between Japanese and Italian experience. Family control over pyramidal groups was eliminated in Japan, and cross-shareholding adopted as a tool to isolate management from owner control. External supervision by the main bank aimed to prevent possible abuses by the managers themselves. In Italy, by contrast, there was no 'managerial revolution'. If anything, family control over pyramidal groups was strengthened. State ownership was also largely used and financial crises were often resolved with injections of public funds or nationalization.

Seen from a Japanese perspective, the Italian experience shows that creating a managerial form of capitalism out of the prewar *zaibatsu* was by no means inevitable. The new organizational equilibrium of the corporate sector that emerged after the war in Japan clearly needed an institutional shock that was absent in Italy at the time. Seen from an Italian perspective, the Japanese postwar settlement shows that an alternative model of corporate governance could have been pursued by the Allies. Unfortunately, perhaps, this was not to be and even today Italy's large private firms still look like an almost stronger version of Japan's prewar *zaibatsu*.

More generally, comparing the Japanese and Italian models shows that within the same legal framework of capitalism it is possible to have very different 'organizational equilibria' which, in turn, depend on the 'institutional shocks' experienced in the histories of the two countries. The very same institutions, such as inter-firm shareholding and main banking (if one wants to classify Mediobanca as a 'main bank' serving the corporate sector),[15] took on very different meanings. In Japan they were the means by which 'managerial capitalism' could organize itself and managers could achieve their autonomy. In Italy, by contrast, the same institutions contributed to the stability of 'family capitalism' beyond the limits of the capitals of the family and helped the local *zaibatsu* to strengthen their control. Postwar Italy and Japan may thus be interpreted as two extreme cases defining an interval within which other corporate governance models are likely to fall.

Notes

1. The following discussion on the diversity of corporate structures draws heavily on Iwai (1999). The discussion of the Italian pyramidal ownership structure is, however, new.
2. For the sake of simplicity we are assuming that all corporations, except those on the bottom layer, function only as holding companies. If they also engage in real economic activities, using part of their capital as a productive asset, then this 'multiplier' has to be adjusted downwards.
3. Let M be the number of corporations each holding company controls and let s be the ratio of the shares mutually held by corporations controlled by the same holding company. If we assume that all corporations are of equal size and ignore mutual shareholdings between firms controlled by different holding companies, then the upper bound of M can be calculated as: $1 = [\frac{1}{2} - (M-1)s]M$, or $M = \frac{1}{2} + \frac{1}{4} + (\frac{1}{4} - \frac{3}{4}s + 1/16s^2)^{\frac{1}{2}}$, as long as $(M-1)s < \frac{1}{2}$ (for the sake of simplicity we assume M to be continuous). The upper bound of the control/ownership leverage ratio of the top shareholder can then be calculated as M^n. Note that when $s = 0$, or there is no cross-shareholding, M becomes equal to 2.

4. If we use the same notation as in note 3, the lower bound of the number of corporations, M, which can insulate a group from outside take-overs by cross-shareholding, is given by the formula: $(M-1)s = \frac{1}{2}$, or $M = 1 + \frac{1}{2}s$.

5. The formal properties of organizational equilibria are examined in Pagano (1993) and in Pagano and Rowthorn (1994 and 1995).

6. The following characterisation of *zaibatsu* owes much to Morikawa (1992).

7. Thus, it appears, for instance that the dividend ratios of *zaibatsu* corporations were both lower and less sensitive to the variations of profit rates than those of non-*zaibatsu* corporations, suggesting the presence of more 'managerial' behaviour (Okazaki (1999), Table 9). Miyajima (1995) also reported that the turnover rates of *zaibatsu* managers appeared to be less sensitive to short-run business fluctuations than that of non-*zaibatsu* managers.

8. As a matter of fact, even during the Tokugawa period, many merchant families, including Mitsui and Sumitomo, had developed a mixture of a family-based and managerial system (the so-called *banto* system). *Banto* were experienced and loyal managers who began their careers as living-in employees at an early age, climbed up the internal promotion ladder and were treated as quasi-members of the family. Indeed, the authority of *banto* could be such that improvident family heads could be forced into retirement by them and substituted with the bright son of a distant relative or, more often, by a promising young employee who, even without blood ties, would be adopted as family head.

9. Indeed, the radical nature of these reforms was vividly described by US Senator Knowland in a end-1947 speech to Congress: 'If some of the doctrine [applied in Japan] had been proposed by the government of the USSR or even by the labor government of Great Britain, I could have understood it' (quoted in Livingstone et al., 1976, p. 113). Similar dismay at the 'imposition of an economic theory far to the left of anything tolerated [in the United States]' was at the time being expressed in the December 1947 issue of the magazine *Newsweek* (ibid., p. 107).

10. In the words of a great Italian thinker of this century:

> The Italian economy was very weak [and] there was no large and powerful economic bourgeoisie; instead there was a great number of intellectuals and petty bourgeois, etc. The problem was not so much to free already developed economic forces from antiquated legal and political fetters as to bring into being the general conditions for these economic forces to develop along the same lines as in other countries. (Gramsci, 1975, p. 57)

11. As Gerschenkron (1962) noted, and as has been confirmed by more recent studies (Federico and Toniolo, 1991), protectionism was, in fact, misdirected, favouring wheat production and basic industries with strong lobbying powers but poor long-term prospects.

12. 100 per cent of Italy's defence-related steel and coal-mining, 90 per cent of its shipbuilding, 80 per cent of shipping and of locomotive manufacture, 30 per cent of electricity generation, and so on. In addition, IRI also controlled the three largest commercial banks, etc. (Castronovo, 1995).

13. Between 1948 and 1952 Italy received transfers of almost $1\frac{1}{2}$ bn, equivalent to 11 per cent of total Marshall Plan aid to Western Europe (Romeo, 1991).

14. The 1936 reform had produced a banking system in which commercial banks were barred from medium- and long-term lending. At the end of the war Mattioli, the chairman of Banca Commerciale, sponsored the formation of a new institute mandated to offer five-year credit to firms. By 1946, this project led to the creation of Mediobanca, an institution which, over the years, transformed itself into a true investment bank for the country's leading private enterprises. For more detail, see Chapter 4 by de Cecco and Ferri in this volume.
15. This similarity should not, however, be carried too far (see de Cecco and Ferri, 1996).

References

Aleotti, A. (1990) *Borsa e industria. 1861–1989: cento anni di rapporti difficili*, Milan, Edizioni di Comunità.

Aoki, M. (1994) 'Monitoring Characteristics of the Main Bank System: an Analytical and Developmental View', in M. Aoki and H.T. Patrick (eds), *The Japanese Main Bank System: Its Relevance for Developing and Trasforming Economies*, New York, NY: Oxford University Press.

Arthur, B. (1989) 'Competing Technologies, Increasing Returns, and Lock-in by Historical Events', *Economic Journal*, 99, 394, 116–31.

Barca, F. (1994), *Imprese in cerca di padrone. Proprietà e controllo nel capitalismo italiano*, Bari: Laterza.

Barca, F. (1995) 'On Corporate Governance in Italy: Issues, Facts and Agenda', Paper presented at OECD Conference on 'The Influence of Corporate Governance and Financing Structure on Economic Performance', Paris, 23–24 February.

Barca, F. (1997) 'Compromesso senza riforme nel capitalismo italiano', in F. Barca (ed.), *Storia del capitalismo italiano dal dopoguerra a oggi*, Rome: Donzelli.

Barca, F., F. Bertucci, G. Capello and P. Casavola (1997) 'La trasformazione proprietaria di Fiat, Pirelli e Falck dal 1947 a oggi', in F.Barca (ed.), *Storia del capitalismo italiano dal dopoguerra a oggi*, Rome: Donzelli.

Barca, F., M. Bianchi, F. Brioschi, L. Buzzacchi, P. Casavola, L. Filippa and M. Pagnini (1994) *Assetti proprietari e mercato delle imprese. Gruppo, proprietà e controllo nelle imprese italiane medio-grandi*, vol. II, Bologna: Il Mulino.

Barca, F. and S. Trento (1997) 'State Ownership and the Evolution of Italian Corporate Governance', *Industrial and Corporate Change*, 6, 3, 533–59.

Berle, A.A. and G.C. Means (1933) *The Modern Corporation and Private Property*, New York, NY: Macmillan

Bottiglieri, B. (1984) 'Linee interpretative del dibattito sulle partecipazioni statali nel secondo dopoguerra', *Economia Pubblica*, 14, 4–5, 239–44.

Brusco, S. and S. Paba (1997) 'Per una storia dei distretti industriali italiani dal secondo dopoguerra agli anni novanta', in F. Barca (ed.), *Storia del capitalismo italiano dal dopoguerra a oggi*, Rome: Donzelli.

Castronovo, V. (1995) *Storia economica d'Italia. Dall'Ottocento ai giorni nostri*, Turin: Einaudi.

Cianci, E. (1977) *La nascita dello Stato imprenditore*, Milan: Mursia.

David, P.A. (1994) 'Why are Institutions the "Carriers of History"? Path Dependence and the Evolution of Conventions, Organisations and Institutions', *Structural Change and Economic Dynamics*, 5, 2, 205–20.

de Cecco M. and G. Ferri (1996) *Le banche d'affari in Italia,* Bologna: Il Mulino.

Federico, G. and G. Toniolo (1991) 'Italy', in R. Sylla and G. Toniolo (eds), *Patterns of European Industrialization,* London: Routledge.

Gerschenkron, A. (1962) *Economic Backwardness in Historical Perspective: a Book of Essays,* Cambridge, MA: Harvard University Press.

Gramsci, A. (1975) *Il Risorgimento, quaderni del carcere,* Rome: Editori Riuniti.

Hadley, E.M. (1970) *Antitrust in Japan,* Princeton, NJ: Princeton University Press.

Hart, O.D. (1995) *Firms, Contracts and Financial Structure,* Oxford: Clarendon Press.

Iwai, K. (1999) 'Persons, Things and Corporations: the Corporate Personality Controversy and Comparative Corporate Governance', *American Journal of Comparative Law,* 45, 101–50.

Livingstone, J., J. Moore and F. Oldfather (eds) (1976) *The Japan Reader 2: Postwar Japan: 1945 to the Present,* Harmondsworth, Middlesex: Penguin Books.

Miyajima, H. (1995) 'Senmon-keieishano Seiha – Nihon-gata Keieisha Kigyono Seiritsu' ('The Domination of Professional Managers – The Coming into Being of the Japanese-style Managerial Corporations'), in H. Yamasaki and T. Kikkawa (eds), *'Nihon-teki' Keieino Renzoku to Danzetsu (The Continuity and Discontinuity of 'Japanese' Management),* Tokyo: Iwanami Shoten.

Morikawa, H. (1992) *Zaibatsu: the Rise and Fall of Family Enterprise Groups in Japan,* Tokyo, University of Tokyo Press.

Okazaki, T. (1999), 'The Corporate System', in T. Okazaki and M. Okuno-Fujiwara (eds), *The Japanese Economic System,* Oxford: Oxford University Press.

Pagano, U. (1993) 'Organisational Equilibria and Institutional Stability', in S. Bowles, H. Gintis and B. Gustafson (eds), *Markets and Democracy,* Cambridge: Cambridge University Press.

Pagano, U. and R. Rowthorn (1994) 'Ownership, Technology and Institutional Stability', *Structural Change and Economic Dynamics,* 5, 2, 221–43.

Pagano, U. and R. Rowthorn (1995) 'The Competitive Selection of Democratic Firms in a World of Self-sustaining Institutions', in U. Pagano and R. Rowthorn (eds), *Democracy and Efficiency in the Economic Enterprise,* London: Routledge.

Romeo, R. (1991) *Breve storia della grande industria in Italia: 1861–1961,* Milan: Il Saggiatore.

Sakudo, Y. (1979) *Sumitomo Zaibatsu-shi (History of the Sumitomo Zaibatsu),* Tokyo: Kyoykusha.

Toyo Keizai (1995) *Kigyo Keiretsu Soran 1995 (Survey on Corporate Groups, 1995),* Tokyo: Toyo Keizai Shimposha.

Yasuda, J. (1970) *Zaibatsu Keisei-shino Kenkyu (Studies of the Historical Formation of Zaibatsu),* Tokyo: Minerva Shobo.

Yasuda, J. (ed.) (1982) *Mitsui Zaibatsu (The Mitsui Zaibatsu),* Tokyo: Nihon Keizai Shinbunsha.

3
Economic Growth: The Role of Demand*

Massimo Di Matteo and Hiroshi Yoshikawa

1 Introduction

Economic growth has always been a major topic in macroeconomics. Why do growth rates differ across countries? Do such growth rates converge? Is the difference in the well-being of rich and poor nations ever going to diminish? These old and important questions still remain crucial today. A fashionable method for an empirical analysis of such problems has recently been put forward – cross-country regression (see, for example, Mankiw et al., 1992; Barro, 1997). Though such regressions shed some light on the issues at hand, they lack robustness. Slightly different periods, country samples or functional forms can produce very different results. In addition, the methodology they use assumes away the historical background of the countries that are studied despite the fact that it is virtually impossible to control for all the important differences between, say, Sweden and Switzerland, let alone Syria, by simply inserting a few ad hoc variables into regression equations. We believe that careful case studies are a fruitful, indeed often better, alternative to cross-country regressions for an understanding of the mechanisms that drive economic growth. In this chapter, we try to provide such a study by looking at the growth experience of Italy and Japan from the end of the Second World War to the early 1990s.

*   This is a modified version of a paper originally published by Physica-Verlag in *Economic Systems* (Massimo Di Matteo and Hiroshi Yoshikawa, 'Economic Growth: The Italian and Japanese Experiences', 23, 1, 11–33, 1999). Both authors would like to thank participants in workshops in Siena and Tokyo as well as Andrea Boltho for helpful comments. The first author is also grateful to P. Rizzi for lengthy discussions and to R.Veneziani for research assistance.

The two standard theoretical (and basically neo-classical) approaches to the study of economic growth are the old Solow model (1956) and the more recent theory of endogenous growth.[1] In both old and new theory growth depends on consumers' time preferences and on countries' factor endowments. Crucial to both approaches is the assumption that production factors are fully employed thanks to factor prices changing in ways that ensure such an outcome. This assumption is usually defended by the contention that in the long run (with which growth is concerned) unemployment cannot persist. In this chapter we maintain, however, that in many real world situations the opposite is much more likely to be the case.

Assume, for instance, that some resource such as labour is underemployed. In such a case, there would be room for 'demand-led' growth. Solow himself, for example, points out that:

> A more interesting question is whether a major episode in the growth of potential output can be driven from the demand side. Can demand create its own supply? The magnitudes suggest that it would be awfully difficult for a surge of aggregate demand to generate enough investment to provide the capacity necessary to accommodate it. In special circumstances it might be done, say, in an economy that has a pool of labor (rural, foreign) that it can mobilize. It might also work if strong aggregate demand can induce a rise in total factor productivity (TFP). This may be less far-fetched than it sounds, if we recognize that a large part of TFP originates not in the research laboratory, but on the shop floor, as production workers figure out how to gain a little efficiency here and a little there. The demand-driven growth story sounds quite implausible to me under current conditions; but it is an example of the kind of question that needs to be asked. (Solow, 1997, p. 232)

Solow is sceptical (presumably in the context of the contemporary American economy) as to the possibility of demand-led growth, but what he terms 'special circumstances' need not be so special. As will be seen shortly, both Italy and Japan had a large pool of underemployed labour that they could mobilize in their high growth period.

Underemployment of labour is often taken to be the same as unemployment above the 'natural rate'. This need not be the case, however. In Japan, for instance, it is well known that the official unemployment rate has been very low and extremely stable over several decades. And yet, many economists believe that underemployment or 'disguised' unemployment has always existed and still exists. One source of such underemployment is provided by 'discouraged workers' who involuntarily quit the labour force because of a lack of job opportunities at times of cyclical slowdown. Another comes from the presence of workers whose marginal product is substantially lower than that in the economy's 'advanced' sector. In the 'full employment' state of neo-classical theory this cannot occur because the *value* marginal product of labour is assumed to be equal in all sectors of the economy. But if this is not the case, underemployment exists and this is important in the context of long-term growth.

The existence of substantial underemployment of this kind in Japan is confirmed by Ohkawa (1975) who estimated the ratio of labour's marginal product in agriculture to that in manufacturing in the 1950s and 1960s (unfortunately, no similar estimates are available for Italy). He found that an agricultural worker's marginal product was at the time equal to between one-seventh and one-tenth that of an industrial worker. It is interesting to note that, according to Ohkawa, this ratio was actually lower in the late 1960s than it had been in the 1950s. This must have happened because differences in productivity growth between the two sectors, due to technical progress and capital accumulation, dominated the effects of the inter-sectoral labour shifts that, according to neo-classical theory, should have narrowed the gap in marginal products between industry and agriculture.

Coming to the postwar growth experience of Italy and Japan, we note that, as of 1950, almost half the labour force in both countries was engaged in agriculture. Even as late as 1970, 19 per cent of Italy's workforce, and 17 per cent of Japan's, were still employed in that sector. Hence, if one accepts Ohkawa's estimates, the marginal product of one out of six workers, in Japan at least, was at the time merely one-tenth that in manufacturing industry. And agriculture is merely an extreme example. Differences in marginal productivities across sectors are likely to be always present. Indeed, at the end of this chapter, evidence will be presented for both Italy and Japan suggesting that significant productivity gaps across industries persisted as late as the early 1990s. Underemployment so defined always exists and so does the room for 'demand-led' growth. In today's circumstances, however, such scope is much more limited than it was in the 1950s, if only because inter-sectoral movements may require the prior acquisition of skills as well as a willingness to move that is clearly less present than in earlier decades, particularly in Italy.

To sum up, substantial underemployment must have existed in both Italy and Japan in the 1950s and 1960s and, arguably, some is present even now. Mobilization of this labour was important for the postwar growth of the two economies, along the lines originally suggested by Lewis (1954) in his well-known model of growth in dualistic economies. This model has usually been applied to developing countries, but the distinction between 'growth' and 'development' is merely a semantic one. Kindleberger, for instance, has argued that the theory can be profitably applied to explain Europe's postwar growth:

> In a previous book, I concluded that economic history suffered from the availability of too many models of economic relationships, all of a certain plausibility but none demonstrably more useful as an explanation of the past than others. After finishing that work, however, I came to think that one model of economic analysis – W. Arthur Lewis' model of growth with unlimited supplies of labor, with its strong affinities to the Marxian system – had much more explanatory power in history than I had allowed. It is helpful in accounting both for the growth of Britain during the Industrial Revolution and for the rise of real income of labor after the slowing down of the rate of growth in the second half of the nineteenth century; it is relevant to the growth of the United States from 1880 to 1913; and in particular, as I seek to demonstrate here, it is useful to explain the very high rates of growth of some countries of Europe in the period since World War II – rates which are higher than can normally be sustained over long periods and are therefore entitled to be called supergrowth. (Kindleberger, 1967, p. 1)

The Lewis model is an appropriate framework for the study of Italian and Japanese postwar growth. However, it has a serious weakness. As Boltho points out: 'abundant labour supply had, after all, been a characteristic of the European economies throughout the nineteenth and early twentieth centuries' (1982, p. 15). The same is, of course, true of Japan. The existence of excess labour cannot, therefore, by itself explain why Italy and Japan in the 1950s and 1960s enjoyed much higher growth than in the prewar period. Lewis took it for granted that low real wages would necessarily bring about high profits and thereby high growth in the modern industrial sector. However, for low real wages to generate high profits and, therefore, investment, demand must continuously expand. In other words, the growth surge of the 1950s and 1960s can only be really explained by a combination of 'abundant labour supply' à la Lewis and a 'demand-led' impulse à la Solow. It is therefore very important to identify what kind of demand made a significant contribution to economic growth.

Section 2 below looks at this issue and provides an explanation of the high growth of the 1950s and 1960s. We find many similarities between Italy and Japan in the mechanisms that propelled growth during this period. High growth, however, came to a halt at the beginning of the 1970s. A number of economists (see, for instance, Bruno and Sachs, 1985; Jorgenson, 1988) have attributed this deceleration to the first oil shock of 1973. We argue, however, that, contrary to this popular view, the end of high growth was caused not by the oil shocks but by internal changes in the two economies. Section 3 considers the Italian and Japanese post-oil shock growth experiences and at the different paths which the two economies followed in the 1970s and 1980s. Finally, Section 4 offers some concluding remarks.

2 The era of 'super growth': 1950–1970

Italy's and Japan's growth experiences in the 1950s and 1960s are well known. Both countries grew very rapidly (Table 3.1), not only by international but also by historical standards. A number of explanations have been provided for this outcome. Thus, postwar reconstruction has often been mentioned as a major reason in both countries. However, the reconstruction period was chaotic in Japan and the average growth rate in the years 1945–52 was actually lower than in the 1950s and 1960s.[2] Therefore, a simple reconstruction story cannot satisfactorily explain a surge in growth that began in the mid-1950s. The same is broadly true for Italy, where reconstruction had been basically completed by 1948–49. A similar problem applies to the standard Ramsey model, according to which the growth rate declines monotonously as capital accumulates. Despite continuous capital accumulation in both countries, growth surged in Japan from the mid-1950s and accelerated in Italy between 1958 and 1963.

There are other explanations. Thus, some economists, such as Lincoln (1988), have attributed Japan's high growth to the adoption of foreign

Table 3.1 GDP growth in Italy, Japan and the OECD area (average annual trend growth rates)

	Italy	*Japan*	*OECD area*[a]
1950–90	4.3	6.8	3.5
1950–70	5.8	8.9	4.1
1970–90	2.9	4.0	2.6

a. Excluding Italy and Japan.
Source: Maddison (1995).

technology which had accumulated during the war, particularly in the United States, and from which the country had been cut off – an explanation which is, of course, equally applicable to Italy. Borrowed technology certainly played a role in the process of postwar growth, but it is not altogether clear whether the technological gap between the United States on the one hand and Italy and Japan on the other was much greater at the beginning of the 1950s than it had been in the late 1920s, or, for that matter, in the late nineteenth century. The gap in, and the borrowing of, technology were clearly favourable factors but not the major causes of high growth (see also Boltho, 1982).

Excess labour supply – or underemployment – is another factor often mentioned. However, as discussed above, excess labour supply alone cannot adequately explain why high growth occurred during the 1950s and 1960s since abundant labour had been present in both countries throughout their earlier industrialization period (1870–1940). The simple Lewis model must be supplemented by demand factors. In both Italy and Japan, high growth during the 1950s and 1960s was basically led by domestic demand. And in this process investment played a central role (Table 3.2). The question then is what brought about such high investment. In what follows, we will focus on internal population flows, accompanying household formation and residential construction and on the diffusion of consumer durables.

Table 3.2   The role of investment in the high growth period (percentages)

	Italy[a]	Japan[b]
Shares in GDP at current prices		
Total fixed investment	21.7	28.4
Residential construction	6.5	4.7
Other construction	6.2	—
	—	23.7
Machinery and equipment	9.1	—
Contributions to real GDP growth		
Total fixed investment	35.4	43.8
Residential construction	16.6	7.7
Other construction	10.6	—
	—	36.1
Machinery and equipment	8.2	—

a.1951–69.
b.1952–69.
Sources: Prometeia, 'Data Bank'; OECD, *National Accounts of OECD Countries, 1950–1968* and *1953–1969.*

2.1 Japan

To understand the high economic growth of the 1950s and 1960s, we must first of all recognize that during this period Japan was a two-sector economy consisting of a backward rural agricultural sector and a more advanced urban manufacturing one. In 1950, 48 per cent of the total labour force was still engaged in agriculture, a figure comparable to that of many developing Asian nations today and the highest among the advanced economies of the time. As mentioned in the introduction to this chapter, labour's marginal product in agriculture was substantially lower than that in manufacturing.

The two decades saw a continuous flow of workers out of farming and into the urban industrial and service sectors. The economy's dual structure enabled manufacturing firms to hire labour at a real wage level which was determined by the agricultural sector with its 'disguised' unemployment and was, therefore, lower than the marginal product in industry. The rapid employment and output growth of manufacturing thus entailed high profits rather than increases in the share of wages in national income. High profits, in turn, must have had a favourable impact on investment. This is, of course, exactly the process that Lewis (1954) describes as being typical of growth in an underdeveloped dual economy.

The Lewis model has been successfully applied to Japan's century-long development by a number of economists (see, for example, Minami, 1973; Ohkawa and Rosovsky, 1973). In the Lewis model, inter-sectoral population flows result entirely from the growth of the modern manufacturing sector and this seems also to have been the case in Japan. Thus, Umemura (1961), Ono (1972) and Minami (1973) demonstrate that internal migration was quite sensitive to the growth of manufacturing – more people left the countryside for the cities in times of boom and vice versa. Yearly fluctuations in migration were therefore a consequence of similar fluctuations in industrial growth. But while in the Lewis model the key factor behind this industrial growth is labour's low real wage, made possible by the existence of 'disguised' unemployment in agriculture, we argue in what follows that in the Japan of the high growth years, it was migration itself that was the crucial force generating strong demand for industrial products and hence stimulating the latters' expansion. In our view, population flows were a *cause* as well as a result of economic growth.

Because of large-scale migration into the main urban areas (Figure 3.1), household formation accelerated dramatically during the 1955–70 years (Figure 3.2), even though the population's growth rate remained quite stable – at about one per cent per year. As a result, over the two decades beginning in 1955, the country's population increased by only 20 per cent

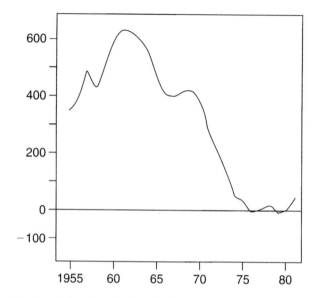

Figure 3.1 Population flows in Japan[a] (thousands)
a. Inflows into, and outflows from, the Tokyo, Osaka and Nagoya metropolitan areas.
Source: Statistical Bureau, Management and Co-ordination Agency, *Annual Report on Internal Migration* (various issues).

(from 90 to 110 million), while the number of households increased by as much as 80 per cent. As one might expect, the number of traditional three-generation merged households hardly increased at all. By contrast, the number of 'core' households (consisting of married couples, possibly with unmarried children, and of unmarried singles) increased dramatically, particularly in urban industrial areas.

When three generations of family members lived in a traditional single household in the countryside, they would have needed only one refrigerator, television set, washing machine or car. But, as young people gave up agriculture and moved from the villages to the cities, they formed new households. This process inevitably generated additional demand for housing, consumer durables and electricity. In this way, the population flow sustained high domestic demand.

Along with the creation of a large number of households, the period was also characterized by the rapid diffusion of new durables. The process was greatly facilitated by the steady price declines of the goods in question and by the buoyant increases in real income. Electric washing machines, for example, first appeared on the Japanese market

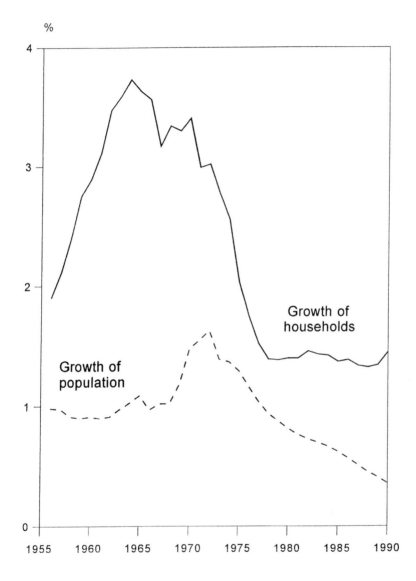

Figure 3.2 Household formation in Japan (percentage changes; three-year moving averages)
Note: the underlying figure for 1970 is affected by the return of Okinawa prefecture to Japan.
Sources: Statistical Bureau, Management and Co-ordination Agency, *Monthly Estimates of Population* and *Annual Report on Households* (various issues).

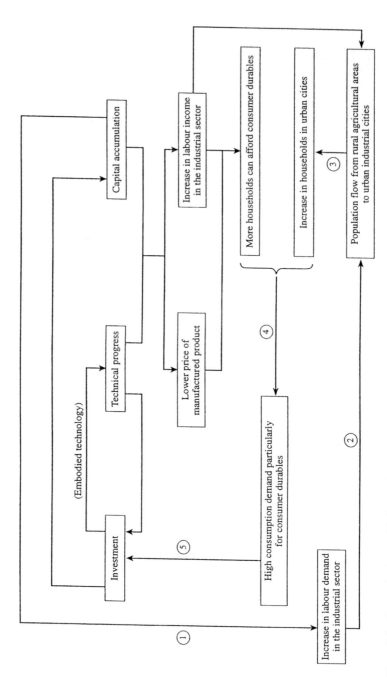

Figure 3.3 Domestic demand-led growth

in 1949. At that time, a machine cost 54 000 yen, while the average annual income was about 50 000 yen. Understandably, only twenty machines were sold each month! However, by 1955, barely six years later, the machines' price had been reduced to 20 000 yen while average annual income had risen above 200 000 yen. Already by this time, more than a third of Japanese households owned a washing machine. The same story holds for other consumer durables. This process, however, could not continue for ever. By the end of the 1960s, household formation was beginning to slow down and the diffusion of most of the then available durables had reached saturation levels.

This process of domestic demand-led high economic growth is schematically summarized in Figure 3.3. Channels 1 and 2 in the diagram are well-known – capital accumulation in the industrial sector, by raising the demand for labour, brings about a population flow from the countryside to the cities. In addition to this well-recognized channel, we emphasize the neglected and yet very important fact that such population flows in turn, by creating new households and raising the demand for consumer durables, ultimately sustained the profitability of manufacturing investment (channels 3, 4 and 5). It must also be remembered that the role of the newly available durables was not confined to their direct demand impact. They greatly expanded the demand for electricity and, through the input-output interrelationships, they raised the demand for intermediate goods such as steel, thereby also stimulating investment in these sectors.

In this virtuous circle of high economic growth, the role of low real wages was much less important than it is in the Lewis model. The profitability of investment was sustained not by low wages but by rapid domestic demand growth. The latter, in turn, grew thanks to the steady rise in real wages which provided the demand for durables, whose production would otherwise have been unable to expand given the insufficient level of international competitiveness at the time. In the prewar period real wages saw little increase and growth in the economy was typically export-led (Shinohara, 1962; Yoshikawa and Shioji, 1990), with low real wages instrumental in achieving international competitiveness, especially in the key cotton industry. Since the war, however, real wages rose rapidly (Table 3.3).

The relationship between household formation and economic growth is well known. The so-called building cycle has a long tradition (see, for example, Hickman, 1974). In that cycle, the link between growth in the number of households and growth in the economy is provided by residential construction. In contrast, we have argued that in postwar Japan,

Table 3.3   Real wage developments in the high growth period (average annual percentage changes)

	Italy[a]	Japan[b]
Growth of real employee compensation per employee[c]	4.6	6.2
Growth of GDP per worker	5.6	7.3

a. 1951–69.
b. 1952–69.
c. Deflated by the consumer expenditure deflator.
Sources: OECD, *National Accounts of OECD Countries, 1950–1968* and *1953–1969*, and *Labour Force Statistics* (various issues).

it was business fixed investment rather than house building that played a crucial role. In the period 1955–70, residential construction's share in total investment was only 17 per cent and its growth rate, at some 15 per cent per annum, while rapid in absolute terms, was eclipsed by that of machinery and equipment. Household formation ultimately sustained the manufacturing sector's high investment rates through its impact on the diffusion of durables rather than through its stimulus to house building. Clearly, the mechanism was one of domestic demand-led growth.[3]

2.2   Italy

The structure of the Italian economy in the early 1950s was also Lewisian, with 45 per cent of the labour force still in agriculture. And the story told for Japan basically applies to Italy as well. The high growth of the 1950s and 1960s was led by domestic demand, with supply forces playing merely a permissive role. Above all, it was led by a spectacular rise in investment whose (constant price) share in GDP rose from 18 per cent in the early 1950s, to close to 30 per cent in the late 1960s.

The driving force behind such high investment was, as in Japan, the flow of population from agricultural employment in rural areas to industrial employment in the cities (in addition to internal population flows, many Italians also emigrated abroad). As a result, the share of the agricultural workforce fell continuously – from 45 per cent in 1951 down to not much more than 6 per cent today. About five million people had left the countryside by 1970, many of whom moved from the Southern half of the country to the Centre-North region. It is difficult to accurately estimate the size of this internal population flow, but two and a half million for the 1950s and 1960s would seem to be a conservative estimate – a figure equivalent to nearly 14 per cent of the South's population in, for instance, 1960 (Figure 3.4). Parallel to such population flows, the number

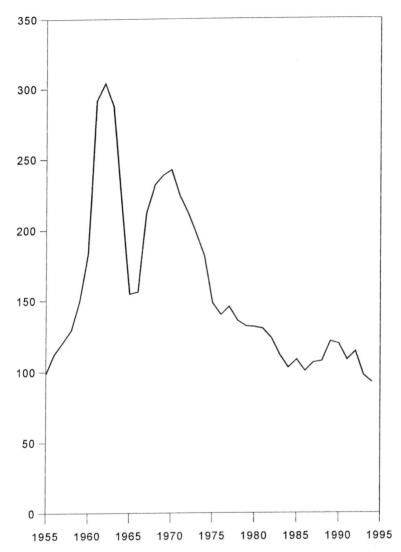

Figure 3.4 South–North migration in Italy (gross flows in thousands)
Sources: ISTAT, *Annuario statistico italiano*; Eurostat, *Regions* (various issues).

of new families also grew, if perhaps not as rapidly as in Japan. The rate of marriages at 6.9 per 1000 inhabitants in 1951, increased to 7.9 in 1961 and then levelled off at 7.5 in 1971 (it has since declined to less than 5 per cent today).[4]

Household formation led naturally to residential construction whose growth was very high throughout the period. This is in contrast to Japan, where it was business investment that led the economy's expansion (Table 3.2). The (volume) share of housing investment in GDP over the two decades rose from some 5 to nearly 12 per cent, a value above that recorded at the time by investment in machinery and equipment. In this sense, perhaps, the building cycle story applies more straightforwardly to high growth in Italy than it does to Japan.

Population flows, household formation and a rise in residential construction were, of course, not the whole story of this period. Thus, non-residential construction was also very buoyant, thanks in part to large infrastructural projects carried out by the public sector. Investment in machinery and equipment, on the other hand, though growing rapidly, maintained a fairly stable share of GDP throughout the 1950s and 1960s. The reasons for the surge in investment differ somewhat between Italy and Japan. An important component in Italy's case was an early 'burst' of entrepreneurship (Fuà, 1965), with increased optimism emerging already at the end of the 1940s (still a period of gloom in Japan) thanks to both external and internal events. On the external side, of great importance was America's economic policy and, in particular, its commitment to Western Europe's development via the Marshall Plan, adopted, at least in part, so as to counter the communist menace. A second crucial factor was the re-establishment of multilateral exchanges within Europe. And, thirdly, the Korean War raised demand everywhere (including, of course, also in Japan).

The internal economic environment was also favourable. The communist party pursued a moderate policy aimed at promoting economic development since, in its perception, it was only in this way that the 'contradictions of capitalism' would emerge. The trade union movement was split and generally weak. Furthermore, some entrepreneurs such as Valletta (general manager of Fiat) were very optimistic about future developments. They saw a niche for Italian products in the world market. Finally, around 1949, the leading Christian Democratic Party shifted its policy emphasis away from a purely 'liberal' towards a more 'social' approach, with greater emphasis put on growth, employment and the satisfaction of basic needs. Indeed, the government pursued a number of interventionist policies. IRI (a state-owned holding company and a legacy of the fascist period) was not dismantled but rather empowered. The same was true for the national oil company which was created in 1953. An agency for the promotion of the South (the *Cassa per il Mezzogiorno*) was established and massive public investment projects were carried out in the electricity, steel, telephone and other basic sectors (Ciocca et al., 1975). These mitigated bottlenecks that would otherwise have choked off growth in this period.

In contrast to Japan, consumption was not a major dynamic force. Its share in GDP fell continuously through the period (the share of durable consumption, on the other hand, rose quite strongly, providing some parallel with Japan). The major reasons for overall sluggishness were a very low growth of employment and modestly growing real wages (Table 3.3). This suggests that Italy's development comes somewhat closer than Japan's to that predicted by the standard Lewis model.

Following external liberalization, exports grew faster than GDP. As a result, their (volume) share in output rose from $4\frac{1}{2}$ per cent in 1951–52 to 15 per cent in 1968–69 (and to 22 per cent by 1989–90). However, exports were not really the driving force behind high growth in these years. True, they grew faster than any other component of aggregate demand but their GDP share still remained relatively small. In addition, net exports were consistently negative for the whole postwar period, with the exceptions of 1978 and the years since 1993. Exports, however, played an important indirect role by stimulating business investment, particularly after the European Common Market was established in 1957 (Campa, 1967). For a few years, between 1958 and 1963, a virtuous circle, the so-called 'economic miracle', set in as exports and investment reinforced each other.

Identifying the end of the high growth period for Italy has been a matter of some controversy. Some economists have chosen the year 1963. However, we follow Vaciago (1970) and put the end of high growth at the turn of the 1960s. Those who take 1963 as the watershed stress the exhaustion of surplus labour at that time. This is not altogether convincing. There were still as many as 100 000 emigrants to other European countries and 200 000 net migrants from the South to the Centre-North in 1963. In fact, it is only by the end of the 1960s that migration slows down and so, partly as a consequence, does the economy as a whole. In addition, fiscal and monetary policies became more restrictive,[5] the GDP share of investment fell sharply, and exports and domestic demand became substitutes rather than complements. All this brought the 'economic miracle' to an end. The twilight of this period can be symbolically associated with the 'Hot Autumn' of 1969 which saw the outbreak of unprecedentedly acute labour disputes across the country. These, in turn, led to a wage explosion and high inflation and paved the way for many of the difficulties that Italy was to face in the subsequent decade.

3   The oil shocks and after: the 1970s and the 1980s

The beginning of the 1970s marked the end of the high growth era for both Italy and Japan. The decade is remembered as a turbulent period when the world economy left the Bretton Woods system for a flexible exchange rates regime, and also experienced two major oil shocks. Like other OECD economies, Italy and Japan were strongly affected by these events. However, the end of high growth was caused by changes in internal factors rather than by exogenous events such as the oil shocks. Unlike the earlier period, when Italian and Japanese developments shared a number of similar features, over these two decades the two countries' experiences were very diverse.

3.1   Japan

The scope for domestic demand-led growth narrowed drastically at the turn of the 1960s. By then, the pool of 'disguised' unemployment in the agricultural sector had been largely exhausted. As a consequence, the population flow from the rural sector and the associated growth in urban households decelerated sharply. At the same time, near-saturation levels were reached for the then available consumer durables. All this brought to an end the domestic demand-led virtuous circle for high growth. Judging from Figures 3.1 and 3.2, we note that this structural change occurred around 1970, a few years in advance of the oil embargo of 1973, and this timing is confirmed by a more formal econometric analysis.[6] The first oil shock, in other words, hit an economy which had already experienced a major structural change making for lower growth.

In contrast, the popular view, associated with such authors as Bruno and Sachs (1985) and Jorgenson (1988), attributes the growth deceleration of the 1970s directly to the 1973 oil shock. This interpretation cannot explain, however, why the second oil shock of 1979 did not bring about a similar fall in the rate of growth – the average growth rates for the periods 1972–80 and 1980–90 are virtually identical (4.1 and 4.2 per cent, respectively). It is true that the oil price quadrupled in 1973–74 while it only doubled six years later, but the real transfers to the Organization of Petroleum Exporting Countries (OPEC) imposed by the terms of trade worsening were very similar in the two episodes (3.8 and 4.1 per cent of GDP respectively). In other words, it is difficult to see how the first oil crisis should have generated a sharp growth shortfall (for analytical details, see Yoshikawa, 1995, Chapter 4). In this respect, we concur with Maddison (1987) who, through careful growth accounting, finds that Japan's GDP growth rate in the period 1973–84 would have been

3.8 rather than the recorded 3.6 per cent 'if it had been possible to maintain the relation between energy growth and GDP growth in the previous period' (Maddison, 1987, p. 672 and Table 15b). In his view, the effect of the oil shocks on growth is plainly minor.

This is not to argue, however, that the oil crisis did not affect the economy's supply side. Importantly, the two oil shocks provided a strong stimulus to the machinery industry which, by the end of the 1970s, had become the economy's leading sector. There were two major reasons for this – one related to domestic price and exchange rate developments, the other to income trends abroad. At home, the cost increase which followed the rise in oil prices was slight in comparison to that faced by other industries such as chemicals, paper or metals, given machinery's much lower dependence on energy. In addition, the machinery sector gained price competitiveness internationally since the yen depreciated by some 10 per cent as a result of Japan's sharp terms of trade deterioration. The gain was particularly marked vis-à-vis Japan's major competitor in this sector – the United States. During the period 1972–76, the wholesale price index of machinery increased by some 25 per cent in Japan as against a 40 per cent increase in the United States. Given the yen's depreciation over the same period, the industry's price competitiveness improved by as much as 25 per cent.

Abroad, the oil price increase led to a huge transfer of money from the oil importing countries to OPEC (about $16 billion in the case of Japan, a figure equivalent to nearly 30 per cent of the country's exports at the time). While some of this money was directly spent by OPEC, a large share was eventually lent on to developing countries, many of which needed to import machinery in order to sustain domestic investment. Hence, and despite the generally depressed state of the world economy, machinery was one of the few products that enjoyed exceptionally high demand. Helped by its competitiveness, Japan's machinery industry emerged as a chief supplier to meet this worldwide demand. The beginning of the 'Japan problem', which has bedevilled US–Japanese economic relations in the 1980s and 1990s, can be found in these developments!

Exports now became a major force generating growth. For example, while the percentage contribution of net exports to GDP growth was –0.8 per cent for the period 1963–73, this figure climbed to an astonishing 35 per cent in the period 1979–84. Similarly, the simple correlation between quarterly growth rates in industrial production and in exports is –0.41 for the period going from 1960 to 1971, but it is 0.56 for the years 1972–1985. The change in the sign of the correlation coefficient is consistent with the view that in the 1960s changes in output were *not* export-led; rather, exports were a 'vent for surplus production' (Boltho, 1996). In contrast, exports led growth in the 1970s and early 1980s.

3.2   Italy

As in Japan, the scope for shifting labour from agriculture to industry, and from the South to the North, had narrowed drastically at the turn of the 1960s. In addition, growth prospects in the early 1970s, well before the outbreak of the oil shock, were also limited by the rigidities that the 'Hot Autumn' had imposed on the flexible use of the workforce. Notwithstanding this, Italian growth decelerated less than did Japan's in the 1970s. But while Japan managed to expand relatively steadily, if much more slowly, through the two decades, Italy's experience was more varied. After recording growth still close to 4 per cent per annum between 1970 and 1980, the country saw a near halving in this rate to little above 2 per cent in the subsequent decade.

The 1970s were marked by the oil shocks and the policies aimed at containing them. As elsewhere, the policy-makers were faced with two conflicting objectives – either the control of inflation or the promotion of growth and employment. Fiscal policy was ready to sacrifice the inflation goal and policies were relatively expansionary in the later 1970s (as was also the case in Japan). Yet, the shrewd action of the Bank of Italy allowed a partial resolution to the dilemma. In the second half of the 1970s, the lira was allowed to depreciate against the deutschmark while remaining stable (or even appreciating slightly) against the US dollar. This enabled Italy to pay less for most of its commodity imports, thereby restraining inflation, while at the same time improving competitiveness boosted exports. The result, not unlike Japan, was a short spell of export-led growth. This policy could not be repeated after the second oil shock, however, since Italy had departed from the floating regime and entered the EMS.

How is one to evaluate the performance of the economy in the decade? Given the constraints (very difficult labour relations, an energy dependence as great as that of Japan, and a much greater dependence on now sluggish foreign demand), overall growth held up very well. And economic policy was undoubtedly successful in offsetting the deflationary effects of the oil crisis. But this success had some in-built costs that heavily affected the economy's subsequent evolution. The two most significant ones were the emergence of high inflationary expectations and the relentless rise in the public sector deficit (by 1978 this had reached 12.4 per cent of GDP).

In the 1980s Italy's economic performance was poor. Though the recession that followed the second oil shock was milder than that of 1974–75,[7] the economy remained depressed thereafter. The average growth rate throughout the 1980s was the lowest of the entire postwar period, with both exports and investments particularly subdued. Monetary and exchange rate policies were largely responsible for this. Thus, EMS membership and dollar appreciation led to a U-turn in Italy's exchange rate movements. In contrast to earlier developments, the lira now depreciated against the dollar while appreciating in real terms against the deutschmark (since the realignments that took place inside the EMS were not sufficient to eliminate continuing inflation differentials). As Italian sales to Western Europe are highly price-elastic, appreciation depressed exports and this effect was reinforced by the enlargement of the European Community to lower-cost countries, such as Greece, Portugal and Spain. At the same time, the monetary authorities were compelled to keep interest rates high to attract foreign capital to finance the trade deficits. High interest rates, in turn, depressed investment and worsened the public deficit.

Those who favoured joining the EMS in 1979 had argued that Italy needed to anchor her currency to the deutschmark – such a commitment would stop firms from relying on devaluation, and would force them to become more competitive. Ostensibly, the policy was successful since industrial firms fired 14 per cent of their labour force in the 1980s though their value-added share in GDP fell by only 1 per cent. Capital deepening progressed in manufacturing, but components of investment declined continuously so that total investment grew at about the same pace as income.

The only dynamic demand component of the period was consumption. This was thanks to rising employment and wages in the tertiary sector. Inflation, however, remained very high throughout the decade, much above that of competitor countries, despite the continuous weakening of the trade unions. It was not until the dramatic devaluation of 1992 and the subsequent highly restrictive fiscal policies that inflation finally started declining to something comparable to the levels found in other European countries.

As this brief description shows, Italy's economic performance during the 1980s was very much affected by policy, and policy was, in turn, almost completely conditioned by external factors – in particular the commitment to Europe, first as a member of the EMS, then as a participant in the 1992 Single Market Project, and finally as a prospective member of EMU.

4   Conclusions

The Italian and Japanese postwar experiences provide some insights into what causes economic growth. First, the high rates of growth in the 1950s and 1960s are best understood through an application of the Lewis model. Abundant labour supply in agriculture was an essential element in the process. The Lewis model, however, fails to explain the particular growth upsurge in those two decades, because excess labour had been present throughout history. To understand this upsurge, demand factors must also be considered. In the 1950s and 1960s, high demand growth was sustained by large population flows and a rapid process of household formation. Clearly, such a 'super-growth' mechanism cannot be repeated. Like Rostow's 'take-off' (1960), it can only be experienced once in the history of each economy.

Second, as Solow (1997) points out, underemployment makes demand-driven growth possible. In the 1950s and 1960s underemployment was widespread in agriculture. In the 1970s and 1980s such abundant labour supplies had dwindled, yet underemployment was still present, be this for cyclical or structural reasons (as argued more fully below). Hence, demand-led growth was still possible. And, indeed, in both Italy and Japan, exports played an essential role in growth during selected periods in these two decades.

Understanding growth depends, of course, on theory. We maintain that the 'full employment of all production factors' assumption is a poor characterization of the economy even in the long run. Underemployment, in the sense that value marginal products differ substantially across sectors, is almost always present. Lewisian underemployment in agriculture is

Table 3.4   Average labour productivity in selected sectors[a] (manufacturing labour productivity = 100)

	Italy[b]			Japan		
	1970–71	1980–81	1990–91	1970–71	1980–81	1990–91
Agriculture	40.5	40.8	34.5	21.6	23.4	24.7
Construction	88.2	89.7	82.9	72.9	78.0	89.8
Distribution[c]	126.7	99.5	89.2	76.2	69.7	68.6
Transportation[d]	107.4	88.0	90.0	85.3	90.9	103.9

a. Value added in current prices, divided by total employment.
b. Manufacturing includes the (very small) mining sector.
c. Wholesale and retail trade.
d. Including communications.
Sources: OECD, *National Accounts of OECD Countries* (various issues).

perhaps historically the most significant form of such underemployment, but it is not the only one. In fact, technical progress is likely to create Lewisian 'backward sectors' repeatedly, unless productivity growth lowers prices in the growing sectors to an extent sufficient to preserve the equality of value marginal products across the whole economy. Table 3.4 suggests that this is highly unlikely, at least in the cases of Italy and Japan. On the basis of a proxy for various sectors' marginal productivities of labour,[8] we observe persistent sectoral differences as late as the early 1990s. These can hardly be regarded as resulting from random 'sectoral shocks'. Rather, they suggest that differences in the pace of technical progress produce underemployment or, at the very least, the potential for continuing inter-sectoral migration. This underemployment is on a much smaller scale than Lewisian underemployment in agriculture. Still, its existence makes growth dependent on demand. And demand is indeed an essential ingredient to an understanding of what caused the postwar growth of both Italy and Japan.

Notes

1. See Grossman and Helpman (1991) and Aghion and Howitt (1998).
2. The Japanese economy was in great difficulty in 1950 (for example, Toyota was on the verge of bankruptcy at that time). The Korean War almost certainly saved Japan from a deep crisis. See Yoshikawa and Okazaki (1993) for an overview of this turbulent period.
3. We can explain this mechanism in an explicit growth model with endogenous investment; the interested reader is referred to Yoshikawa (1995, ch. 10).
4. It should be noted, however, that the number of marriages had become a poor proxy for family formation by the late 1970s because of the increasing incidence of divorce and of unmarried households.
5. This applies particularly to the investment of state-owned firms, as noted by Sylos Labini (1974).
6. The approach involved the search for a turning point in GDP via the estimation of a regression with a piecewise linear trend. Rolling the turning point from 1969 Q.3 to 1974 Q.2, it was found that the minimum standard error is attained in 1971 Q.4; see Iwamoto and Kobayashi (1992).
7. The story is, of course, different if one looks at inflation. This was above 20 per cent in 1980 and remained at a two-digit level until 1984.
8. The proxy used is labour's average productivity. This is perfectly adequate if the production function is of a Cobb-Douglas form since then average productivity is proportional to marginal productivity. Assume a production function of the form:

$$Y = AK^{\alpha}L^{1-\alpha}$$

The marginal product of labour (dY/dL) is then equal to:

$$dY/dL = (1 - \alpha)AK^{\alpha}L^{-\alpha} = (1 - \alpha)Y/L.$$

In other words, the marginal product of labour is equal to the average product times $(1 - \alpha)$. Therefore, even if α differs across sectors, as one would expect, changes in marginal productivity will be equal to changes in average productivity as long as α is stable in each sector.

References

Aghion, P. and P.W. Howitt (1988) *Endogenous Growth Theory*, Cambridge, MA: MIT Press.

Barro, R. (1997) *Determinants of Economic Growth: a Cross-country Empirical Study*, Cambridge, MA: MIT Press.

Boltho, A. (1982) 'Growth', in A. Boltho (ed.), *The European Economy: Growth and Crisis*, Oxford: Oxford University Press.

Boltho, A. (1996) 'Was Japanese Growth Export-led?', *Oxford Economic Papers*, 48, 3, 415–32.

Bruno, M. and J.D. Sachs (1985) *Economics of Worldwide Stagflation*, Cambridge, MA: Harvard University Press.

Campa, G. (1967) 'Progresso tecnico ed esportazioni nello sviluppo economico italiano', Economia internazionale, 20, 2, 297–333.

Ciocca, P.-L., R. Filosa, and G.M. Rey (1975) 'Integration and Development of the Italian Economy', *Banca Nazionale del Lavoro Quarterly Review*, 28, 114, 284–320.

Fuà, G. (1965) *Notes on Italian Economic Growth, 1861–1964*, Milan: Giuffrè.

Grossman, G.M. and E. Helpman (1991) *Innovation and Growth in the Global Economy*, Cambridge, MA: MIT Press.

Hickman, B.G. (1974) 'What Became of the Building Cycle?', in P.A. David and M.W. Reder (eds), *Nations and Households in Economic Growth*, New York, NY: Academic Press.

Iwamoto, Y. and H. Kobayashi (1992) 'Testing for a Unit Root in Japanese GNP', *Japan and the World Economy*, 4, 1, 17–37.

Jorgenson, D.W. (1988) 'Productivity and Economic Growth in Japan and the United States', *American Economic Review*, 78, 2, 217–22.

Kindleberger, C.P. (1967) *Europe's Postwar Growth: the Role of Labor Supply*, Cambridge, MA: Harvard University Press.

Lewis, W.A. (1954) 'Economic Development with Unlimited Supplies of Labour', Manchester School of Economic and Social Studies, 22, 5, 139–91.

Lincoln, E.J. (1988) *Japan: Facing Economic Maturity*, Washington, DC: Brookings Institution.

Maddison, A. (1987) 'Growth and Slowdown in Advanced Capitalist Economies: Techniques of Quantitative Assessment', *Journal of Economic Literature*, 25, 2, 649–98.

Maddison, A. (1995) *Monitoring the World Economy, 1820–1992*, Paris: OECD.

Mankiw, N.G., D. Romer and D.N. Weil (1992) 'A Contribution to the Empirics of Economic Growth', *Quarterly Journal of Economics*, 107, 2, 407–37.

Minami, R. (1973) *The Turning Point in Economic Development: Japan's Experience*, Tokyo: Kinokuniya.

Ohkawa, K. (1975) 'Kajo Shugyo Sairon' ('Underemployment Revisited'), in K. Ohkawa and R. Minami (eds), *Kindai Nihonno Keizai Hatten* (*Economic Development of Modern Japan*), Tokyo: Toyokeizai.

Ohkawa, K. and H. Rosovsky (1973) *Japanese Economic Growth: Trend Acceleration in the Twentieth Century*, Stanford, CA: Stanford University Press.

Ono, A. (1972) 'Senzen Sengono Rodo Ido' ('Labour Mobility in Pre-war and Post-war Japan'), *Gendai Keizai (Contemporary Economics)*, 7, 140–55.

Rostow, W.W. (1960) *The Stages of Economic Growth*, Cambridge: Cambridge University Press.

Shinohara, M. (1962) *Growth and Cycles in the Japanese Economy*, Tokyo: Kinokuniya.

Solow, R.M. (1956) 'A Contribution to the Theory of Economic Growth', *Quarterly Journal of Economics*, 70, 1, 65–94.

Solow, R.M. (1997) 'Is there a Core of Usable Macroeconomics that We Should All Believe in?', *American Economic Review*, 87, 2, 230–2.

Sylos Labini, P. (1974) *Trade Unions, Inflation, and Productivity*, Lexington, MA: Lexington Books.

Umemura, M. (1961) *Chingin, Kogyo to Nogyo (Wages, Employment and Agriculture)*, Tokyo: Taimeido.

Vaciago, G. (1970) 'Alternative Theories of Economic Growth and the Italian Case', *Banca Nazionale del Lavoro Quarterly Review*, 23, 93, 180–211.

Yoshikawa, H. (1995) *Macroeconomics and the Japanese Economy*, Oxford: Oxford University Press.

Yoshikawa, H. and T. Okazaki (1993) 'Postwar Hyper-inflation and the Dodge Plan, 1945–50: An Overview' in J. Teranishi and Y. Kosai (eds), *The Japanese Experience of Economic Reforms*, London: Macmillan.

Yoshikawa, H. and E. Shioji (1990) 'Senzen Nihon Keizaino Makurobunseki' ('A Macroeconomic Analysis of the Pre-war Japanese Economy'), in H. Yoshikawa and T. Okazaki (eds), *Keizai Rironeno Rekshiteki Paasupekuchibu (Economic Theory in Historical Perspective)*, Tokyo: University of Tokyo Press.

4
Italy's Financial System: Banks and Industrial Investment

Marcello de Cecco and Giovanni Ferri

1 Introduction

Unlike the situation in most industrialized countries, banks and other financial institutions have traditionally played only a minor role in the corporate governance of Italian firms in the postwar period (for more detail see de Cecco and Ferri, 1996) For all practical purposes, Italy has not had proper merchant banks. There have only been two partial exceptions to this. For the financing and corporate governance of major firms, an important role was played by Mediobanca – the biggest private special credit institution, which specialized in marshalling control by families and coalitions at large private corporations. For the financing and corporate governance of small and medium-sized enterprises (SMEs), an active role was played by local banks and by the so-called *commercialisti* – a business professional peculiar to Italy, only partially translatable by the English words 'accountant' or 'individual business consultant'. These *commercialisti* were often closely acquainted with the firm's fortunes, offered tax advice and acted as a liaison between the enterprise and financial intermediaries.

The inherent weakness of such a system of corporate governance did not jeopardize Italy's growth potential in the first two decades after the Second World War. Thereafter, however, the organization of production in large firms began to suffer because of the absence of the corporate governance that merchant banks normally provide. That growth was still able to remain relatively high in the 1970s and 1980s was thanks to the expansion of innovative and export-oriented manufacturing SMEs, mostly located in the North-Eastern and Central regions of the country, away from the North-Western area of initial industrialization at the turn of the century.

Section 2 of this chapter looks at the changing industrial and financial landscape of Italy, concentrating in particular on two features – the switch from a growth model led by large companies to one dominated by SMEs, and the historical origins of the present-day corporate governance system. Section 3 then considers the institutions that have been most active in the financing of large-scale firms, while Section 4 shifts the attention to SMEs and to the two most important actors in the provision of advice and finance in that area – the *commercialisti* on the one hand, local banks on the other. A brief concluding section summarizes the main arguments.

2 Changing patterns in industrial and financial structure

2.1 A 'downsized and downsizing' industrial structure

The long period of rapid growth experienced by the Italian economy after the Second World War shows a major break around 1970. Until that point, growth had been mainly led by large-sized manufacturing firms, mostly located in the so-called 'industrial triangle' centred on Turin, Genoa and Milan, and specializing in heavy and/or technology-oriented production. Since then, Italy has experienced major changes in the nature and in the regional distribution of its industrial activities. These followed a number of events – the oil price shocks of the 1970s, the floating of the currency and the emergence of significant rigidities in the unionized labour market. The development of a dense network of light manufacturing SMEs, gaining and holding niches in the international market for high-quality consumer goods, was the most noticeable signal of the change (Goodman and Bamford, 1989; Pyke et al., 1990).

That a major break occurred is shown by the changing composition of Italian exports. From the earlier concentration on heavy and/or technology-oriented goods these shifted towards more traditional light industrial production (see, among others, Gros-Pietro and Sembenelli, 1993, and, for early detection, de Cecco, 1971 and Bank of Italy, 1979). The break is also apparent in the shrinking average size of firms. The 1961 Census assigns 46 per cent of the total labour force to establishments with 50 or more employees and 25 per cent to those with 500 or more employees; 20 years later these shares had dropped to 37 and 19 per cent respectively. In the manufacturing sector the rate of downsizing was even greater (Table 4.1). An important question in this context is whether the trend towards small firms is an Italian peculiarity or whether this phenomenon is also observable in other major economies. We address this question by following two different approaches.

Table 4.1   Manufacturing employment by establishment size class (percentage shares)

	1951	1961	1971	1981	1991
Number of employees:					
< 50	46.4	46.9	42.0	48.9	57.8
> 50	53.6	53.1	58.0	51.1	41.2
of which:					
> 500	25.1	21.5	24.0	19.7	13.0

Source: ISTAT, *Censimento industriale* (various years).

First, we look at how large Italian firms rank among the world's largest non-financial corporations. Such a comparison, drawing on the rankings regularly published by *Fortune* magazine and reported in Table 4.2, shows that Italian companies are currently underrepresented with respect to their position in the mid-1960s. Between 1966 and 1998, for instance, while the share of Italy's GDP in the total output of the G7 countries rose, the presence of Italian firms among the (non-US) world's 200 largest non-financial companies declined both in number and, especially, in share of sales/revenues.[1] This trend can also be observed for the United Kingdom, but not for Japan nor for France and Germany. By and large, we can therefore confirm that the trend is peculiar to the Italian economy.

Table 4.2   Italy's share in G7 GDP and in non-US 200 world's largest non-financial corporations

	1966	1998
	Share in GDP of G7 countries	
Italy	5.3	7.9
Japan	7.8	25.3
France	7.9	9.6
Germany	10.1	14.3
United Kingdom	7.9	9.1

	Share in non-US world's largest non-financial corporations			
	Number	*Share of total sales*	*Number*	*Share of total revenues*
Italy	7	5.3	6	3.3
Japan	38	14.6	66	39.0
France	23	10.8	29	12.3
Germany	26	16.7	27	17.4
United Kingdom	58	33.8	23	10.5

Sources: Authors' calculations based on OECD, *National Accounts of OECD Countries* (various issues) and *Fortune* magazine data.

Table 4.3 Industrial employment by firm size class in selected countries, early 1990s (percentage shares)

	Italy (1991)	France (1992)	Germany (1992)	United Kingdom (1993)	United States (1991)	Japan (1991)
Number of employees:						
< 250	71.4	47.0	37.5[a]	44.5	36.6[b]	74.1[c]
of which:						
< 50	52.5	25.8	21.7	22.8	—	—
> 250	28.6	53.0	62.5	55.5	63.4	25.9

Note: The small firm threshold is not the same across all countries
a. Less than 200 employees.
b. Less than 500 employees.
c. Less than 300 employees.
Source: Eurostat, *Enterprises in Europe, Fourth Report*, Brussels, 1996.

The second approach draws on additional and more detailed comparisons between the distribution by size of firms in Italy, France and Germany. According to Cannari et al. (1993), in the 1980s there were only 128 companies with 500 or more employees in Italy, as against 345 in France and 336 in Germany. Furthermore, the shares of employees in firms with fewer than 10 and more than 500 employees were 42.8 and 18.5 per cent respectively in Italy, as opposed to 24.8 and 34.3 per cent in Germany. The comparison can be extended to the early 1990s by using the data published by Eurostat and reported in Table 4.3. Although firm size classes are not fully comparable across countries, Italy and Japan stand out as economies relying very heavily on smaller-sized establishments. In Japan, however, this goes hand in hand with a considerable presence among the world's largest firms, something that is hardly the case in Italy.

The existence of widespread intra-group links, more prevalent in Italy than elsewhere, modifies but does not overturn the overall conclusion. Thus, an adjustment for this factor – following Barca et al. (1994) – increases the share of employees in large firms by approximately 10 percentage points while decreasing that of small firms by 5 percentage points. Thus, the conclusion that the industrial structure in Italy is visibly downsized vis-à-vis that of other major economies seems to be based on relatively firm ground and appears to be due primarily to the limited individual growth of Italian firms.

This 'shrinking' of the industrial structure reflected a number of features. It is well known, for instance, that, as in other countries, downsizing in manufacturing, particularly during the 1970s, went hand in hand with decentralization in production as well as with the outsourcing of services previously produced in-house. It is also well known that downsizing in Italy was fostered by the rapid growth of SMEs, particularly in the so-called 'industrial districts' in the North-Eastern and Central regions of the country. Growing rigidities in the labour market facing large-scale firms and tax avoidance also contributed to the phenomenon.

It is our contention, however, that in addition to such forces, the changes that took place must be linked with parallel trends in the country's financial structure. Old approaches (Gerschenkron, 1962; Cameron, 1972) and new theories (Pagano, 1993) lead us to believe that economic growth requires a financial system able to support the growth of single firms. Accordingly, a crucial factor accounting for the relative lack of large corporations in Italy might be the insufficient supply of those sources of finance that are particularly conducive to growth. It is precisely in this context that the role performed by merchant banks becomes paramount in building the complex arrangements needed to provide both guarantees for investors and incentives for proper firm behaviour. Being an insider, the merchant bank is in the best position to evaluate the firm's prospective profitability. By taking a stake in the firm, the merchant bank signals to the market its positive evaluation of that firm. Should the merchant bank deliberately send 'wrong' signals, its reputation would be spoiled and its signals would no longer be trusted. Exerting this role means, according to current terminology, 'enforcing the corporate governance of firms'.

As is clear by now, our working hypothesis is that it was the lack of merchant banks – that is, the lack of insiders taking stakes, and therefore exercising corporate governance – that was one of the major reasons for Italy's industrial downsizing. This is the proper point to turn to a full exposition of how and why this happened.

2.2   The lack of corporate governance: How could it happen?

An outside observer comparing Italy's industrial and financial structure with that of its major neighbouring economies in the first decade of the twentieth century, would find fewer differences than today. The scale of industry and finance were much smaller at the time than in France and Germany, but differences between the processes involved in establishing companies were less noticeable. Thus, universal banks played a large role, assisting directly in the birth of industrial firms. They also worked in symbiosis with a stock exchange which, until 1907, developed rapidly and seemed destined to acquire features similar to those of the

German stock exchange. Nevertheless, a closer look reveals that some of the ingredients accounting for future developments were already in place.

First, a clear difference with Germany could be detected in company law, with Italy's legal arrangements paying little attention to the safeguard of minority shareholders and being particularly lenient to the limited disclosure of information by firms.

Second, the Italian state's role in the financial system was more pervasive, not only as an issuer of, but also as a guarantor for, commercial and industrial debt. This role as guarantor was crucial in ensuring the connection between the two components of a dual credit circuit. On the one hand, the financial savings of the public accrued mostly to savings banks and to the postal system and, through them, were invested in treasury securities. On the other, the major universal banks were instead linked to corporate financial transactions. They attempted to solve their structural funding problem by means of short-term inter-bank borrowing on international markets because the domestic stock exchange, as was soon to be seen, was inadequate for fulfilling their needs.

Third, a further difference concerned the role of this stock exchange. In Italy, the stock exchange was hardly the place to enforce corporate governance on firms given that company law was not conducive to this. It could, nonetheless, have provided the means to free the mixed banks that had been established in the 1890s from excessive illiquid investments in corporate shareholdings (Baia Curioni, 1991). Yet, rather than seeking the development of private financial markets, Italy used their relative underdevelopment as a scapegoat to justify the need for state ownership and control in the financial system. This occurred, in particular, at the time of the Great Depression – an era which magnified the fragility of the universal banks.

Major changes began after the deep recession of 1907 which had revealed the fragility and instability of the existing arrangements. Banks became progressively locked into their industrial investment and suffered from serious liquidity problems. This prompted an intense debate on how to improve the access of industry to finance, as alternatives were sought for what was considered an inadequate stock exchange (Conti, 1993; Pace and Morelli, 1984). This debate provides the real start for the system's transformation, a transformation that was finally completed in the 1930s when a new financial set-up was put in place, based on virtual state ownership and direction.

By and large, this transformation took place according to the blueprint envisaged by Alberto Beneduce, a highly influential technocrat who became the central mover in the reshaping of the country's financial system. Beneduce firmly opposed the so-called 'maturity transformation mechanism' by which commercial banks collected short-term deposits and re-lent them long-term to industry, or even purchased industrial shares, since he had seen that system collapse and be rescued three times in his lifetime. The logic of the system he favoured was that of directly linking final savers and final users of financial savings. Since final savers operated in conditions of great uncertainty and of seriously deficient information, only state guarantees could convince them to lend their money to financial institutions. Thus, special credit institutions (SCIs), managed by an elite of technocrats, were to be entrusted with issuing bonds and then using the proceeds to finance industrial and infrastructural investment, while commercial banks had to be excluded from the business of financing capital formation.

The coming to power of fascism and the crisis of the 1930s allowed Beneduce's vision to be broadly realized. A number of newly created SCIs issued bonds backed by public sector guarantees and provided long-term credit under general directives coming from the 'corporatist' planning apparatus. Interestingly, however, these various institutions did not become overly involved in the governance of customer firms. As a consequence, their lending became increasingly bureaucratic, and state guarantees were overstretched. In this new system, the state had replaced universal banks to bridge the trust gap between savers and entrepreneurs, and to provide some co-ordination for the various agents operating in the financial system. Though the universal banks did not vanish, their ability to provide for corporate financial needs was curtailed. Their supply of long-term finance had, for instance, to be disguised under the form of the rolling-over of short-term loans.

The outcome of these various trends was that Italy acquired a unique position among industrialized countries – it had a financial system quite capable of providing long-term finance, but rather unfit to accompany this with an active role in corporate governance. Indeed, the relationship between banks and industry in Italy turned out to be both weak and fragile. This was quite the opposite of the advantageous lasting relationships between banks and firms that, according to the dominant strand of the theory of intermediation, are conducive to the efficient screening and monitoring of investment projects.

The old debate over the financing of industry did not, however, die with the inception of direct state intervention in the banking system in the 1930s. It only smouldered and was rekindled in the aftermath of the Second World War by the discussions on the future of the economy held at the Constituent Assembly between 1946 and 1947. The debate acquired new force in the 1960s, when the country's 'economic miracle' lost some of its glitter. Finally, it raged in the 1970s and 1980s, as the Italian economy, and particularly Italian industry, underwent the radical transformation briefly described in Section 2.1 above.

Many have suggested that, despite the absence of merchant banks throughout the country's modern history, the alternative institutions that had performed their functions had been able to lead Italian industry onto a path of relatively rapid growth. This had been the case with the universal banks already at the turn of the century and had also been true of the state-run financial system that had subsequently emerged and that had continued to operate without many formal changes after the Second World War.

This seems, implicitly, the view that was taken at the Constituent Assembly. The debate that took place there started from a firm denial of any practical possibility that the Milan Stock Exchange might play a significant role in channelling new savings to industrial firms. This denial was explained by the 'very reduced savings capacity of (our) country' (de Cecco and Ferri, 1996, p. 59). Having dispensed with one of the pillars of traditional finance, the Assembly's Economic Commission expressed the opinion that the system of compulsory savings which had been put in place in the 1930s to finance the war (and which was commonly known under the name of 'monetary circuit') might also finance postwar reconstruction.

The so-called 'double intermediation' method had to be preserved. Special banks would issue bonds to be bought by commercial banks and resold to the public. Long-term loans to industry were to be made with the proceeds of these bond sales. The acquisition of industrial shares was considered a secondary activity for these special banks. The Commission deemed that any such shares the special banks might have acquired would remain on their balance sheets forever, as the stock exchange had no capacity to relieve them of the burden. Again, as at the time of universal banks, the Italian stock exchange was the deficient institution which prevented the Italian system from acquiring the features and following on the tracks of the more established forms of capitalism, whether of the Anglo-American or German variety.

While most institutional aspects of the earlier system were, thus, preserved, its substance changed radically in the absence of the planning provided by the 'corporatist' machine. The state maintained its role as guarantor of private savings. Investment and financing decisions, however, became increasingly decentralized, as the state withdrew from its role as allocator of financial resources.

With the exception of common shares and private bonds, all other savings were protected by a state guarantee, but the state did not bother to exercise any control on how the system was run in practice. Commercial banks were given an incentive to develop lending methods more akin to insurance than to banking. Since they were supposed to stay away from the running of non-banking firms, they refrained from exercising any financial supervision of the enterprises to which they lent money. As for long-term industrial financing this was to be performed by long-term special banks. The latter, however, were given no specific role as financial advisors to firms, nor as co-ordinators of corporate governance.

If the Constituent Assembly had nothing to say on the role of banks in corporate governance, several people in Italy took those problems very much to heart. Among them was Raffaele Mattioli, head of Banca Commerciale Italiana (or Comit), the largest of the former universal banks that had been rescued by the state in the 1930s. Mattioli was convinced of the need to separate short- from long-term credit. He agreed with the Banking Reform of 1936, which had imposed that separation, but also believed that firms must be given continuous financial assistance and advice by SCIs. Expecting that after the war Comit would wish to revive its corporate finance business, he sought to create a friendly long-term lending SCI exclusively connected with his own bank. With the help of this institution, Comit would have been able to offer a full corporate finance menu, spanning from short- to long-term credit, to advice, and to underwriting in the stock exchange. In view of the opposition this attempt generated, the new industrial credit bank (Mediobanca) escaped from his full control and was launched under the auspices of the three former universal banks: Comit, Credito Italiano and Banco di Roma.

Since Mediobanca ended up outside the terms of reference Mattioli had first stipulated, he resigned himself to impersonate a peculiar type of universal banker. He would provide long-term finance to industrial firms by rolling-over short-term credit. In this compromise solution he found the tacit connivance of the central bank, which allowed Comit to perform the functions of relationship banking vis-à-vis the companies of the industrial triangle of Northern Italy. Mediobanca, on the other hand, was taken out of the hands of the man who had designed it, and went its own way, becoming for four decades, virtually the only institution in Italy worthy of the name of merchant bank. Several other institutions fulfilled the role of industrial banks, especially in connection with the ample funds the state made available for concessionary credit, but only Comit and Mediobanca performed all the roles usually performed by merchant banks.

The morphology of industrial firms in Italy, especially as they have developed in recent decades, suggests they clearly need the services of merchant banks. These services have remained largely unavailable, despite the various efforts made to provide them. Though SCIs, created for this purpose, extended ample industrial credit, the methods followed in granting such credits did not facilitate the transformation of the granting institutions into merchant banks. Industrial credit was always regulated by extremely detailed laws which specified the requirements that borrowers had to fulfil in order to qualify. In many cases, central or regional governments were given the power of ultimately supervising credit allocation. This primacy of legal over banking methods drastically reduced the SCIs' ability to acquire merchant banking skills. Credit was allocated much as it was in the then socialist countries of Eastern Europe. Borrowers, together with their technical advisers, were ultimately in charge of the whole procedure. A large role was thus reserved for the *commercialisti* who, together with local banks, performed the role of the missing merchant banks for the majority of Italy's SMEs.

During the last half-century, the financial system thus evolved along two directions, neither of which was particularly favourable. On the one hand, banks became less and less willing to lend on the basis of their own screening and monitoring functions and more and more prone to lending on the basis of collateral. They also relied increasingly on the insurance principle of the pooling of risks whereby multiple banking (in which firms borrow from more than one bank) became a common feature even for lending to SMEs – a unique case among industrialized countries. On the other hand, state involvement in the allocation of credit grew rapidly. In this area too, loans, even when subsidized, were extended on the basis of collateral. Bank–firm relationships – which, according to recent theory, are the keystone of a solid financial structure – became increasingly weak and fragmented.

This being said, the so-called 'Macmillan Gap' (that is, the shortage of finance to support investment, particularly for SMEs) was filled, if in a peculiar way. SCIs doled out industrial credit with the proceeds of the long-term bonds they issued, and with concessionary loans directly financed by the government budget, while commercial banks lent short-term funds, largely with the backing of real guarantees. With the exceptions of Mediobanca and Comit on the one hand, and of local banks on the other, the role of relationship banking was played by a myriad of *commercialisti*, who personally had no funds to lend, but who orchestrated the whole activity of structuring the borrowing needs of the firms that had entrusted themselves to them.

Before examining this peculiarly Italian system of a corporate governance exercized in small firms by *commercialisti* and local banks, it is necessary to provide more detail on our claim pertaining to the corporate governance of large firms – namely, that Mediobanca (the largest Italian private SCI) was virtually the only fully-fledged merchant bank operating in the country in the postwar period. Other SCIs with stronger links to the government (such as IMI or Istituto Mobiliare Italiano, the largest Italian SCI) did not engage in the same business.

3   A real and a 'would-be' merchant bank

3.1   Mediobanca and the care-taking of large private firms

As was mentioned above, the Mediobanca that emerged in the late 1940s was not along the lines that Mattioli had envisaged. Given Mediobanca's lack of vertical integration with Comit, the institution had to re-focus its own business. Rather than gaining information by managing the payments of borrowing firms and observing their day-to-day financial situation, Mediobanca had to rely on information acquired as a shareholder and thanks to its own links with selected customers. This helps explain why, under the stable guidance of Enrico Cuccia (its head from the beginning), the institution deviated from Mattioli's original blueprint to become, over time, a merchant bank of the French type.

The fact that Mediobanca turned out to be the only fully-fledged merchant bank in Italy is not enough to blame it for having gained a monopolist position. After all, several other institutions could have entered the field and provided merchant banking services. That none did during this period must have been due to either a lack of ability, or to a lack of demand, or to a combination thereof. One consideration that is relevant in this context is the small number of large private firms in Italy (small also because of the important role of state ownership and control, much enlarged after the rescues of the 1930s). In addition, the most dynamic part of Italian industry was represented by SMEs, and it is not clear whether these firms needed a merchant banker rather than a venture capitalist. In other words, and for both reasons, the potential role for any merchant banker was limited.

3.2 IMI and the financing of large-scale enterprises

IMI was established in 1931 to help solve the problems that Italian universal banks had faced during the 1920s. IMI was part of the whole strategic design of an alternative financial structure, based on state guarantees; it was supposed to be the primary channel for industrial investment financing. Instructed with this generic mission, it did not overlap with the other SCIs created by Beneduce to assist Italian development. The consensus among economic historians is that, until the Second World War, IMI did not wholly fulfil its purpose. In the first years of its activity, it shunned the purchase of industrial shares and showed a preference for granting long-term credit backed by mortgages on existing assets. This prevented IMI from participating in the mobilization of the illiquid industrial assets piled up in the balance sheets of the universal banks. Nor did IMI do anything to close the 'Macmillan Gap'. This is why the Constituent Assembly expressed doubts on the ability of an industrial credit system exclusively based on IMI to assist the growth of SMEs.

Between 1936 and the end of the war, the governor of the Bank of Italy became chairman of IMI (Cesarini, 1982). After the war, it is reasonable to assume that Donato Menichella – former director of IRI (a public-sector industrial holding conglomerate) and then governor of the Bank of Italy from 1947 to 1960 – wanted to keep IMI under the control of the central bank in order to direct industrial investment towards sectors he considered as strategic. We have evidence of the central bank's provincial managers recommending individual firms to IMI as likely borrowers. We also know that it was Menichella who insisted on giving IMI the monopoly of control over the disbursement of those Marshall Plan funds which had been ear marked for Italian investment. Between 1949 and 1957, available data show how IMI concentrated its financing on large-scale industry.

Around 40 per cent of the credit IMI extended went to IRI companies, and the rest to other large-scale firms. It was, however, all debt; IMI refrained from purchasing the shares of any of the companies it liberally financed with special credits or with concessionary credits supplied by the state. IMI had clearly decided to maintain an arm's length attitude vis-à-vis the companies it financed, even vis-à-vis those to which it provided most of the funds.

There was never an attempt on IMI's part to offer its clients the services of a merchant bank. In contrast to Mediobanca, it did not introduce companies to the stock exchange, nor did it supply them with financial advice. IMI had virtually no role in corporate governance. The way long-term credit was supplied never strayed far from mortgage banking, thereby distancing IMI from its clients. Mortgages would always guarantee IMI's loans. As far as small firms were concerned, IMI seemed uninterested in their fate, except in those limited instances in which it managed, in the most impersonal manner, the funds assigned to them by special laws. In particular cases – for example, when it was allotted a fund to assist the development of the engineering sector – IMI's strategy seems to have been that of granting funds to firms that, while economically unviable, were politically sensitive. This is indirectly confirmed by the fact that when the special funds were exhausted, such firms ended up being salvaged by some infamous state-run rescue operation or other.

The main industrial credit experiment conducted by IMI in the 1960s – the financing of a large chemical group – ended in disaster. In order to prevent IMI from going bankrupt, the state had to refinance it directly in the 1970s. Since the early 1980s, IMI has developed a new activity, and with much greater success. It has become a manager of trust and pension funds, tapping the market for the management of private savings which emerged in Italy in the 1980s and which has steadily grown since then. Until very recently, however, in common with all other Italian investment funds, IMI generally invested in Italian public debt. Very little has been invested in common stock. Moreover, IMI seems to have wanted to play no part in the corporate governance of those companies whose shares it owns. In more recent years, IMI has also become an advisor in the privatization of state-owned companies, a programme that began in earnest in the 1990s. Here, the institution has acquired valuable experience, having been put in charge of very large operations.

4.   The second tier: *commercialisti*, local banks and the financing of small firms

As was suggested above, the vibrant development of SMEs kept Italy growing at a relatively rapid pace even after its large firms, starting in the 1970s, met with increasing problems and began a process of downsizing. Thus, this section briefly looks at the peculiarities of finance for the country's SMEs.

We had earlier concluded that Italian financial intermediaries have been unable to enforce satisfactory corporate governance. We have also claimed that this has been a key factor in limiting the growth of Italy's large firms. Accordingly, one may ask how a financial environment not conducive to such growth could instead support, or at least allow, the rapid growth of SMEs. An answer can be provided along at least two different lines. First, it could be that external finance is relatively less important for the growth of SMEs. Second, the financial institutions charged with providing adequate arrangements for funding and for the corporate governance of SMEs could be different from those required by large corporations. In line with the predictions made by the prevailing strand in the theory of financial intermediation (see, for instance, Bhattacharya and Thakor, 1993), we do not share the former interpretation. We will, therefore, follow the latter view and argue, in particular, that two types of institutions seem to have played an important role in satisfying the financial needs of SMEs:

(i)   *Commercialisti*, that is accountants or individual business consultants. In order to provide much-needed fiscal advice, the *commercialisti* became insiders to the SMEs they were helping and used this position to act as a liaison between customer firms and financial intermediaries;

(ii) Local banks (often, though not exclusively, cooperative banks) that could provide informed lending to local entrepreneurs who happened to be part of their own constituency, if not their own shareholders.

4.1   The special role of the '*commercialisti*'

Most Italian firms are still private, and owned by a single family; indeed, many of them are still run by the individuals who founded them. Accordingly, the *commercialista* was ideally suited to play the part of a very peculiar merchant banker. He became a commanding figure of the country's economic landscape following the tax reform of the early 1970s, which made income tax returns compulsory for almost every individual in Italy. Subsequent tax reform laws also contributed to imposing on an unwilling, but by and large law-abiding, population a heavy weight of complex fiscal duties. The fiscal administration had no experience of providing friendly advice to taxpayers; in addition, tax rates were from the start rather high, thus stimulating partial avoidance. This was the juncture at which the *commercialisti*, who had hitherto worked for a minority of Italian entrepreneurs, stepped in and soon became indispensable to most businessmen.

As the only people who really knew the financial situation of their clients – a situation that they had to master in every detail in order to give proper tax advice – the *commercialisti* were also the only ones who could give proper financial advice. Italian firms had always possessed two sets of accounts (as Attilio Cabiati, a highly respected economist, had noted as early as 1911)[2] and both were concocted by the family's *commercialista*. The *commercialista* thus possessed the inside knowledge of the client's business that no banker could acquire. Being a non-banking banker, he could also be trusted with non-partisan advice. He thus could, and did, develop the skills to master the intricacies of the application forms necessary to obtain industrial credit on concessionary terms. Specialized knowledge of a legal nature was required – the *commercialista* had acquired such skills at university and in his practice. In many ways he became a small-scale merchant banker. The comparison is far from being inappropriate.

Merchant banks perform most of the functions we have just outlined. They need to know the real accounts of their clients; they give fiscal advice; they provide specialized financial consulting services. Here, however, the comparison ends. The other tasks performed by merchant bankers are not performed by the *commercialisti*. Merchant bankers tell their clients how to structure their financial requirements, and this the *commercialista* does. But the latter mostly advises his clients on how to obtain credit from other institutions, while merchant bankers help clients to place common stock either privately or through the stock exchange. The Italian *commercialista* will go as far as finding takers of privately placed shares, but it is only extremely seldom that he will advise clients on a public quotation. He certainly does not buy shares to resell them on the stock exchange at a later date. In other words, the *commercialista* works within the context of the Italian financial, legal and fiscal systems, and these systems are not conducive to an enlargement of the functions of the stock exchange.

Apart from that, the *commercialista* has several advantages over bankers, whether merchant or commercial. He is much nearer to the client, since he first acquires his trust as a solver of fiscal problems. The fact that the client is somebody fully occupied in building up his company and has no time for complex fiscal analysis does, of course, help in establishing a relationship of complete trust on which the *commercialista* can then build to become his client's financial adviser. The relationship between the *commercialista* and the entrepreneur is by definition non-adversarial, unlike that of a lender and his borrower. Using a terminology derived from game theory, we could claim that the *commercialista*, unlike the bank, does not play a zero-sum game with his client. Rather, he plays a positive-sum game, and it is well known that co-operative strategy equilibria are more likely to result in these circumstances than in a zero-sum game.

There are other advantages. The *commercialista* has very few overheads to amortize and is usually his own master. Most merchant banks depend on salaried personnel, are typically too big relative to the size of Italian firms and charge far too much for their services. They thus intimidate the small entrepreneur, in a way in which the *commercialista* does not. He is embedded in the same environment as his clients, and is often linked to them by a complex network of social and even family relationships.

It is thus not surprising that *commercialisti* have become intermediaries between foreign merchant banks which have started operating in Italy and medium-sized Italian firms. More often, however, the *commercialista* will work to keep the client he advises from becoming too big. He will advise him to clone his companies, rather than allow them to grow to a level where they will develop an independent, in-house, financial function.[3] The *commercialista* is by definition not very conversant with matters of the stock exchange, which has so far involved only large companies that do not seek his services. Why should he give his client the advice to go public? Being first and foremost a tax adviser, his prime skills are those which allow firms to show the taxman as little as possible. This is, after all, the very opposite of going public, which is everywhere an operation based on disclosure.

For the greater part of the last two to three decades, given the structure of long-term credit, of company law, and of fiscal legislation, the *commercialista* has been the ideal agent for Italy's SMEs. The proliferation of this profession, and the growing esteem in which it is held (like medical doctors they are loved and hated at the same time), means that the *commercialista* is useful for his clients. As long as credit has been on tap, he has been the one who learnt how to open the tap, and to maximize the flow for his clients – all on the best conditions available.

4.2 What's different about local banks?

Fama (1985) entitled his paper 'What's Different about Banks?' and came to the conclusion that the information embodied in their lending activity provides the main rationale for their existence. If it were not for banks overcoming the asymmetric information problem they face, Fama argues, most businesses would have no access to external finance, and would instead have to rely exclusively on self-financing. Mimicking Fama's approach, others have tried to provide a rationale for the existence of local banks. Nakamura (1993) argues, for instance, that, in spite of the presence of scale economies, small banks (and, in general, local banks are small) can still exist because large banks undergo diseconomies of scale in lending to small/local firms.[4] This argument would jointly explain why small/local banks exist together with large/national banks and why they specialize in lending to small/local firms, whereas large/national banks tend to lend more to larger firms.[5]

If, for the reasons given above, small/local banks are more efficient in lending to small/local firms, the presence of this type of intermediary might have favourable consequences for the growth of SMEs. More generally, we might expect that local banks would engage in more 'relationship lending' – even in the context of the Italian banking system that we have characterized as being rather prone to 'arm's length lending'. This expectation finds some support in various recent studies of local economic development in Italy that have tried to assess the role of well-run local banks in assisting the production and investment of SMEs. For brevity, we will make reference to only a few of them.

According to Conti and Ferri (1997), the proliferation and strengthening of minor and local banks in Italy was, at least in part, the fruit of deliberate efforts by small enterprise to create a rudimentary capital market. Local banks would be able to mobilize the community's savings for either the transformation of pre-existing productive arrangements or the launch of new lines of local economic activity. In many cases, local banks gave the nascent class of small businessmen the necessary confidence to take the first steps and to face difficulties. As members of the same community, these banks possessed better information than outside banks on local loan applicants. They were also better placed to monitor the use of the funds and to act in the event of loan recovery proceedings.

Conti and Ferri (1997) also refer to the geography of the development models of the 'Three Italies' (the three areas into which Italy is often divided according to the different characteristics of their productive structures – the North-West area of first industrialization, dominated by large corporations, the North-East and Centre area of second industrialization, dominated by SMEs, and the South, where industrialization is still lagging). The two authors show that these geographic divisions have, to some extent, coincided with those of the banking system. Figure 4.1 clearly identifies marked regional differences – in spite of the changes that have happened over time, the North-West is characterized by larger firms and larger banks, whereas the opposite holds for the North-East and Centre.

Cosci and Mattesini (1997) show that growth of per capita income was higher in those Italian provinces where bank intermediation was better supplied and where co-operative banks, typically local banks, prevailed. Other essays contained in Cesarini et al. (1997) also shed light on the beneficial link between small/local banks and small/local firms.

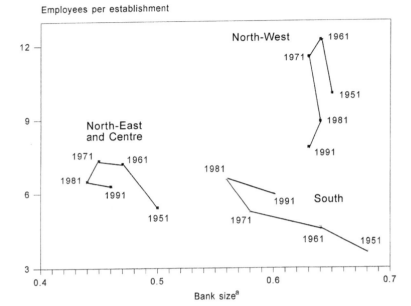

Figure 4.1   Establishment and bank size by geographical area

a. The bank size indicator is obtained by calculating the average number of bank branches present in each town, weighting each branch according to the size class of the bank to which it belongs under the Bank of Italy's classification in force until 1992 (the weights are $\frac{1}{5}$ for very small banks, $\frac{2}{5}$ for small banks, $\frac{3}{5}$ for average-sized banks, $\frac{4}{5}$ for large banks and 1 for very large banks), and then calculating the simple average of the indicators for each individual town. The indicator ranges from 0 to 1; the larger the banks that are present, the closer it will be to 1.

Sources: Authors' calculations based on ISTAT, *Censimento industriale* (various years) and Banca d'Italia, 'Data Bank'.

5   Conclusions

The major conclusion of this chapter is that banks have traditionally been absent in the corporate governance of Italian firms. The interaction between banks and firms that occurred can be described as an 'arm's length' relationship. The origins of such a relationship go back to some particular factors that prevailed in Italy after the Second World War. The first reason was the extensive use of family and coalitions to ensure corporate control and the demand by these groups for more confidential services than banks could offer. The second was the regulatory ban on banks' corporate shareholding and the large-scale state ownership and control of banks. The third was the fact that, partly in response to the above, the 'information content' of banks' lending shrank, as reliance on real collateral, on state guarantees and on multiple bank borrowing all increased.

We have been able to identify only two exceptions to this pattern. First, one particular private SCI, Mediobanca, was the major player in the financing and corporate governance of the largest private firms. Second, *commercialisti* (defined by us as a special type of individual business consultants) and local banks played important roles in the financing and governance of smaller-sized firms. Despite this unusual set-up, growth did not suffer, at least until the early 1960s.

Subsequently, however, weak corporate governance began to have negative repercussions. And it was large firms that were most affected in terms of an inefficient organization of production. Faced with growing difficulties, they responded by downsizing and by relying increasingly on seclusive hierarchical group links that insulated them from the scrutiny of financial markets.

Nevertheless, recounting this inward evolution of large corporations does not tell the whole story of postwar Italy. After all, the country continued to grow relatively rapidly through the 1970s and 1980s, despite the difficulties encountered by its large manufacturing conglomerates. We have argued that this was thanks to a network of small, innovative and export-oriented manufacturing firms, mostly located in the North-Eastern and Central regions. Their buoyant development meant a double redeployment of production – a geographical shift away from the North-West and towards the North-East-Centre, and a structural shift away from large corporations toward small-sized businesses.

In addition, this change implied a reliance on a different system of corporate governance. Indeed, the corporate governance that established itself for these small firms, based as it was on fiduciary networks in local communities, on *commercialisti* and on local banks, proved more solid and durable than that for large firms. However, this system also had some limitations. In particular, while it nurtured small businesses, it was unable to further their growth by launching them onto the financial or the stock markets.

Profound changes are now under way in Italy's system of corporate governance. Various factors contribute to challenging the existing linkages between finance and industrial investment – the widespread privatization of state-owned companies, amendments to company law, EMU, and the growing integration of the Italian financial system with international markets. While it would be presumptuous to foretell what the new set-up will be, we can reasonably forecast that it will have to build on the distinctive features of the existing two-tier system that we have described.

Notes

1. This share declines even if one takes into account the whole group structure of Italian companies (a procedure that would probably overestimate their size); see de Cecco and Ferri (1996).
2. Cabiati noted at the time:

   Frankly, who can trust company statements published in Italy? One of the most harmful consequences of the reprehensible excessive tax burden on industrial income is to induce companies – almost all law abiding because of a natural instinct of self-preservation – to make up statements in a way that these statements represent as vaguely as possible the true situation of the company. (our translation from the original, reprinted in Pace and Morelli, 1984, p. 77)

3. De Cecco and Ferri (1996) report two interesting findings. First, the presence of *commercialisti* in 1991 across Italy's 95 provinces (as measured by their share in the province's total employment) shows a negative and statistically significant correlation ($r = -0.25$) with average provincial firm size. Second, in a regression equation having as dependent variable the change in average firm size per province between 1981 and 1991 (and controlling for this size in 1971 and 1981), the introduction of a variable based on the presence of *commercialisti* in 1991 (no figures are available for earlier dates) delivers a negative and significant coefficient.
4. According to Nakamura (1993), small/local banks enjoy superior information in lending to small/local borrowers because they can observe the liquidity position of those firms that tend to concentrate their banking business with them. Focusing on relatively small loans to small firms would not be profitable for larger banks and could generate moral hazard problems. Thus, branch managers could engage in opportunistic behaviour vis-à-vis their headquarters – since the cost of monitoring them is assumed to increase with the distance between headquarters and branch, small/local banks would have a comparative advantage in this area of business. Ferri (1997) corroborates this hypothesis: the turnover of branch managers is higher for large than for small Italian banks and the higher the turnover, the worse the quality of the loan portfolio.
5. Berger et al. (1995) find such a specialization in lending for the United States; Angeloni et al. (1995) show that this also holds in Italy.

References

Angeloni, I., L. Buttiglione, G. Ferri and E. Gaiotti (1995) 'The Credit Channel of Monetary Policy across Heterogeneous Banks: The Case of Italy', Banca d'Italia, *Temi di discussione*, No. 256.

Baia Curioni, S. (1991) 'Sull'evoluzione istituzionale della Borsa valori di Milano (1898–1941)', *Rivista di storia economica*, ns, 8, 1, 41–80.

Bank of Italy (1979) *Annual Report*, Rome.

Barca, F., M. Bianchi, L. Cannari, R. Cesari, C. Gola, G. Manitta, G. Salvo and L.F. Signorini (1994) 'Proprietà, modelli di controllo e riallocazione nelle imprese industriali italiane', in *Assetti proprietari e mercato delle imprese. Gruppo proprietà e controllo nelle imprese italiane medio-grandi,* vol. I, Bologna: Il Mulino.

Berger, A.N., A.K. Kashyap and J.M. Scalise (1995) 'The Transformation of the U.S. Banking Industry: What a Long, Strange Trip It's Been', *Brookings Papers on Economic Activity,* 2, 55–218.

Bhattacharya, S. and A.V. Thakor (1993) 'Contemporary Banking Theory', *Journal of Financial Intermediation,* 3, 1, 2–50.

Cameron, R.E. (ed.) (1972) *Banking and Economic Development: Some Lessons of History,* New York, NY: Oxford University Press.

Cannari, L., G. Marchese and M. Pagnini (1993) 'Forma giuridica, quotazione e struttura proprietaria delle imprese italiane: prime evidenze comparate', Banca d'Italia, *Temi di discussione,* No. 202.

Cesarini, F. (1982) *Alle origini del credito industriale. L'IMI negli anni '30,* Bologna: Il Mulino.

Cesarini, F., G. Ferri and M. Giardino (eds) (1997) *Credito e sviluppo. Banche locali cooperative e imprese minori,* Bologna: Il Mulino.

Conti, G. (1993) 'Finanza di impresa e capitale di rischio in Italia (1870–1939)', *Rivista di storia economica,* ns, 10, 3, 307–32.

Conti, G. and G. Ferri (1997) 'Banche locali e sviluppo economico decentrato', in F. Barca (ed.), *Storia del capitalismo italiano dal dopoguerra a oggi,* Rome: Donzelli.

Cosci, S. and F. Mattesini (1997) 'Credito e sviluppo nelle province italiane', in F. Cesarini, G. Ferri and M. Giardino (eds), *Credito e sviluppo. Banche locali cooperative e imprese minori,* Bologna: Il Mulino.

de Cecco, M. (1971) 'Lo sviluppo dell'economia italiana e la sua collocazione internazionale', *Rivista internazionale di scienze economiche e commerciali,* 18, 1, 973–93.

de Cecco, M. and G. Ferri (1996) *Le banche d'affari in Italia,* Bologna: Il Mulino.

Fama, E.F. (1985) 'What's Different about Banks?', *Journal of Monetary Economics,* 15, 1, 29–39.

Ferri, G. (1997) 'Branch Manager Turnover and Lending Efficiency: Local vs. National Banks', *Banca Nazionale del Lavoro Quarterly Review,* 50, Supplement to No. 200, 229–47.

Gerschenkron, A. (1962) *Economic Backwardness in Historical Perspective: a Book of Essays,* Cambridge, MA: Harvard University Press.

Goodman, E. and J. Bamford (eds) (1989) *Small Firms and Industrial Districts in Italy,* London: Routledge.

Gros-Pietro, G.M. and A. Sembenelli (1993) 'La struttura industriale europea: un'analisi descrittiva basata sulle quote di produzione', in Istituto Nazionale per il Commercio Estero (ed.), *Rapporto sul commercio estero 92,* Rome: Edisi.

Nakamura L.I. (1993) 'Commercial Bank Information: Implications for the Structure of Banking', in M. Klausner and L.J. White (eds), *Structural Change in Banking,* Homewood, IL: Irwin.

Pace, C. and G. Morelli (1984) *Origini e identità del credito speciale,* Milan: Franco Angeli.

Pagano, M. (1993) 'Financial Markets and Growth: an Overview', *European Economic Review,* 37, 2/3, 613–22.

Pyke, F., G. Becattini and W. Sengenberger (eds) (1990) *Industrial Districts and Inter-firm Co-operation in Italy,* Geneva: International Institute for Labour Studies.

5
Japan's Financial System: A Failure of Corporate Governance?*

Akiyoshi Horiuchi

1 Introduction

The Japanese banking sector has been struggling for nearly a decade with huge amounts of non-performing loans, without much success. The problem arose in the early 1990s with the bursting of a major speculative asset price bubble. At first, both the banks and the government tried to conceal the difficulties, hoping that economic recovery would resolve the issue. But the recovery did not materialize, in part because the non-performing loan problem seems to have prevented banks from supplying credit to industry, thereby aggravating the economic setback. This, in turn, worsened the business environment, added to the amount of bad loans and generated a vicious circle between the banking crisis and virtual economic stagnation.

The huge amount of non-performing loans, variously put at ¥30 to ¥75 trillion, or 6 to 14 per cent of GDP (OECD, 1998), is synonymous with a capital shortage for the banks. Responding to this capital shortage, the government introduced a major policy package consisting of some ¥60 trillion in October 1998. Two long-term credit banks have been temporarily nationalized and capital is being supplied to banks that agree to drastically restructure their management.

However, these various injections will not, by themselves, solve the fragility of the sector because the origins of these problems are much

* This chapter is a by-product of my joint research with Masaru Hanazaki of the Research Institute on Capital Formation of the Japan Development Bank. Constructive comments on an earlier version have come from Andrea Boltho, Patrick Bolton, Michael Gibson, Shinichi Hirota, Anil Kashyap, Hugh Patrick, Eric Rosengren and Yoshiro Tsutsui. Financial support from the Japan Ministry of Education Scientific Research Grant is gratefully acknowledged.

deeper. This may sound surprising. After all, it has been commonly believed that the Japanese financial system, centred on banks, had worked very efficiently to promote industrial development after the Second World War. In particular, banks have been considered as an important player in the Japanese framework of corporate governance, thanks to the effective monitoring they have exercised on borrowing firms. From this perspective, the 1990s crisis appears somewhat of a mystery.

The purpose of this chapter is to provide a possible answer to this mystery from the perspective of corporate governance theory. According to this theory, banks must play an essential monitoring role if an efficient corporate governance is to be realized in a financial system centred on the banking sector. However, the bank is itself a corporation that needs to be monitored and disciplined. There is, therefore, an issue of 'who monitors the monitor'. This chapter will examine the hypothesis that Japan has not succeeded in resolving this issue. In other words, the country has suffered from a vacuum of governance in bank management. It is this that accounts for the fragility of the banking sector and the prolongation of the non-performing loan problem.

The chapter is organized as follows. Section 2 briefly explains the formation of the bank-centred financial system in postwar Japan. Section 3, which is the chapter's core part, discusses the governance issues. The section looks, in turn, at the disciplinary effects on bank management of the capital market, of market competition, and of supervision by the regulatory authorities. We emphasize that these mechanisms have been prevented from working effectively mainly by government policy. Section 4 explains how the financial market has responded to the bank crisis, a crisis that can be understood as a market attack on the vacuum of governance. Finally, Section 5 summarizes the main arguments and briefly looks at the future.

2   Preconditions for the bank-centred financial system

During the so-called high growth era of the two decades from the early 1950s, bank credit was dominant in Japanese corporate finance. Seen from a longer-term perspective, however, this dominance was a new phenomenon. Table 5.1 shows changes in the composition of fund-raising by non-financial firms since the 1930s. From this table, it can be seen that bank loans were not particularly important in the 1930s, a period in which the stock market played a much larger role (in the 1920s corporate bond issues had played a similar role).[1]

Table 5.1 Sources of funds for Japanese non-financial firms (period averages; percentages)

	1931–40	1941–44	1946–55	1956–65	1966–75	1976–85
Internal funds	37.0	28.8	37.0	41.1	43.8	58.8
Loans from private financial institutions	27.3	41.8	45.4	43.7	45.8	32.4
of which:						
from banks	21.1	45.8	31.7	26.1	23.9	20.3
Bonds	4.3	8.6	2.3	2.6	2.0	1.4
Shares	31.0	19.5	8.7	8.3	3.4	3.1
Other[a]	0.4	1.3	6.6	4.3	5.0	4.3

Note: The data on 'internal funds' are derived from the National Income Statistics and are, therefore, not entirely compatible with the other data in the table which are estimated by the Bank of Japan.

a. Mainly loans from the public sector and trade credit.

Sources: Bank of Japan, *Economic Statistics Annual* (various issues); EPA, *Annual Report on National Income Statistics* (various issues).

2.1 Prewar consolidation and wartime controls

Following a major bank panic in 1927, Japan's banking sector underwent drastic structural changes under the influence of a new banking law that prescribed a rather high minimum capital requirement. If banks were not able to satisfy the requirement within five years, they were forced either into liquidation or into mergers with other banks. Even after the five years, grace period, the Ministry of Finance (MoF) continued this policy with a view to producing a sector characterized by fewer, larger banks. As a consequence, during the 19 years from 1926 to 1945, the number of commercial banks fell from 1420 to 61. This drastic reduction was associated with a substantial increase in size. The sector's restructuring was one of the important preconditions for the dominance of banks in Japanese corporate finance after the war.

Some scholars argue that, for better or for worse, wartime controls also contributed to this postwar dominance. For example, as early as 1937 the government had begun to limit firms' ability to raise funds in the securities market, and to control the industrial allocation of bank credit. This restrictive policy weakened the function of the capital market for corporate finance. Moreover, in 1944 the government introduced a system under which each ammunitions company was assigned a major bank that cared for the firm's every financial need. The designated banks were to supply credit to the assigned enterprises and to monitor their management.

Though this system was abolished in 1946, it has been argued that it was at the origin of the postwar's main bank relationships (Teranishi,

1994; Hoshi et al., 1994). However, from the perspective of corporate governance, the validity of this argument seems doubtful. It is widely recognized that the main bank relationship is important because it allows banks to closely monitor their client firms (Horiuchi et al., 1988; Aoki, 1994). The wartime system, however, by explicitly or implicitly ordering banks to provide credit to the ammunitions' companies did not enhance their surveillance abilities. The designated banks did not need to worry about the creditworthiness of their major borrowers and were not given any incentive to monitor them[2]

Indeed, there is some evidence suggesting that the banks' involvement in the wartime economy worsened their financial intermediation capacity. Figure 5.1 shows the sharp wartime and postwar fall in the ratio of bank loans to the amount of Bank of Japan (BoJ) notes circulating in the economy (with the latter standing as a proxy for the level of nationwide economic activities). The ratio only returned to the average prewar level in the late 1950s, thereby suggesting that wartime controls seriously damaged the banks' financial mediation capacity. The argument that controls were an important precondition for the dominance of banks in postwar corporate governance thus seems somewhat farfetched. It should also be pointed out that the August 1946 suspension of government compensation of wartime expenses (which amounted to as much as 17 per cent of GNP at the time) was damaging to banks.

2.2   Postwar reconstruction of financial institutions

The government was quick to reconstruct the banking sector immediately after the war. In particular, it is noteworthy from the corporate governance perspective that the De-concentration Law of December 1947 made an exception in the case of the financial sector. This law, introduced under the guidance of the occupation authorities, aimed at dissolving the *zaibatsu* groups and the monopolistic companies that had played important roles in the wartime economy. In February 1948, 300 non-financial companies became targets for dissolution. However, the government decided that this law would not be applied to banks and financial institutions.

Not only were banks protected from dissolution; the concomitant break-up of the *zaibatsu* also enhanced their role. The dissolution of 83 holding companies, which constituted the central nervous system of the *zaibatsu* organizations, radically altered the governance structure of the country's large companies and allowed the major banks to install themselves in the position of essential controllers of Japan's postwar

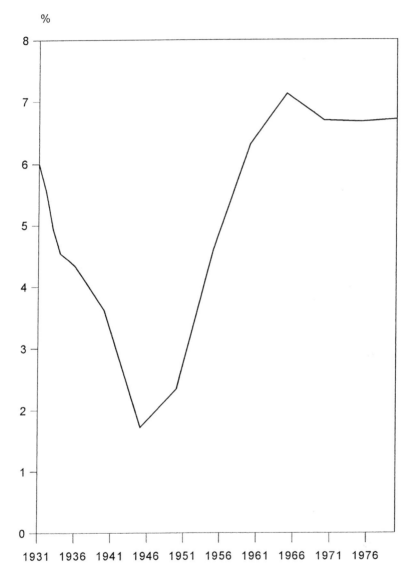

Figure 5.1 Bank credit/bank notes ratio (percentages)
Source: Bank of Japan, *Economic Statistics Annual, 1982.*

corporate sector (Miyajima, 1994; Okazaki, 1997). Clearly, this promoted the formation of a bank-centred corporate governance system. As Table 5.1 shows, the reliance of non-financial companies on bank credit was particularly significant during the high growth period from the mid-1950s to the early 1970s.

Japanese banks are permitted to hold the shares of their client firms up to a 5 per cent ceiling prescribed by the Anti-Monopoly Law. Thus, the banks should be able to mitigate the agency problem inherent in the conflict of interest between debt-holders and shareholders since they hold both statuses simultaneously (Stiglitz, 1985). It should also be noted that the banks played a leading role in the practice of mutual shareholding among firms and financial institutions.[3] This practice made it difficult for outsiders to threaten incumbent managers through hostile take-overs, thereby weakening the disciplinary mechanism of the capital market. Many scholars argue, however, that mutual shareholding has promoted the investment of managers and employees into firm-specific human capital.

3   The shortcomings of governance in bank management

The previous section has explained how the corporate governance structure centred on the banking sector was formed immediately after the Second World War. Many have argued that this structure worked efficiently to mitigate the agency problems associated with corporate finance (see, for example, Hoshi et al., 1991). It should be noted, however, that there is no unanimous agreement about the efficiency of Japan's financial system. In particular, since the mid-1990s crisis, which revealed the banks' fragility, there has been a growing tendency to reconsider both its advantages and disadvantages (Weinstein and Yafeh, 1998; Morck and Nakamura, 1999).

A corporate governance based on a bank-centred financial system is likely to be inefficient if banks are not motivated to perform their monitoring role. For this role to be fulfilled, and given that banks are themselves corporations, somebody must monitor and discipline them. This section will argue that Japan has not succeeded in resolving the issue of how to motivate banks to be good monitors. The fundamental cause of the current bank crisis lies in this failure.

In general, bank management could be disciplined by either of the following three means:

(i)   The capital market, in which either investors (including depositors) would monitor performance, or the threat of hostile take-overs would discipline managers for their poor performance;

(ii) Market competition in the banking industry that would force inefficiently managed banks to leave the industry;

(iii) Supervision by the regulatory authorities that would either prevent banks from taking excessive risk in the ex ante stages of their business, or force managers of distressed banks to restructure their businesses in the ex post stages.

In what follows, it will be shown that these disciplinary mechanisms have been ineffective in Japan. There has been a vacuum in bank governance, which has led to management inefficiency and, in particular, to a delayed response to the substantial restructuring necessitated by the non-performing loan problem of the 1990s.

3.1 Lack of capital market discipline

The Anglo-American view of corporate governance stresses the importance of the disciplinary effect of the capital market on management. As far as Japanese banking is concerned, however, this effect did not work mainly because of the existence of a comprehensive safety net which suppressed the incentives of investors to carefully monitor bank management. In addition, capital market pressures were muted because of the practice of mutual shareholding. As was noted above, Japanese banks have constituted the core part of this tradition, the purpose of which was to protect managers of corporations, including banks, from possible hostile take-over bids.

The safety net mechanism. The presence of some safety net mechanism is widely recognized as indispensable to minimize the spill-over effects arising from the failures of banks and other financial institutions on the financial system as a whole. However, such mechanisms decrease the monitoring incentives of depositors and other investors because, either explicitly or implicitly, they protect them from losses associated with bank failures. Thus, in order to keep the safety net viable, appropriate incentive mechanisms are required to reinforce the monitoring of bank management. The wider the safety net's scope, the stronger are the moral hazard incentives given to the bank's management and, thus, the more energetically the regulatory authorities must monitor banks to prevent excessive risk-taking.[4]

The Japanese financial system operates under an extensive safety net implemented by the regulatory authorities. In the past, the MoF has rescued distressed financial institutions in tight collaboration with the BoJ and private financial institutions, particularly major banks. Before 1990, however, the number of bank failures was quite small.[5] In some instances the MoF guided (or, more precisely, ordered) private banks to rescue their distressed peers. In other cases, the MoF placed its officers on the board of the distressed banks with a view to reorganizing their management. Dispatching officials to a distressed bank may be an effective way of signalling to the public that the government has made a commitment to rescue the bank at any cost. This signal might have helped the MoF to persuade other banks to collaborate with the bailing-out programme. In reality, however, this signalling does not seem to have always been successful. A recent case was Hyogo Bank, to which the late chief of the Banking Bureau of the MoF was sent to reorganize its management. Despite this intervention, Hyogo finally went bankrupt in October 1995.

Side-effects of a comprehensive safety net. Since the actions taken by the authorities to rescue troubled banks have been covert, it is difficult to estimate the social costs of the safety net and the exact distribution of the burden among the various agents. However, the safety net was comprehensive in the sense that not only depositors, but also most other debt holders (except for some financial institutions) were exempted from the burdens associated with bank failures. In most cases even shareholders of failed banks seem to have been protected. For example, when credit co-operative banks went bankrupt, their equity holders were not required to share the costs of failures.[6] The burden of preserving financial stability has fallen disproportionately on sound private banks, particularly the major ones. In some cases, the BoJ may have extended loans to distressed banks at the official discount rate, which was substantially lower than money market interest rates, but it is impossible to obtain any information about these unofficial rescue programmes (whose costs would, ultimately, have been borne by the taxpayer).

Dangers of forbearance policy. The MoF's implementation of the safety net was essentially covert, with no explicit rules that the authorities were expected to obey. It has, thus, been almost impossible for outsiders to evaluate the MoF's performance in operating this net. Herein lies a danger of the forbearance policy, in the sense that the authorities postpone taking determined actions to liquidate de facto insolvent banks. The bureaucrats in charge of monitoring the management of individual banks have significant incentives to postpone any definite decision that would reveal their incompetence. It is well known that a forbearance policy is likely to generate large social losses when the troubled banks finally fail, having remained in business for a long time due to the policy's operation (Kane, 1985; 1993).

It is easy to understand why the forbearance policy tends to increase the social cost of dealing with bank failures. A bank on the brink of bankruptcy has a particularly strong incentive to take extreme risks because it stands to lose almost nothing when it fails. On the other hand, depositors and most other investors fail to monitor the bank's management because of the safety net's existence. Insufficient disclosure is likely to worsen the situation. Therefore, unless the authority stops its operation, the distressed bank continues to increase its liabilities, most of which will finally be transferred to the safety net.[7]

Deposit insurance in Japan. The experience of the US financial system suggests that deposit insurance should be an important element of any safety net. However, this has not been the case in postwar Japan. A system of deposit insurance was introduced in 1971, but it was not actually used until 1992. The MoF continued to implement the traditional safety net to avoid straightforward bankruptcies, and gave priority to the protection of weak (and therefore inefficient) banks over the promotion of competition, even after the introduction of deposit insurance. Indeed, in December 1997, following the bankruptcy of two major financial institutions, the government declared that all deposits and other bank debts such as bank debentures would be protected from bank failures.

Inevitably, this commitment by the government is likely to produce further moral hazard on the part of bank management by weakening the monitoring incentives of depositors and investors. However, even before the commitment, the long-standing implementation of the comprehensive safety net had produced a perception among these depositors and other investors that they would never be required to share any burden should their banks go bankrupt. Because of this widespread perception, the government adoption of a policy of paying off insured deposits without rescuing investors (along the lines of a deposit insurance scheme) would have resulted in an unexpected shock to the financial system, thereby making the difficulties even more serious. Thus, at the end of 1997, the Japanese government could not but make a commitment to ensure that the widespread perception about the safety net was still valid.

Japan's safety net may have had the merit of freeing people from the need to concern themselves about the soundness of an individual bank's management. However, it has also deprived investors of incentives to monitor the performance of individual banks and hindered the development of market mechanisms to discipline bank management. The lack of such mechanisms, in turn, has made it quite difficult for the government to abandon the traditional safety net. We learn from this experience how dangerous it is for the authorities to have the public believe in the effectiveness of too comprehensive a safety net.

3.2 Disciplinary influence of market competition

As has been shown for manufacturing (Nickell et al., 1997), market competition can exert a strong disciplinary influence on corporate management by weeding out inefficiently managed firms. Many Japanese believe that Japan's manufacturing firms have achieved worldwide excellence because they have faced fierce competition over many years. Though this belief requires empirical testing, it seems, prima facie, plausible. By contrast, Japan's financial services industries, including banking, have been protected from market competition by a web of regulations. Thus, competition has not worked to discipline management in banking and other financial services.

Role of regulations restricting competition The primary purpose of the MoF's administrative guidance was to suppress competition in the financial sector so as to protect less competitive and small-scale banks. The regulations that were used to this effect included interest rate controls, limitations on the numbers of branch offices,[8] and restrictions on new entry into banking and other financial business, which served to segment and compartmentalize the industry. These regulations conferred handsome rents on existing banks and other financial institutions. These rents, in turn, contributed to the stabilization of the banking system. First, as economic theory shows, the existence of rents provides private banks with incentives to refrain from excessive risk-taking in order to continue enjoying such rents, even in the absence of effective prudential regulation (Hellman et al., 1997). In addition, thanks to the protection offered by the MoF's regulations, even inefficient banks rarely found themselves in situations of difficulty that are particularly likely to induce moral hazard behaviour.[9]

Second, the monetary authorities were able to use the rents accumulated in the banking sector as a means of dealing with banks in financial distress. Specifically, the regulators relied on the collaboration of private banks in implementing the safety net, and the major banks faithfully bore a disproportionate share of the costs involved. This mechanism would not have worked had these banks not enjoyed the rents stemming from the competition-restricting regulations. The MoF also used regulations to give private banks an incentive to accept its initiatives when dealing with bank failures. Regulations were manipulated to favour those banks that toed the line and to penalize those that failed to heed official guidance. In other words, the restriction of competition was strategically important for the MoF to determine the distribution of rents among banks and to maintain the safety net's viability.

Delayed financial market deregulation. The regulations restricting competition have, however, gradually weakened the capacity of Japanese banks and other financial institutions to adapt themselves to changes in the environment since the mid-1970s. The most important of these was financial deregulation, urged upon Japan by foreign, and in particular American, pressures. In practice, however, the government has tightly controlled the process and has followed a policy of gradualism so as to prevent what it called the 'unduly destabilizing' effects of financial deregulation. In reality, this gradualism suppressed the disciplinary effects that deregulation was expected to exert on management and was synonymous with a policy of protecting vested interests in the financial sector. It was only in November 1997 that the government abandoned its policy of gradualism, with the announcement of a 'big bang' financial reform – a shock therapy belatedly making up for lost time.

Despite its gradualism, the deregulation of the 1980s did have some impact on domestic financial markets. In particular, major companies reduced their dependence on bank borrowing by issuing a large amount of corporate bonds on international markets. This 'internationalization' of corporate finance led to some deregulation of the domestic corporate bond market from the mid-1980s (Horiuchi, 1996). Yet, the impact of this 'internationalization' on the overall operations of the financial sector remained modest – most banks and other financial institutions went on basing their business on the huge amount of wealth accumulated by Japanese households.

3.3 The role of government in bank governance

The previous sections have argued that neither the capital market nor competitive forces were effective in disciplining bank management in Japan, mainly because government intervention (through the provision of a safety net and through pervasive regulation) suppressed those disciplinary influences. Efficient surveillance could, however, have been achieved through government supervision. The current legal framework allows this, since it assigns responsibility for monitoring bank management to the MoF, to the BoJ and, since 1998, to the Financial Supervision Agency. The following will examine how the government has implemented prudential regulations, and provide evidence to show that the weakness of monitoring by the regulatory authorities has contributed to the fragility of the banking industry.

Capital adequacy regulations. Capital adequacy requirements, accompanied by rigorous monitoring, are a typical means of prudential regulation and such requirements were imposed in Japan after the war. Thus, the occupation authorities insisted that banks increase their capital base and the MoF in 1953 instructed banks to reduce current expenses to 78 per cent

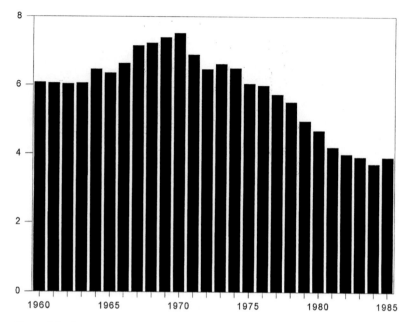

Figure 5.2 Commercial banks' capital/deposits ratios
Source: Japan Bankers' Association, *Analysis of Financial Statements of All Banks* (various issues).

or less of current revenues. A formal capital adequacy regulation was introduced in 1954. This required banks to increase broadly defined capital to more than 10 per cent of total deposits, and could be regarded as a forerunner of the capital adequacy regulation introduced by the Bank for International Settlements (BIS) in 1987. However, some depository financial institutions were not covered by this regulation until the late 1980s.[10]

Moreover, the regulation seemed to be ineffective. Figure 5.2 shows that, from 1960 to the mid-1970s, the average of the (broadly defined) capital/deposits ratio for 'city' banks and regional banks, remained almost constant at 6 per cent, far below the MoF's requirement of 10 per cent. Furthermore, the average capital/deposits ratio dropped abruptly to below 4 per cent during the 1980s.

Bank capital and 'amakudari'. Since bank management was disciplined neither by the capital market nor by competition, and since prudential regulation by the MoF was not seriously implemented, it would seem that a major vacuum existed in the governance of Japan's financial institutions. However, Aoki et al. (1994) have argued that the financial authority has been able to monitor bank management through the so-called *amakudari* system, a system in which private banks (and other firms) appointed retired government officials to their executive boards.[11] According to their argument, this system has given regulatory officers the incentive to rigorously monitor bank management, since failure to do so would have lessened their chances of obtaining good jobs in the private sector after retirement. In other words, *amakudari* should have had a positive influence on bank performance.

There is an agency problem, however, with the *amakudari* system, because bureaucrats supervise the management of banks that are likely to employ them after their retirement.[12] If these bureaucrats and banks collude to increase their own benefits, the *amakudari* system could undermine the effectiveness of monitoring by the financial authority and allow banks to engage in unsound management at the expense of depositors and/or taxpayers (Kane, 1995; Horiuchi and Shimizu, 2000). In other words, banks accepting *amakudari* officials could, in practice, show a below-average performance, in sharp contrast with the hypothesis advocated by Aoki et al. (1994).

In what follows, the hypothesis of whether or not the *amakudari* system undermines the prudence of the Japanese banking sector is tested by a simple statistical method. We take a sample of 125 regional banks existing as of March 1996 and classify them into four categories according to whether or not they accepted *amakudari* officers from the regulatory

Table 5.2 *Amakudari* and the performance of regional banks, 1985–1989

| | Regional bank category: | | | |
	MoF & BoJ (41)	MoF (43)[a]	BoJ (21)	NON (20)
Capital/asset ratio[b]	2.85*	3.01*	3.39	3.41
Total asset growth[c]	10.95	9.93	10.53	9.82
Profits/equity capital[b]	8.91	9.09	8.64	8.61
Non-performing loan/ total loan ratio[d]	4.15*	4.15*	2.21	2.20

Note: for an explanation of the regional bank categories used, see text; figures in brackets denote the number of regional banks in each category.
* Denotes that the figures are different from those of the 'NON' category at the 1 per cent statistical significance level.
a. Excluding Daiko Bank because of its abnormal performance in the 1980s.
b. Annual averages.
c. Average annual percentage changes.
d. As of March 1996.
Source: Author's calculations on data in Japan Bankers' Association, *Analysis of Financial Statements of All Banks* (various issues).

authorities in the mid-1980s. The first group (MoF and BoJ) contains banks that accepted *amakudari* bureaucrats from both these institutions; the second and third ones (groups MoF and BoJ) consist of banks taking officers only from the MoF or the BoJ respectively, while the fourth (group NON) is composed of those banks that did not hire *amakudari* officers at all. Table 5.2 compares the performances of these four categories of regional banks in four selected areas: the capital/asset ratio; the growth of total assets; the current profits per equity capital ratio; and the non-performing loan/total loan ratio. The latter is measured at March 1996; the other three are the averages of the sample period 1985–89.

No major differences emerge in the performances of the four groups of banks for two of the indicators chosen (growth of assets and profitability). Large differences appear, however, in capital/asset ratios, with categories MoF&BoJ and MoF showing significantly lower ratios than the group NON. Since lower capital/asset ratios imply higher levels of risk (Keeley, 1990), these results suggest that banks accepting *amakudari* officials from the MoF tended to behave less prudently.[13] While the equity/asset ratio could be regarded as an ex ante measure of risk-taking, the bad loan ratio could be seen as an ex post measure. Comprehensive data on non-performing loans were only first disclosed in March 1996. Taking these figures as a measure of the amount of risk taken by banks in the second half of the 1980s and in the first half of the 1990s, it can be shown that groups MoF&BoJ and MoF had bad loan ratios that were almost twice as high as those of banks totally independent of the *amakudari* relationship. These results too are consistent with the hypothesis that the relationship undermines MoF monitoring.Some may call into question the causality between *amakudari* and bank performance by stressing the fact that the MoF more often than not will dispatch officials to banks in financial distress in order to rehabilitate them. This has certainly been the case in some instances. However, almost all of the banks in distress had accepted *amakudari* officials long before they had faced managerial difficulties.

It would appear, on the basis of this evidence, that, contrary to what Aoki et al. (1994) have argued, *amakudari* was not effective in improving the performance of those banks that accepted the relationship. We conclude that the lack of effective monitoring by outsiders is the most conspicuous feature of the governance of Japanese banks. This feature has generated inflexibility in management and has contributed to the non-performing loans crisis of the 1990s.[14]

4 A vacuum of governance and delayed responses

When corporate managers run their firms independently of outsiders' control, as has been the case for Japanese banks, they will tend to: (i) engage in expansionism to display their managerial capability (Gorton and Rosen, 1995); and (ii) delay structural changes after their policy is found to have failed (Boot, 1992). This second point is particularly important in explaining why the Japanese banking crisis is so serious. In our opinion, the real problem arose not so much from the accumulation of non-performing loans, but from the delayed response on the part of bank management to this issue. Bank crises, after all, are not peculiar to Japan – as many as 133 were recorded in IMF member countries between 1980 and 1995 (Lindgren et al., 1996). What is special about Japan is the inordinately long time taken to tackle the crisis. Japanese banks have hesitated to take the necessary restructuring action. As for the govern-

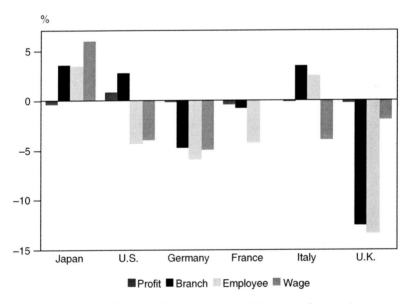

Figure 5.3 Restructuring in the banking industry: international comparison
Note: 'Profit' (total profits per asset) shows the difference between average profits in 1992–94 and 1986–88; 'Branch' shows the growth in the number of branches between 1990 and 1995; 'Employee' shows the growth in the total number of employees between 1990 and 1994; 'Wage' shows the difference in the ratio of total wage payments to total revenues between 1992–94 and 1986–88.
Source: BIS, 66th *Annual Report*, Basel, 1996.

ment, it did not take measures forcing banks to quickly strengthen their capital base because it hoped that the banks themselves would act. More importantly, it wanted to preserve the status quo in the financial sector for as long as possible.

An indication of this delay is provided by Figure 5.3, which presents an international comparison of bank restructuring in the first half of the 1990s. It will be seen that bank profitability decreased at the time in all the major industrialized countries, except the United States. Yet, while banks elsewhere acted to downsize their scale of business (by reducing, for instance, the number of bank branches or of employees, or by cutting the growth of wages), Japanese banks did not undertake any of these measures.

Market responses to the crisis. Initially, there were no responses from the financial markets either. Though investors had recognized the deterioration in bank performance, they believed in the government's capacity to implement the traditional safety net and trusted that this would protect them from any losses associated with possible bank failures. Thus, they felt no need to differentiate good banks from bad ones. However, as the non-performing loans problem dragged on, belief in the government's capacity to bail-out distressed banks began to wane.

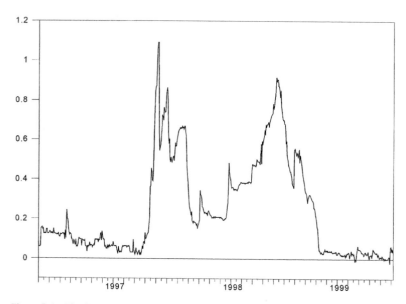

Figure 5.4 The 'Japan premium'[a] (January 1997–October 1999)
a. Difference between the Tokyo and London inter-bank borrowing rates.
Source: Nikkei Needs Money 'Data Bank'.

This is shown by the rise in the 'Japan premium' (Figure 5.4) which measures to what extent Japanese banks pay higher interest rates than foreign banks in the international inter-bank money markets. The premium was virtually non-existent until the end of September 1995. In October 1995, however, it jumped to more than 50 basis points, following what was felt to be the awkward reaction of the MoF to the disclosure of wrongdoings by the New York branch of Daiwa Bank. It then rose to a full percentage point in late 1997, following the failure of two significant financial institutions. These various events triggered off scepticism about the government's ability to stabilize the banking system by means of the traditional safety net.

This loss of confidence in the government finally prompted investors to monitor and discipline banks directly. This is shown, for instance, by the fact that banks began to face differential interest rates in line with investors' perceptions of their performance and contrary to earlier practice which had seen virtually no discrimination for various subsets of financial institutions. In short, the capital market at long last began to fill the vacuum that had hitherto existed in the governance of bank management. It did so, however, at the worst possible time, just when most banks were suffering from a high level of bad loans.

A number of emergency policy measures (injecting substantial public funds into the banking sector) were taken in 1998 and 1999. Yet, the 1998 injections did not tackle the root of the problem since help was provided to banks without consideration of their true performance. Investors were not convinced that the government would truly part with the old forbearance policy, and the capital market saw the injection as nothing but a continuation of the policy of protecting inefficiently managed institutions. As a consequence, the 'Japan premium' was not eliminated, since the markets clearly felt that only through drastic restructuring would the Japanese banking system be rationalized. Following the 1999 injection of public funds, by contrast, the 'Japan premium' has virtually disappeared. The emergency policy package enacted in October 1998, which allowed the government to temporarily nationalize two long-term credit banks, apparently convinced the capital markets that a substantial restructuring of bank management had finally begun.

5 Conclusions

This chapter has reviewed the governance structure of Japan's banking industry and stressed the fact that banks have been independent from outsiders' control. Even the Ministry of Finance has been ineffective in its monitoring and disciplining of bank management. The issue of 'who monitors the monitor' has thus not been solved and a vacuum exists in the governance of the country's financial system.

This vacuum of governance was responsible for the delayed response of the banking sector to the bad loan problem of the 1990s. It was only in the late 1990s that the government introduced a 'prompt corrective action rule' intended to put a halt to the previous forbearance policy. This measure seems to have at last induced hesitant banks to start restructuring their businesses. This fact in itself shows us that the banks had no strong incentives to reform on their own initiative.

To establish an efficient and robust financial system, Japan needs to fill the vacuum of governance. Fortunately, this process has now started. First, the government has promoted full-scale deregulation with the 1998 plan of 'big bang' financial reform. Although some uncertainties still surround this plan, it should create conditions that bring the financial industry nearer to those of a contestable market. Second, the government has made a commitment to start a pay-off of failed banks' deposits through the deposit insurance system in April 2001. This implies a reduction in the extent of the safety net. Large-scale depositors and other sophisticated investors will no longer be protected from bank failures. Thus, the capital market will be more active in monitoring bank management. Third, both the 1998 establishment of a Financial Supervisory Agency and the introduction of the 'prompt corrective action rule' have signalled a substantial change in government policy. In essence, prudential regulation will become more transparent, the notorious policy of forbearance will be discontinued and bank managers will be forced to reshape their ways of doing business.

Thus, the current policy is correctly directed at filling the governance vacuum that has long existed in Japanese bank management. A well-balanced combination of market competition, a limited safety net, capital market pressures, and effective monitoring by the supervisory authority should bring stability banks to the country's financial system and promote efficiency in financial intermediation.

Notes

1. Thus, 'in contrast to post-World War II years, Japanese corporations in the 1920s and 1930s had relied heavily on bond finance. Even in 1931 bonds provided 29.9 per cent of external corporate funding and bank loans only 13.6 per cent' (Calder, 1993, p. 29).
2. The recent theoretical literature on bank-firm relationships predicts that asymmetric information between lenders and borrowers will autonomously

produce long-term relationships between the two parties (Sharpe, 1990; Rajan, 1992). Thus, even if there had been no government-designated banks, intimate long-term relationships would have still been created. The wartime policy can, at most, explain why a specific firm chose a specific bank as its main bank.

3. *Zaibatsu* dissolution forced the disposal of large blocks of shares of *zaibatsu* related companies among many small investors, thereby exposing these companies to the dangers of hostile take-overs or 'green-mailing'. Responding to these dangers, the companies instituted mutual shareholding so as to block stock market pressures on management (Sheard, 1991).

4. Total abolition of the financial safety net would greatly strengthen the incentives of depositors and investors to monitor and discipline bank management. However, most depositors are only small wealth-holders enjoying no economies of scale in collecting and analysing information on bank performance. Thus, exclusive reliance on market discipline would not necessarily ensure the stability of the banking system. As argued by Dewatripont and Tirole (1994), some financial safety net is needed to protect small depositors.

5. The protection given to shareholders may be seen as a form of compensation for their silence on the issue of bank management. In reality, shareholders have been rather similar to debtholders in the banks' governance structure. This is indirectly shown by the great stability of dividend payments, regardless of bank performance. Thus, while 'city' (or major) bank profits were negative to the tune of ¥1.8 trillion (or some $ 15bn) in the five year period 1993–97, the amount of dividends paid out to shareholders remained almost constant at ¥1 trillion.

6. Unfortunately, a number of cases suggest that the forbearance policy continued in the 1990s. The most recent example is provided by the bail-out scheme implemented to salvage Nippon Credit Bank. In 1997, the MoF forced some financial institutions to supply capital to Nippon Credit, although it was recognized by the authorities that the bank was already virtually bankrupt. Ultimately, Nippon Credit was nationalized in late 1998.

7. The MoF's administration of branch offices was a particularly significant area of regulation. During the high growth period, when almost all interest rates were fixed by the authorities, the establishment of branch offices was the most important means for banks to compete for deposits. The MoF regulated the location of such offices and gave preferential treatment to small banks, whose numbers of branches increased more rapidly than that of the 'city' banks (Horiuchi, 1984). This regulation was only finally abolished in 1995.

8. Assuming asymmetric information about banks' monitoring activities, Aoki (1994) argues that the rents were necessary to motivate the banks to efficiently monitor their borrowers. He suggests that Japan's long-term bank–firm relationships (or 'main bank relationship') were crucially dependent on regulations restricting competition. However, regulations are not the only means by which to motivate banks to a supply a 'high quality' level of monitoring. A laissez-faire market would ensure a similar outcome (see Klein and Leffler, 1981).

9. For example, the *sogo* banks (medium-sized financial institutions, forerunners of today's regional banks) were, until 1989, required only to maintain more

than the prescribed minimum amount of equity capital (book value). Thus, they could have increased their leverage ratio without limit had they wished to do so. Similarly, the *shinkin*, or co-operative, banks, were free from capital adequacy requirements until 1986.

10. The MoF amended the capital adequacy regulation in 1986 when the accounting rules governing bank financial statements were changed. The new rules required banks' broadly defined capital to be equal to at least 4 per cent of total assets – hardly a stringent requirement. Since 1987, banks with branches or offices abroad have been subject to the BIS capital adequacy rule, but other banks continue to face only the domestic 4 per cent requirement.

11. *Amakudari* means the 'descent of gods from heaven'. In the present context, gods are retired officials and heaven is the bureaucracy. For an overview of some of the hypotheses of why the Japanese financial system has accepted *amakudari* officials, see Blumenthal (1985) and Rixtel (1994).

12. A similar agency problem has existed in the US banking system [Kane, 1989] and has apparently been responsible for the difficulties encountered by the Savings and Loans institutions in the 1980s.

13. Since the BoJ has not played a significant role with respect to prudential regulation, this result seems plausible (Horiuchi and Shimizu, 1998).

14. Since 1997, the bank crisis has, in fact, been centred not on smaller banks, but on the major 'city' banks whose non-performing loan problems have been most serious. The latter have, on the whole, been independent from the *amakudari* relationship. By contrast, regional banks appeared relatively sound in the later 1990s because the weakest ones had disappeared by 1997. Thus, the negative influence of *amakudari* on the soundness of bank management cannot explain the whole story of Japan's 1990s crisis.

References

Aoki, M. (1994) 'Monitoring Characteristics of the Main Bank System: an Analytical and Developmental View', in Aoki and Patrick (1994).

Aoki, M. and H.T. Patrick (eds) (1994) *The Japanese Main Bank System: Its Relevance for Developing and Transforming Economies*, New York, NY: Oxford, University Press.

Aoki, M., H.T. Patrick and P. Sheard (1994) 'The Japanese Main Bank System: an Introductory Overview', in Aoki and Patrick (1994).

Blumenthal, T. (1985) 'The Practice of *Amakudari* within the Japanese Employment System', *Asian Survey*, 25, 3, 310–21.

Boot, A.W.A. (1992) 'Why Hang on to Losers? Divestitures and Takeovers', *Journal of Finance*, 47, 4, 1401–23.

Calder, K.E. (1993) *Strategic Capitalism: Private Business and Public Purpose in Japanese Industrial Finance*, Princeton, NJ: Princeton University Press.

Dewatripont, M. and J. Tirole (1994) *The Prudential Regulation of Banks*, Cambridge, MA: MIT Press.

Gorton, G. and R. Rosen (1995) 'Corporate Control, Portfolio Choice, and the Decline of Banking', *Journal of Finance*, 50, 5, 1377–1420.

Hellman, T., K. Murdock and J.E. Stiglitz (1997) 'Financial Restraint: Toward a New Paradigm', in M. Aoki, H.-K. Kim and M. Okuno-Fujiwara (eds), *The Role of*

Government in East Asian Economic Development: Comparative Institutional Analysis, New York: NY, Oxford University Press.

Horiuchi, A. (1984) 'Economic Growth and Financial Allocation in Postwar Japan', Brooking Discussion Papers in International Economics, No. 18.

Horiuchi, A. (1996) 'An Evaluation of Japanese Financial Liberalization: a Case Study of Corporate Bond Markets', in T. Ito and A.O. Krueger (eds.), *Financial Deregulation and Integration in East Asia*, Chicago, IL. University of Chicago Press.

Horiuchi, A., F. Packer and S. Fukuda (1988) 'What Role has the "Main Bank" Played in Japan?', *Journal of the Japanese and International Economies*, 2, 2, 159–80.

Horiuchi, A. and K. Shimizu (1998) 'The Deterioration of Banks' Balance Sheets in Japan: Risk-taking and Recapitalization", *Pacific Basin Finance Journal*, 6, 1–2, 1–26.

Horiuchi, A. and K. Shimizu (2000) 'Did *Amakudari* Undermine the Effectiveness of Regulatory Monitoring in Japan?', *Journal of Banking and Finance* (forthcoming).

Hoshi, T., A. Kashyap and D. Scharfstein (1991) 'Corporate Structure, Liquidity, and Investment: Evidence from Japanese Industrial Groups', *Quarterly Journal of Economics*, 106, 1, 33–60.

Hoshi, T, A. Kashyap and G. Loveman (1994) 'Financial System Reform in Poland: Lessons from Japan's Main Bank System', in Aoki and Patrick (1994).

Kane, E.J. (1985) *The Gathering Crisis in Federal Deposit Insurance*, Cambridge, MA: MIT Press.

Kane, E.J. (1989) 'Changing Incentives Facing Financial-services Regulators', *Journal of Financial Services Research*, 2, 3, 265–74.

Kane, E.J. (1993) 'What Lessons should Japan Learn from the US Deposit-insurance Mess?', *Journal of the Japanese and International Economies*, 7, 4, 329–55.

Kane, E.J. (1995) 'Three Paradigms for the Role of Capitalization Requirements in Insured Financial Institutions', *Journal of Banking and Finance*, 19, 3–4, 431–59.

Keeley, M.C. (1990) 'Deposit Insurance, Risk, and Market Power in Banking', *American Economic Review*, 80, 5, 1183–1200.

Klein B. and K.B. Leffler (1981) 'The Role of Market Forces in Assuring Contractual Performance', *Journal of Political Economy*, 89, 4, 615–41.

Lindgren, C.-J., G. Garcia and M.I. Saal (1996) *Bank Soundness and Macroeconomic Policy*, Washington, DC: International Monetary Fund.

Miyajima, H. (1994) 'The Privatization of Ex-*zaibatsu* Holding Stocks and the Emergence of Bank-centered Corporate Groups in Japan', EDI Working Papers, No. 94–52.

Morck, R. and M. Nakamura (1999) 'Banks and Corporate Control in Japan', *Journal of Finance*, 54, 1, 319–39.

Nickell, S., D. Nicolitsas and N. Dryden (1997) 'What Makes Firms Perform Well?', *European Economic Review*, 41, 3–5, 783–96.

OECD (1998) *Economic Survey of Japan, 1998*, Paris.

Okazaki, T. (1997) 'The Government-firm Relationship in Postwar Japanese Economic Recovery: Resolving the Coordination Failure by Coordination in Industrial Rationalization', in M. Aoki, H.-K. Kim and M. Okuno-Fujiwara (eds), *The Role of Government in East Asian Economic Development: Comparative Institutional Analysis*, New York: NY, Oxford University Press.

Rajan, R.G. (1992) 'Insiders and Outsiders: The Choice between Informed and Arm's-length Debt', *Journal of Finance*, 47, 4, 1367–1400.

Rixtel, A. (1994) 'The Change and Continuity of *Amakudari* in the Private Banking Industry: Patterned Equalization, Bureaucratic Intervention and Career Management', paper presented at the seventh Conference of the European Association of Japanese Studies.

Sharpe, S.A. (1990) 'Asymmetric Information, Bank Lending, and Implicit Contracts: A Stylized Model of Customer Relationships', *Journal of Finance*, 45, 4, 1069–87.

Sheard, P. (1991) 'The Economics of Interlocking Shareholding in Japan', *Ricerche economiche*, 45, 2–3, 421–48.

Stiglitz, J.E. (1985) 'Credit Markets and the Control of Capital', *Journal of Money, Credit and Banking*, 17, 2, 133–52.

Teranishi, J. (1994) 'Emergence of Loan Syndication in Wartime Japan: an Investigation into the Historical Origin of the Main Bank System', in Aoki and Patrick (1994).

Weinstein, D.E. and Y. Yafeh (1998) 'On the Costs of a Bank-Centered Financial System: Evidence from the Changing Main Bank Relations in Japan', *Journal of Finance*, 53, 2, 635–72.

6
Foreign Trade Performance: From Early Similarities to Present Diversity*

Andrea Boltho

1 Introduction

As in many other areas explored in this book, Italy and Japan share similarities as well as differences in their foreign trade structure and evolution since the Second World War. Both countries have a low natural resource endowment and have therefore traditionally imported raw materials and foodstuffs. These accounted for well over 50 per cent of the Italian import bill in the early 1950s and for as much as 90 per cent of the Japanese one. By the later 1990s, these shares had declined to some 33 and 45 per cent respectively, yet these figures were still much above the 15 to 25 per cent shares that are commonly found elsewhere in the OECD countries. Conversely, their exports have been overwhelmingly manufactured products – 65 per cent for Italy and 85 per cent for Japan at the beginning of the period under examination; 90 and 95 per cent respectively by 1996–97. These figures too are among the highest in the world, matched in the OECD area only by Germany and Switzerland.

Paralleling their rapid growth rates in output, both countries have also experienced rapid growth in foreign trade flows, with their shares of the world market for manufactures doubling (Italy), or more than trebling (Japan), between the early 1950s and the late 1990s. Interestingly, however, after sharing a relatively similar commodity specialization pattern at the outset, the two economies have subsequently diverged.

* The author would like to thank Wendy Carlin for numerous helpful comments.

Japan's exports have shifted from labour-intensive to high-skill and high-tech products; Italy's sales abroad have changed less – even today the country is still specialized in consumer goods that, on the surface at least, appear to be low-tech. An even starker difference emerges on the import side – while import shares in output have risen rapidly in Italy, they have remained stable and very low in Japan.

Finally, both countries have experienced growing integration into their surrounding areas. In Italy this trend had already begun in the 1950s in the wake of Europe's trade liberalization. In Japan, by contrast, the 1950s and 1960s saw trade diversification away from Asia – in particular, towards North America. The very buoyant growth of East and South-East Asia over the last two decades has, however, led to a gradual reorientation. By now, this area accounts for nearly 40 per cent of Japan's trade, well below the 60 per cent or more of Italy's exchanges with Western Europe, but well above the low point (20 per cent) of the mid-1960s.

The following pages explore some of these differences and similarities. Sections 2 and 3 look at foreign trade trends in greater detail, concentrating, in particular, on the structural changes that have occurred in export composition, with Section 4 providing some possible interpretations. A brief conclusion summarizes the main arguments and gives a tentative look at the future.

2   Trends

The introduction to this chapter has mentioned the rapid postwar growth of Italian and Japanese foreign trade. This section looks at the phenomenon in greater detail, examining in turn trends in the shares of trade in domestic output and in world markets and the changing commodity composition of trade flows.

2.1   Trade shares

In the early 1950s, Japan's degree of openness to foreign trade (measured by the current price share of exports and imports of goods and services in GDP) was slightly above Italy's (Table 6.1). Since then, developments in the two countries have been starkly divergent. Apart from some temporary upward fluctuations dictated by the terms of trade shocks of the 1970s, Japan's share has, if anything, declined, in contrast to regular increases in Italy's share. By the late 1990s, the value of foreign trade was equal to roughly half of Italy's GDP, but to only one fifth of Japan's.

Table 6.1   Foreign trade share in output (exports plus imports of goods and services in per cent of GDP at current prices)

	Italy	Japan
1951–52	21.6	24.2[a]
1970–71	33.0	20.5
1996–97	49.2	20.2
Memorandum item:		
Annual trend change in share, 1951–97[b]	0.63	–0.03[a]
	(12.6)	(0.7)

a. 1951 calendar year data were obtained for Japan by applying fiscal year 1951–52 percentage changes to 1952 calendar year figures.
b. Obtained from fitted linear trends; figures in brackets are t-ratios.
Sources: OECD, *National Accounts of OECD Countries* (various issues) and EPA, *Revised Report on National Income Statistics (1951–1967)*.

Despite stability in output shares, Japan's exports grew more rapidly than Italy's. Figure 6.1 illustrates the two countries' penetration of the world market for manufactures. Both economies recorded a broadly similar growth in market shares in the 1950s and 1960s, reflecting in part a process of catch-up. Thereafter, however, and until the mid-1980s, Japan continued to register impressive gains, while the growth of Italy's inroads abroad slowed down sharply. Japan's overall performance is particularly striking since, through a good deal of the period, the country laboured under three major handicaps that were not (or were much less) present in Italy.

First, Japanese exports have, since the mid-1950s, suffered from a plethora of restrictive practices abroad. Tariffs, quotas and ubiquitous 'voluntary' export restraints were imposed on, inter alia, Japanese textiles in the 1950s, steel in the 1960s, durable consumer goods in the 1970s, and cars in the 1980s and 1990s (Argy and Stein, 1997). Italian exports, on the other hand, have encountered virtually no specific discrimination. In its major Western European markets, in particular, Italy has increasingly enjoyed barrier-free entry.

Second, Japan faced for the first three decades of the period a less favourable commodity and geographic export structure than did Italy. Table 6.2 provides rough estimates of the growth of the two economies' export markets. Until the late 1970s, both the demand for the kinds of goods that Japan sold and the countries to which they were destined, expanded more slowly than did world trade as a whole,[1] while the opposite was the case for Italy. In other words, the rise in market shares achieved by Japan implied a much greater competitive effort than that made by Italy. It was only from the later 1970s onwards that the

%

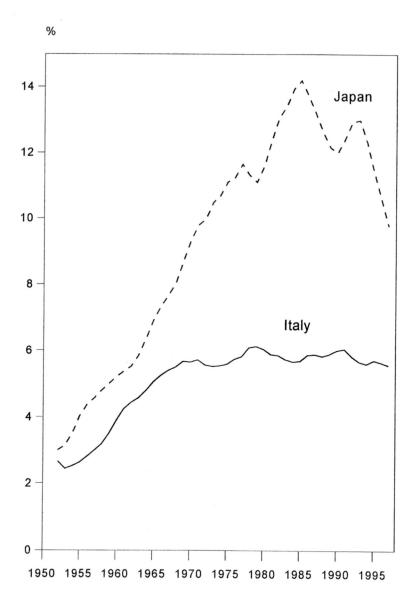

Figure 6.1 Manufactured export market shares (in per cent of world exports of manufactures; three-year moving averages)
Sources: GATT, *International Trade* and WTO, *Annual Report* (various issues).

Table 6.2 Growth of export markets for manufactures[a] (average annual percentage changes)

	World trade[b]	Growth of: Italian markets	Japanese markets
1955–63	7.7	8.2[c]	6.0[c]
1963–73	9.8	10.1	8.5
1973–80	5.9	5.8	5.8
1980–90	5.6	5.0	6.4
1990–96	6.4	6.0	8.0

a. Obtained by applying to Italian and Japanese area and commodity trade matrices for each base year the export growth rates from the major industrialized countries over the period. The size of the matrices varies depending on period; for 1955–63, the matrix is only geographical and contains 8 areas; for the later periods, they contain from 6 to 12 commodity groups and from 6 to 10 geographical areas. The data were deflated by the single unit value index for total manufactured exports.
b. Growth of world exports of manufactures.
c. Market growth is based on a geographical breakdown only.
Sources: General Agreement on Tariffs and Trade (GATT), *International Trade* (various years); World Trade Organization (WTO), *Annual Report* (various years); OECD, *Foreign Trade Statistics, Series B* (various years) and *Foreign Trade by Commodities, 1996*.

commodity composition of Japan's trade flows became more favourable, thanks to the country's move towards the frontier of technology. Italy's more stable pattern of comparative advantage (discussed further below) implied instead that no similar transformation was forthcoming – market growth was regular in the earlier decades, but the country missed out on the more recent acceleration in the demand for high-tech products. Furthermore, while Japan has in the last two decades benefited from the buoyant expansion of East and South-East Asia, Italy found that its heavy reliance on a now more sluggish Western Europe could be a handicap.

Third, and equally importantly, Japan's real exchange rate has often been above its equilibrium level (Figure 6.2).[2] This was almost certainly the case through the 1950s (though not the 1960s), a period for which most estimates of the yen's real value suggest a measure of overvaluation (Nakakita, 1993). Floating led to pronounced currency fluctuations along an underlying steeply rising trend. In part this reflected Japan's rapid productivity growth (Yoshikawa, 1990); on several occasions, however, the currency overshot its equilibrium value. Italy, by contrast, began the period with an exchange rate that seemed at least 10 to 15 per cent undervalued relative to the dollar (Boltho, 1996a). Moreover, real undervaluation vis-à-vis both the dollar and Europe's other currencies is likely to have increased in the course of the 1950s and 1960s in view of the country's subdued price and cost developments at the time (ibid.). Some

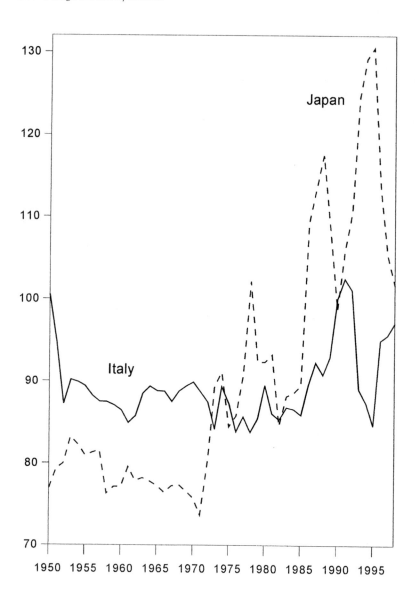

Figure 6.2   Real exchange rates (indices; 1990 = 100; based on relative wholesale prices)
Source: Author's estimates based on data in IMF, *International Financial Statistics* (various issues).

real appreciation occurred under floating, particularly in the second half of the 1980s, but this pales in comparison with what happened to Japan.

Major differences in trends are also apparent on the import side. The shares of manufactured imports in GDP, which were broadly similar in the early 1950s, have since diverged – Japan's experienced near constancy, Italy's very rapid growth (Figure 6.3). This last development has been common to virtually the whole of the industrialized world as a consequence of liberalization and of the growth of intra-industry trade.[3] Japan shared in the first of these two features but, partly because of its distance from Western Europe and North America, partly for other reasons looked at in Section 3 below, it has largely shunned intra-industry trade.[4] Only in the 1990s has the country increased its purchases of foreign manufactures, largely from neighbouring Asia. Yet, even now, such imports are overwhelmingly simple manufactures primarily produced by Japanese subsidiaries abroad (Katz, 1996).

2.2 Commodity composition

In the 1950s Italy and Japan had a relatively similar commodity composition of trade. Primary products loomed large in import bills, simple manufactures in sales abroad. Thus, ranking exports by indices of revealed comparative advantage (RCA)[5] shows that in 1955 in both economies the top Standard International Trade Classification (SITC) three-digit product groups consisted overwhelmingly of clothing and semi-manufactures, such as intermediate textiles and products of the chemicals and leather (Italy) or pottery (Japan) industries. Rank correlations between the two countries' RCA indices show positive and statistically significant coefficients, particularly if the RCAs are weighted by the various products' shares in total exports (Table 6.3).

Forty years later the correlation is, if anything, negative. Japan's top ten export products, when ranked by RCA, come now overwhelmingly from the machinery sector (seven from SITC section 7 and one from precision instruments), while Italy's are still to be found in semi-manufactures (five in SITC section 6) and in consumer goods (four in SITC section 8). In other words, while Italy's initial comparative advantage was broadly maintained, Japan's was radically transformed. Italy's three top SITC three-digit export earners in 1995 (cars, office machinery and clothing) were also Italy's three top export earners in 1965. In Japan, by contrast, there was not one product in common between these two years. Textiles and steel loomed large in the 1950s and 1960s, ships and cars in the 1970s, and cars and machinery in the 1980s and 1990s. More formally, there is clear evidence of a strong positive correlation between the specialization

%

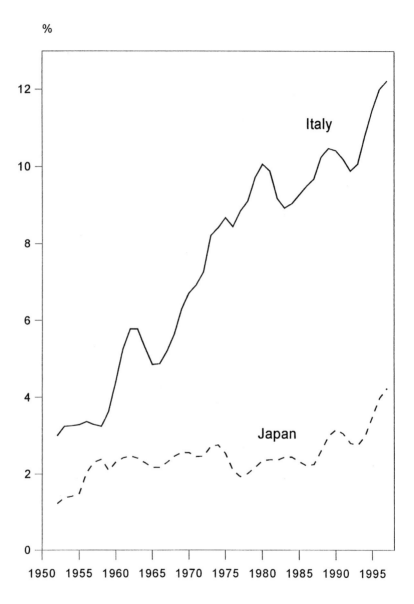

Figure 6.3   Manufactured imports share in GDP (percentages; three-year moving averages)
Sources: GATT, *International Trade* and WTO, *Annual Report* (various issues); OECD, *National Accounts of OECD Countries* (various issues).

Table 6.3   Rank correlation coefficients for indices of revealed comparative advantage

	SITC 2-digits		SITC 3-digits	
	Simple[a]	Weighted[b]	Simple[a]	Weighted[b]
Italy with Japan				
1955	0.25*	0.57***	0.16*	0.38***
1995	–0.12	–0.39**	0.12	–0.31***
Italy				
1955 with 1995	0.31**	0.68***	0.22**	0.44***
Japan				
1955 with 1995	–0.09	–0.37**	0.03	–0.56***

Note: the SITC nomenclature has undergone two changes between 1955 and 1995. An attempt was made to make the 1995 data comparable with the 1955 ones. Inevitably, however, some discrepancies still remain and the through-time results here shown are based on not fully comparable statistics.
* Significant at the 10 per cent level.
** Significant at the 5 per cent level.
*** Significant at the 1 per cent level.
a. Spearman coefficient of rank correlation.
b. The coefficient weighs rank differences by the product's importance in exports (and is equal to $1 - [(6\Sigma d_i^2 w_i)/(n^2 - 1)]$; where d_i are the differences in ranks, w_i the weights of each product group and n the number of observations (see, for instance, Hufbauer, 1970).
Source: Author's estimates based on Organisation for European Economic Co-operation (OEEC) and OECD, *Foreign Trade Statistics* (various series and issues) and GATT, *International Trade* and WTO, *Annual Report* (various issues).

patterns of 1955 and 1995, as measured by the RCA indices, in Italy, as against a non-existent or negative correlation in Japan (Table 6.3).

An indicator of these differing trends is provided by data on trade balances by technological categories which show almost mirror images of each other (Figure 6.4).[6] Japan, whose surplus in low-tech products, in per cent of GDP, was much larger than Italy's at the beginning of the 1960s, moved into growing deficits as the yen began its secular appreciation. Italy, by contrast, switched from rough balance into rising surplus. Trade in high-tech goods saw almost opposite trends – Japan strengthened its position, at least until the mid-1980s, while Italy recorded a growing deficit, at least until the early 1990s. Not surprisingly perhaps, in the light of this, it turns out that Italian exports come to a much larger extent than Japanese ones from small firms. The data in this area are not strictly comparable, but a recent OECD study suggests that, in the late 1980s, more than 50 per cent of Italy's sales abroad originated in enterprises with fewer than 200 employees (OECD, 1997). In Japan, by contrast, firms with fewer than 300 employees were responsible for less than 15 per cent of total exports (ibid.), sharply down from significantly higher shares in

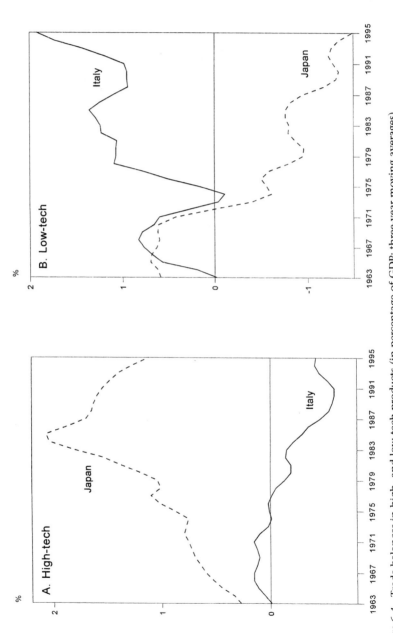

Figure 6.4 Trade balances in high- and low-tech products (in percentage of GDP; three-year moving averages)
Sources: OECD, 'Data Bank' and *National Accounts, Vol. I, 1960–1997*.

earlier years (some 25 per cent in 1970, for instance, or as much as 60 per cent in 1956) (Rapp, 1976).[7]

A further characteristic that distinguishes Italian from Japanese exports is the latters' much greater concentration on a few products. In 1995, for instance, Japan's three top exports earners (cars, electric and office machinery) accounted for as much as 40 per cent of the value of the country's industrial sales abroad. The corresponding figure for Italy was less than one-quarter. More formally, Hirschman indices of concentration show that from rough similarity in 1955, the two countries have since sharply diverged. At the outset of the period, the indices (for an SITC three-digit breakdown) stood at 0.129 for Italy and 0.126 for Japan. By 1995, the Italian index had declined to 0.097 while that for Japan had climbed to 0.199.[8]

3 Some explanations

Section 2 has pointed to a number of areas in which Italian and Japanese trade performances have differed over the last half-century. Of particular importance would seem to be the following:

(i) Japan's export performance appears to have been superior to that of Italy, and this despite the country having had to cope with more protectionism, a stronger exchange rate and a less favourable commodity and geographic composition of its sales abroad than Italy through much of the period;

(ii) Within this performance, Japan experienced a much faster pace of structural change, a much greater concentration on a few key products (that have changed from decade to decade), and a much higher presence of high-tech and investment goods than Italy;

(iii) On the import side, the penetration of foreign manufactures has grown much more rapidly in Italy than in Japan, as has the importance of intra-industry trade; other than for primary products, Japan has seemed an almost closed economy through much of the period.

The reasons for these differences are, no doubt, numerous. At a risk of oversimplification, two major sets of factors will be considered below: macroeconomic forces and enterprise behaviour.

3.1 Macroeconomic forces

Standard export or import demand functions can shed light on the behaviour of the two countries' trade flows in the short run (Table 6.4).

Table 6.4   Manufactured export and import shares – main determinants, 1951–1997

| | Exports | | Imports | |
	Italy	Japan	Italy	Japan
	Dep. variable: Xsh		Dep. variable: Msh	
Constant	3.70	3.99	–3.61	–1.48
	(4.0)	(4.5)	(2.2)	(3.5)
RER_{t-1}	–0.035	–0.035	0.019	0.021
	(3.6)	(4.1)	(1.0)	(5.5)
ChY/ChY_{mf}	–0.037	–0.090	0.186	0.034
	(2.1)	(2.4)	(9.5)	(4.4)
Xsh_{t-1}/Msh_{t-1}	0.92	0.98	1.16	0.75
	(25.4)	(26.5)	(35.6)	(7.1)
$\bar{R}^2$	0.96	0.97	0.97	0.74
SE	0.25	0.63	0.46	0.31

Xsh = Share in world exports of manufactures;
Msh = Share of manufactured imports in GDP;
RER = Real exchange rate (relative wholesale prices);
ChY = Percent change in GDP;
ChY_{mf} = Percent change in manufacturing output;
Figures in brackets are *t*-ratios.

On the basis of an, admittedly simple, specification, the equations shown suggest that performance was very similar, with the responsiveness of the world market share to the real exchange rate virtually identical. Demand pressures (proxied by the growth rate of GDP) also matter. The effect is particularly pronounced in Japan and confirms the well-known counter-cyclical role that exports have often played in the country. A similar specification on the import side (substituting only the growth of manufacturing value added for that of GDP to proxy demand pressures) generates similarly reasonable results for Japan, but is unable to unearth a statistically significant link between the import share and the real exchange rate for Italy.

Yet, such variables, while able to explain year-to-year changes, say very little about the longer-run trends which show much larger export gains and much lower import penetration for Japan than for Italy. More structural explanations are needed. For exports, a plausible interpretation might link the success of Japanese goods abroad to the country's very rapid economic growth. Over the half-century from 1950, Japan's GDP trend growth rate has been close to 6 per cent per annum, as against Italy's $3\frac{3}{4}$ per cent. This difference in supply performance may well have generated different export responses, in line with an approach explicitly put forward by Krugman (1989) (and implicitly by Kaldor [1981]). In this approach, the explanation for a positive correlation between rapid domestic and export growth is based on a model in which, thanks mainly to the operation of scale economies: 'fast growing countries expand their shares of the world market by expanding the range of goods they produce' (Krugman, 1989, p. 1039).

The same explanation, however, can hardly be applied to the import side. Rapid growth leads to rising import penetration through short-run demand spill-overs (as, indeed, confirmed by the evidence presented in Table 6.4), and through longer-run taste diversification likely to privilege manufactured imports (Barker, 1977). Yet, as shown by Figure 6.3, this has hardly happened in Japan in contrast to the experience of Italy (and of virtually all other developed market economies). The reasons for Italy's trends are well known – trade liberalization carried out with vigour from the late 1940s onwards[9] was a major import stimulating force. And this process was powerfully helped by the concomitant expansion of intra-industry trade, which greatly diminished the costs of (and hence the resistance to) liberalization from import-competing sectors. Japan, on the other hand, began to open its economy only in the mid-1960s and carried out this process more slowly. Protectionism, in other words, was both more pronounced, and present for much longer, than in the case of Italy.

By today, ostensibly at least, both countries are equally open to foreign goods. Neither formal trade barriers, nor the incidence of those non-tariff barriers that can be roughly measured, differ much – if anything, the latter may be higher in Italy.[10] Despite this, the share of Japanese manufactured imports in GDP is only one third that of Italy. This issue has generated a voluminous literature (see, inter alia, Lincoln, 1990; Lawrence, 1993; Saxonhouse, 1993; Argy and Stein, 1997) which has pointed to a number of structural reasons for Japan's low manufacturing import propensity, such as the country's distance from major trading partners and the importance of its primary product imports. In addition, however, it also appears that Japan has managed to remain relatively closed to foreign manufactures. A long tradition of mercantilism may play some role in inhibiting imports,[11] but such cultural influences are now declining. More important reasons for implicit protectionism come from cumbersome wholesale and retail trade structures which make selling in Japan expensive for foreigners (interestingly, this feature could also play a role in Italy, given the country's fragmented commercial system,[12] yet is rarely evoked when discussing the difficulties of entering that market). Others have to do with the purchasing practices of the public sector and of the *keiretsu* conglomerates which appear to privilege intra-group purchases at the expense of imports (Lawrence, 1991; Noland, 1997).

3.2   Firm behaviour

This latter explanation leads to a further important reason for why Japanese and Italian trade performances have differed – that of firm behaviour. On the import side, as just argued, the presence of conglomerates in one country, their virtual absence in the other, made for different purchasing policies abroad. Similarly, Japan's large and powerful trading companies may well have helped export successes through their market research, advertising, financing and other activities. In Italy, by contrast, Japanese-style trading companies are absent – even though Italian exporters are in greater need of such services than their Japanese counterparts, given the much larger weight in exports of small firms, usually less familiar with foreign markets.

A second area of difference lies in the private sector's investment efforts in both human and physical capital. Throughout the half century under examination, Japanese firms have almost certainly devoted many more resources than Italian ones to on-the-job training. Similarly, their investment in machinery and equipment has constantly outstripped, and by a significant margin, that made by Italian firms (Table 6.5).

Thirdly, expenditure on R&D has been large and has risen rapidly in Japan; in Italy, by contrast, it has been small and sluggish (Figure 6.5). This must have influenced the high-tech exporting performance of the two countries. The plethora of small Italian exporting firms, while clearly spending on the upgrading of their products' quality and design, has found (formal) R&D either impractical and/or too expensive. Largely as a consequence, Italy's presence on world high-tech markets is much smaller than Japan's (the former country accounted for $3\frac{1}{2}$ per cent of total OECD exports of high-tech products in the mid-1990s, the latter for $19\frac{1}{2}$ per cent).

Table 6.5   Share of machinery and equipment investment in output (in per cent of GDP at current prices)

	Italy	Japan
1951–96	9.5	11.6[a]
1951–60	9.3	9.8[a]
1961–70	8.8	14.4[a]
1971–80	10.4	11.6
1981–90	9.9	11.0
1991–96	8.7	10.8

a. The investment data for the years 1951–69 are for fiscal years.
Sources: OECD, *National Accounts of OECD Countries* (various issues); Prometeia, Data Bank; EPA, *Revised Report on National Income Statistics (1951–1967)* and *Annual Report on National Income Statistics, 1974.*

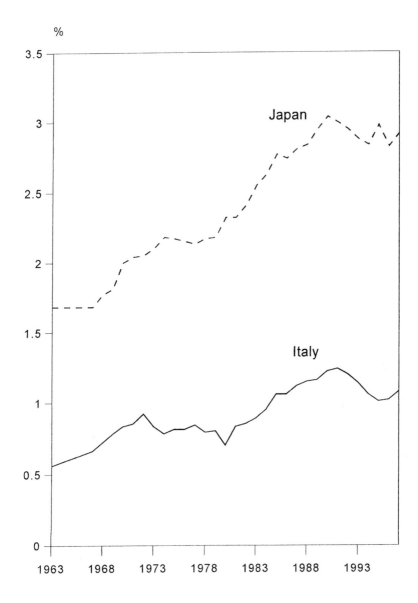

Figure 6.5   R&D expenditure (in percentage of GDP)
Sources: National Science Foundation, *National Patterns of Science and Technology Resources*, 1982; OECD, 'Data Bank' and *Pattern of Resources Devoted to Research and Experimental Development in the OECD Area, 1963–1971*, Paris, 1975.

Finally, the FDI flows of Japanese firms over the last quarter century have reached nearly $350 billion, as against some $75 billion for Italy. Not all FDI generates greater exports. Some (especially in Japan) is made to ensure raw material supplies. More importantly, recent Japanese FDI has often taken place to circumvent foreign protectionism, a process likely to reduce exports. Yet, it is also well known that FDI, initially at least, stimulates sales abroad by generating a rising demand for machinery and intermediate inputs. On balance, the strength of Japan's FDI relative to Italy's is likely to have contributed to the country's exports, as confirmed by estimates made of its effects on net trade in the first half of the 1990s (Yoshitomi, 1996).

Ultimately, many of these differentiating features can be linked to a behavioural characteristic that has often been associated with Japanese enterprises and that seems much less present in the Italian corporate sector – 'long-termism'. Large R&D efforts, significant investments in capital formation, long-standing relationships with other firms, and a growing involvement in production overseas, are all features likely to encourage market share growth and (at times at least) to discourage purchases from outside one's established network of suppliers, even if all this may come at some cost in terms of immediate profitability (Saucier, 1987).

4   An interpretation

The foregoing may provide some proximate explanations for the two countries' trade performances, but does not answer the question as to why the 'natural' evolution of Italy's and Japan's comparative advantage should have moved along such very different paths despite rather similar starting points. Not only was there similarity in initial RCA indices; most of the available evidence assembled for the 1950s or the 1960s suggests that, in addition, the two countries' factor endowments were also broadly comparable. Thus, estimates of total capital or technological endowments made for 1962, put Italy at levels only slightly above those of Japan (Aquino, 1981). In the same vein, calculations of the capital per worker, or of the skilled manpower contents, of the two countries' exports in 1965 give very similar values (Hufbauer, 1970), a finding broadly confirmed in other investigations (such as that of, Keesing, 1968).

By the mid-1990s, however, the structure of the two economies and of their export bundles, was radically different. Japan stood at the frontier of technology in a number of important areas, its capital–labour ratio was much above Italy's and its export structure was heavily concentrated in R&D-intensive activities. By contrast, Italy's high-tech presence was limited, its exports continued to heavily depend on small firms, and their structure was much more skewed towards consumer goods. To be sure, there is a world of difference between the simple shirt or leather bag exported in the 1950s and the Armani or Gucci products sold on world markets today, but there is surely an even greater difference between the cheap consumer goods or crude steel that Japan exported in the early postwar years and the videos, semiconductors or numerically controlled machine tools it sells nowadays. One country, much more than the other, seems to have been able to 'create' comparative advantage in new areas.

'Catch-up' can hardly provide a sufficient explanation. It is true that Japan lagged behind Italy in the 1950s. Already by 1970, however, incomes per capita (measured in purchasing power parity terms) were quite similar and today Japan is some 15 per cent ahead.[13] Cultural explanations seem similarly wanting – Confucian Japan is a country with a high saving ratio, but so is Catholic Italy (with household saving ratios in the two countries roughly similar over the 1960–95 years), and both save a good deal more than Protestant Britain or Sweden; 'animal spirits' appear to have prospered in individualistic Italy just as in more group-oriented Japan, and so on.

Section 3 above pointed to the importance of differing company behaviour. The latter, in turn, could be partly linked to a corporate governance structure that, since the war, has been very different from Italy's,[14] and that seems to have fostered a much greater degree of 'long-termism'. Italy's corporate governance model could have done the same since the country's state enterprises or family-controlled pyramidal groups have hardly been subject to the short-term pressures said to be characteristic of Anglo-American capitalism. Yet, 'long-termism' was not much in evidence. A broader explanation would thus seem required, an explanation that is able to distinguish between the largely spontaneous evolution of Italy's export performance and the more policy-guided inroads made by Japan's on world markets.

Government intervention has, of course, been present in both economies.[15] In Italy, nearly as much as in Japan, the authorities have interfered in sectoral matters, have laid out industrial plans and policies, have strived to 'defend' or 'improve' their firms' external competitiveness, and so on. It is only very recently that a gradual withdrawal from such interventionist practices has tentatively begun. Yet, looking at the comparative experience, there would seem to have been more careful planning and greater consistency in Japan's case than in Italy's.

Officially, three criteria have guided Japanese industrial policy – sectors were selected for help if they were associated with high future income elasticities of demand, a high potential for productivity growth and, increasingly, a high use of advanced technologies (Itoh et al., 1988). Looking at outcomes, these criteria seem to have been broadly followed. In the move through time from the steel and shipbuilding of the 1950s, to the cars and electronics of the 1960s and 1970s and to the more recent knowledge-intensive sectors, Japan's bureaucracy has shown an apparent continuity of purpose that was absent in Italy. It has also used a panoply of instruments going well beyond the mere protection or subsidization of particular activities (for example, provision of imported technology, organization of 'recession cartels', so-called 'administrative guidance'). Particularly important may have been the announcement effects of choosing certain sectors. These indicated a tacit public commitment to provide an implicit safety net to the chosen sector's large-scale firms in case of difficulty.

Italy has had its fair share of industrial policies, but, according to most observers, these have lacked a coherent strategy (Prodi and De Giovanni, 1990). Implementation has been hindered by the division between private and state industry (ibid.), while effectiveness was increasingly sacrificed to the overriding aim of preserving employment in large-scale enterprises through the indiscriminate granting of subsidies (Gros-Pietro, 1990). In the 1970s and 1980s, in particular, funds were distributed in line with various sectors' weights in industrial production, a policy clearly favouring the status quo (La Noce, 1989). Aid was given to smaller firms, with apparently favourable effects in the 1950s and 1960s (Arrighetti and Seravalli, 1997), but this aid seldom aimed at creating new establishments and never at strengthening the country's dynamic 'industrial districts' (Becattini, 1998).

The overall impression is that intervention seems to have fallen prey to special interest groups to a larger extent in Italy than in Japan. In part, this probably reflects the fact that many of the privileged Italian sectors were dominated by one, or a few, large-scale firms, in contrast to the more competitive Japanese markets. And this points to what is probably the most crucial difference between Italian and Japanese industrial policies. Japanese policies encouraged competition at home (Boltho, 1985), Italian ones much more readily accepted the existence and preservation of dominant positions. In Japan, for instance, when licensing imported technologies, MITI shared these out to several competing firms, be this in synthetic fibres (Ozawa, 1980), polyethylene (Peck, 1976), steel (Vestal, 1993) or television production (Lynn, 1994). In Italy, by contrast, the vast public industry sector, in particular, enjoyed continuous monopoly positions and preferential access to state banks.

Interestingly, while Japan encouraged competition at home, it discouraged it from abroad. Italian policies were almost opposite. As mentioned earlier, Japan sheltered its domestic industry from foreigners for much longer and with much greater determination. Italy, by contrast, had, already in the late 1940s, reacted against the semi-autarchy of the interwar years and had, by the 1950s, joined the move towards freer intra-European trade. That the latter was welfare-enhancing can hardly be doubted. Benefiting from a relatively low real exchange rate and from the opening of neighbouring countries, and stimulated by foreign competition, Italy was able to raise the quantity and quality of its exports, diversify its consumption and grow rapidly, but its comparative advantage changed little. Japan, on the other hand, opened much less, yet transformed its industrial structure and, ultimately, grew even more rapidly.

An illustration of comparative developments for one particular product (passenger cars) is provided by Figure 6.6. In this sector Italy possessed a revealed comparative advantage in 1955 while Japan did not. By 1995, the positions had been reversed – Japan's RCA index was its fifth highest, Italy's was well below unity. If only very impressionistically, the chart points to one major difference – Japan had, in 1951 already, opted to pursue an import substitution policy (Mutoh, 1988), along the lines of the 'flying geese' approach pioneered by a Japanese economist in the 1930s (Akamatsu, 1961). Italy, in partial contrast, after following similar developments in the early 1950s, had opened its doors to imports.[16] Japan, particularly in the 1950s and early 1960s, appears as an almost textbook case of the Krugman (1984) model of 'import protection for export promotion', in which privileged access to the domestic market allows the exploitation of scale economies, lowers costs and facilitates sales abroad. Italy, on the other hand, shows how comparative advantage can change under the pressure of international competition and in the absence of conscious policy efforts designed to preserve or strengthen an existing advantage.

The developments shown in Figure 6.6 do not prove that industrial policies lead to welfare-enhancing outcomes compared to what the unfettered play of market forces would have delivered. Whether this is so or not has been much debated, notably in connection with Japanese intervention (see, inter alia, Saxonhouse, 1983; Komiya et al., 1988; Vestal, 1993; Beason and Weinstein, 1996). A consensus on the issue has hardly been reached. Yet, when looking at foreign trade, there would seem to be little doubt that most of the sectors targeted by Japanese industrial

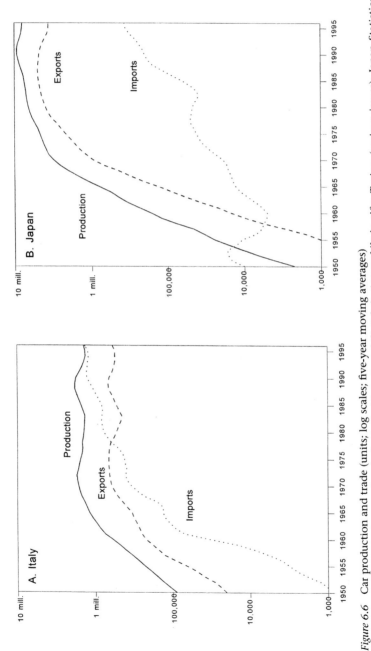

Figure 6.6 Car production and trade (units; log scales; five-year moving averages)
Sources: ANFIA (Associazione nazionale fra industrie automobilistiche), *Automobile in cifre*, Torino (various issues); Japan Statistical Association, *Historical Statistics of Japan*, Tokyo, 1988; *Japan Statistical Yearbook and Monthly Statistics of Japan* (various issues).

policies turned out to be successful, something that can hardly be said of Italy. Here, the best export performance was recorded by sectors that were often ignored by the policy-makers and by firms that were too small to be noticed in Rome. It is true that Japan's successes could have been achieved despite the policies and that the (relatively small) public funds that were spent could have been better employed in alternative uses. Yet, a study attempting to test for the effects of industrial policies on foreign trade performance concluded that this influence had been positive (Noland, 1993).[17] In the present context, looking just at the comparison with Italy, it would seem plausible to argue that the higher physical and R&D investments of Japan's private sector and its greater trade successes, must, to some extent at least, have been linked to a more determined and better administered policy effort.

Japan, in other words, would seem to provide an example of the application of a new strand in the modern theory of international trade – 'strategic trade policy' (Krugman, 1986). Domestic protection gave Japanese companies the possibility of benefiting from scale economies and, more importantly, of engaging in massive investments that raised productivity and turned them into successful exporters. A corporate governance structure that encouraged 'long-termism' clearly helped, as did a competitive market structure. But the new comparative advantages that were created also relied on a policy that had selected certain sectors and credibly committed itself to helping them. In Italy, on the other hand, 'long-termism' was less in evidence and protectionism was ruled out by trade liberalization (in any case, had it been applied, it would almost certainly have been much less effective than in Japan, given greater bureaucratic inefficiencies and a much lower degree of domestic competition).

Yet, Italian exports still grew relatively rapidly through much of the period as the country's traditional sectors generated if not scale economies then externalities in the industrial districts located in the peninsula's Centre and North-East. The size of these districts is substantial. Rough estimates suggest that, by the early 1990s, they may have accounted for 30 to 40 per cent of manufacturing employment (up from perhaps only 10 per cent in the 1950s) (Brusco and Paba, 1997); parallel estimates show that over 50 per cent of Italian exports come from sectors (such as fashion, furniture and machine tools) that are largely located in these districts (ibid.).[18] Significant external benefits seem to have arisen in these areas from the presence of trained labour forces and know-how, of specialized local financial intermediaries, of common research, marketing and advertising services, of producers of purpose-made machine-tools and intermediate inputs, of resulting backward and forward linkage effects, among other factors (Becattini, 1998; Onida, 1998). Not unlike Silicon Valley, the districts appear to be a mixture of extreme competition, yet also implicit co-operation thanks to so-called 'social networks'. Indeed, quantitative estimates suggest that the mere belonging to a district contributes to the productive efficiency of firms specialized in that district's main activity (Fabiani and Pellegrini, 1998). This would seem to confirm the significance of such externalities and provides an illustration of another strand in the modern theory of international trade – the importance given to the beneficial effects coming from the geographic clustering of economic activities (Krugman, 1991).

5 Conclusions

The foregoing has looked at the diverging trade performances of Italy and Japan over the last five decades. At the outset, the two countries' foreign trade structures were rather similar. Today, however, they are very different. On the import side, the major reasons for the diverging trend in the penetration of manufactured goods in the two economies are mainly structural and institutional – Italy is fully integrated in a large and free-trading European environment; Japan, while ostensibly equally open, is in practice less so for numerous reasons, some linked to its distance from other major trading nations, some to the practices of its firms (and, possibly, of its government).

On the export side, Japan experienced rising market shares abroad via a radical transformation of its export mix. Italy experienced, initially at least, a similar increase in its world market share with many fewer changes in its comparative advantage pattern. Japanese successes have been linked to two main features – a corporate governance model allowing managers to take a long-term view of their firms' prospects and an industrial policy committed to help certain domestic sectors achieve international competitiveness, while at the same time ensuring that within these sectors companies competed against each other. Italian successes, on the other hand, have had more to do with spontaneous small firms' responses to market challenges. Often, these took the form of clustering in highly specialized industrial districts, with policies playing very little part in such developments.

Italy's successes clearly owe little to the fashionable arguments based on the importance of R&D and high-tech. Japan fits this story much better. Yet, there is no certainty that Japan will necessarily continue to outperform Italy. For one thing, Japanese firms, while active in some high-tech activities, seems absent from what, at present at least, is considered the really dynamic end of the sector – software, telecommunications and biotechnology. For another, Japan's strength has been mainly based on the large-scale manufacturing of extremely reliable products, using 'just-in-time' subcontracting to cut costs and well-trained workers to ensure quality. Neither of these advantages is necessarily permanent. 'Just-in-time' techniques are being supplanted by so-called 'information technology outsourcing' to which US companies are increasingly turning (Yoshitomi, 1996); the strength of Japan's training and educational system could be subverted should the changing nature of technology give a greater premium to less formal forms of learning and to greater inventiveness as it, arguably, may be doing.[19] Finally, 'long-termism' is under threat, as Japan's corporate governance model begins to creak.

Despite the often voiced fears that Italy's industrial structure is ill-suited to trends in world demand (for example, Modiano, 1984; Guerrieri, 1990), the industrial districts could represent a source of strength in an environment in which scale economies are no longer as important as they used to be. High-tech in the production process rather than in final products (through, for instance, the use of microprocessors and numerically controlled machine tools) may not make 'small' beautiful, but has clearly made 'small' increasingly economical. And in such a world, the growing differentiation of tastes which comes from affluence gives a premium to firms in which sunk costs in physical assets are low and production can be quickly and flexibly switched towards shorter fashion cycles and/or more sophisticated goods, something which the firms operating in the Italian industrial districts have amply shown to be capable of doing.

This is not to underestimate Japan's capacity to adapt and change. In fact, both countries provide vivid examples of how firms competing on world markets have successfully established and then defended their positions. Japanese firms have, over the last three decades, had to cope with relentless upward pressures on their currency; Italian ones with continuous threats from lower-cost competitors in Asia and, more recently, in Eastern Europe. Both sets of producers have been able, if in different ways, to enhance their non-price competitiveness. Doubtless, this process will continue. Even if future growth will be relatively subdued, if only because of very rapid ageing, on the export front both countries can be expected to maintain the strong presence on world markets that they have established over the last half century.

Notes

1. The data shown in Table 6.2 for the period 1955–63 provide only a geographic breakdown; it is, however, well known that the commodity composition of Japanese exports was at the time unfavourable, both in absolute terms (Boltho, 1996b) and relative to Italy (NIESR, 1963).
2. The real exchange data shown in Figure 6.2 apply relative wholesale price developments to trade weights for 18 countries. Unit labour costs would have been a more appropriate indicator, but data were not available for the whole period. In any case, the present estimates do not differ markedly from the real exchange rate measure published by the IMF which uses relative normalized unit labour costs (but is available only since 1975; see Figure 8.2). Between 1975 and 1998, for instance, the correlation coefficient between year-to-year changes in the two sets of indices is of 0.84 for Italy and 0.92 for Japan.
3. In fact, if anything, such trends have been even more buoyant elsewhere – Italy's share of manufactured imports in GDP in the late 1990s was, after Japan and the United States, the third lowest in the OECD area.
4. Earlier estimates of the share of intra-industry in total trade show that this rose from a relatively high 61 per cent in 1970 to 64 per cent in 1987 in Italy, while it declined, over the same time-period, from a very low 33 per cent to an even lower 28 per cent in Japan (Stone and Lee, 1995). Adjustment for trade imbalances (which tend to depress the calculated values of intra-industry trade) would leave Italy's figures broadly unchanged, but would show an increase for Japan from 0.28 to 0.35. These adjustments do not substantially change the picture and are, in any case, controversial (ibid.).
5. Indices of revealed comparative advantage measure the ratio between a country's share of world exports in a particular product and its share of total world exports. For 1955, the 'world' is defined as the OECD less Finland, Spain and Switzerland.
6. The definition of technological intensity is based on the share of R&D spending in value added. Very broadly, low-tech activities include textile, clothing, leather, food, wood and paper products, while the high-tech sector includes pharmaceuticals, precision instruments, aeronautics and computing equipment.
7. These figures are likely to underestimate the total contribution of small firms to Japan's exports since many such firms work as subcontractors for larger exporters. Allowance for this might boost the (direct and indirect) contribution of small firms to Japanese sales abroad in the late 1980s to about 35 per cent (OECD, 1997).
8. This index varies between 0 and 1, with the latter value indicating that one product alone would account for a country's total exports.
9. Italy, for instance, had removed all its quantitative barriers on intra-OEEC trade already by 1952, faster than any other Western European country bar Portugal. Liberalization vis-à-vis the dollar area was somewhat slower and Italy's tariffs remained high in the decade, but the 1955 Messina Treaty, which announced the coming of the Common Market, was a clear signal of impending tariff dismantlement. After 1958, Italy's trade policy was made in Brussels and the country shared in the general opening of the European and world economies.

10. Tariffs on manufactures are by now very low both in Japan and in the European Union. Non-tariff barriers continue to exist, with the available (if tentative) estimates of their coverage suggesting that Italy is more protectionist than Japan (Nogués et al., 1986; Laird and Yeats, 1990; Lee and Swagel, 1997).

11. A vivid example of some of the obstacles to the opening of the Japanese market is provided by the following quote: 'it took nearly 10 years of pressure to get liberalization of [Japan's] cigarette market, longer than it took to negotiate SALT I, SALT II, or the INF treaties with the Soviets' (Noland, 1991, p. 48).

12. See Chapter 9 by Nishimura and Punzo in this volume.

13. The simplest possible test of the 'catch-up' hypothesis confirms this. Linking the growth of GDP per capita, expressed in PPPs (data from Maddison, 1995, updated with OECD figures), over the period 1950–97 to the initial levels of this GDP per capita for 22 OECD countries, results in an estimated value for Italy only marginally below what was achieved, but to an underestimation of Japanese growth of as much as 1.8 percentage points per annum.

14. See Chapter 2 by Barca et al. in this volume.

15. Indeed, in aggregate terms, it has been more pervasive in Italy than in Japan. Thus, Italy's public sector expenditure, revenue or employment are all larger, in relative terms, than in Japan. The same is even truer of nationalized industry.

16. It is true that Italy's car industry greatly benefited in the 1970s and 1980s from a strict quota on the imports of Japanese cars (these were limited to 2000 a year). Yet, it turns out that the quota in question had originally been asked for by Japan (oral communication from Franco Bernabè, formerly head of Fiat's research unit). Worried in the 1950s by possible Italian competition for its fledgling car industry, MITI obtained a reciprocal quota that seemed of little importance to Italy at a time at which the Japanese market was very small.

17. A more detailed sectoral attempt at trying to estimate all the repercussions of an industrial policy favouring semiconductors came to the conclusion that protecting the industry had almost certainly had negative effects on Japan's welfare, but that without such protection the industry would never have achieved its comparative advantage (Baldwin and Krugman, 1988).

18. A recent study suggests that the districts account for only 22 per cent of Italy's exports, but this estimate uses a conservative definition of the districts' geographic and productive coverage (Becattini and Menghinello, 1998).

19. See Chapter 10 by Brunello and Ishikawa in this volume.

References

Akamatsu, K. (1961) 'A Theory of Unbalanced Growth in the World Economy', *Weltwirtschaftliches Archiv*, 86, 2, 167–79.

Aquino, A. (1981) 'Changes over Time in the Pattern of Comparative Advantage in Manufactured Goods', *European Economic Review*, 15, 1, 41–62.

Argy, V. and L. Stein (1997) *The Japanese Economy*, London: Macmillan.

Arrighetti, A. and G. Seravalli (1997) 'Istituzioni e dualismo dimensionale dell'industria italiana', in F. Barca (ed.), *Storia del capitalismo italiano dal dopoguerra a oggi*, Rome: Donzelli.

Baldwin, R.E. and P.R. Krugman (1988) 'Market Access and International Competition: a Simulation Study of 16K Random Access Memories', in R.C. Feenstra (ed.), *Empirical Methods for International Trade*, Cambridge, MA: MIT Press.

Barker, T. (1977) 'International Trade and Economic Growth: an Alternative to the Neoclassical Approach', *Cambridge Journal of Economics*, 1, 2, 153–72.

Beason, R. and D.E. Weinstein (1996) 'Growth, Economies of Scale, and Targeting in Japan (1955–1990)', *Review of Economics and Statistics*, 78, 2, 286–95.

Becattini, G. (1998) *Distretti industriali e 'made in Italy'*, Turin: Bollati Boringhieri.

Becattini, G. and S. Menghinello (1998) 'Contributo e ruolo del *made in Italy* "distrettuale" nelle esportazioni nazionali di manufatti', *Sviluppo locale*, 5, 9, 5–41.

Boltho, A. (1985) 'Was Japan's Industrial Policy Successful?', *Cambridge Journal of Economics*, 9, 2, 187–201.

Boltho, A. (1996a) 'Convergence, Competitiveness and the Exchange Rate' , in N. Crafts and G. Toniolo (eds), *Economic Growth in Europe since 1945*, Cambridge: Cambridge University Press.

Boltho, A. (1996b) 'Was Japanese Growth Export-led?', *Oxford Economic Papers*, 48, 3, 415–32.

Brusco, S. and S. Paba (1997) 'Per una storia dei distretti industriali italiani dal secondo dopoguerra agli anni novanta', in F. Barca (ed.), *Storia del capitalismo italiano dal dopoguerra a oggi*, Rome: Donzelli.

Fabiani, S. and G. Pellegrini (1998) 'Un'analisi quantitativa delle imprese nei distretti industriali italiani: redditività, produttività e costo del lavoro', *L'industria*, 19, 4, 811–31.

Gros-Pietro, G.M. (1990) 'La ristrutturazione dei grandi gruppi industriali', *Rivista di politica economica*, 80, 5, 149–69.

Guerrieri, P. (1990) 'Gli scambi mondiali di prodotti high-tech e il caso italiano', in P. Guerrieri and E. Sassoon (eds.), *La sfida high-tech*, Milan: Il Sole-24 ore.

Hufbauer, G.C. (1970) 'The Impact of National Characteristics and Technology on the Commodity Composition of Trade in Manufactured Goods', in R.Vernon (ed.), *The Technology Factor in International Trade*, New York, NY: Columbia University Press.

Itoh, M., K. Kiyono, M. Okuno and K. Suzumura (1988) 'Industry Promotion and Trade', in R. Komiya, M. Okuno and K. Suzumura (eds), *Industrial Policy of Japan*, Tokyo: Academic Press Japan.

Kaldor, N. (1981) 'The Role of Increasing Returns, Technical Progress and Cumulative Causation in the Theory of International Trade and Economic Growth', *Économie appliquée*, 34, 4, 593–617.

Katz, R. (1996) 'From Growth Superstar to Economic Underachiever', *Japan Economic Studies*, 24, 2, 3–72.

Keesing, D.B. (1968) 'Labor Skills and the Structure of Trade in Manufactures', in P.B. Kenen and R. Lawrence (eds), *The Open Economy: Essays on International Trade and Finance*, New York, NY: Columbia University Press.

Komiya R., M. Okuno and K. Suzumura (eds) (1988) *Industrial Policy of Japan*, Tokyo: Academic Press Japan.

Krugman, P. (1984) 'Import Protection as Export Promotion: International Competition in the Presence of Oligopoly and Economies of Scale', in H. Kierzkowski (ed.), *Monopolistic Competition and International Trade*, Oxford: Oxford University Press.

Krugman, P. (1989) 'Differences in Income Elasticities and Trends in Real Exchange Rates', *European Economic Review*, 33, 5, 1031–46.

Krugman, P. (1991) *Geography and Trade*, Cambridge, MA: MIT Press.

Krugman, P.R. (ed.) (1986) *Strategic Trade Policy and the New International Economics*, Cambridge, MA: MIT Press.

Laird, S. and A. Yeats (1990) 'Trends in Non-tariff Barriers of Developed Countries, 1966–1986', *Weltwirtschaftliches Archiv*, 126, 2, 299–325.

La Noce, M. (1989) 'Linee di intervento delle politiche di incentivazione industriale dal 1970 al 1987', in A. Battaglia and P. Valcamonici (eds), *Nella competizione globale. Una politica industriale verso il 2000*, Bari: Laterza.

Lawrence, R.Z. (1991) 'How Open is Japan?', in P. Krugman (ed.), *Trade with Japan: Has the Door Opened Wider?*, Chicago, IL: University of Chicago Press.

Lawrence, R.Z. (1993) 'Japan's Different Trade Regime: An Analysis with Particular Reference to *Keiretsu*', *Journal of Economic Perspectives*, 7, 3, 3–19.

Lee, J.-W. and P. Swagel (1997) 'Trade Barriers and Trade Flows across Countries and Industries', *Review of Economics and Statistics*, 79, 3, 372–82.

Lincoln, E.J. (1990) *Japan's Unequal Trade*, Washington, DC: Brookings Institution.

Lynn L.H. (1994) 'MITI's Successes and Failures in Controlling Japan's Technology Imports', Center for International Studies, Massachusetts Institute of Technology, Working Paper MITJP 94–11.

Maddison, A. (1995) *Monitoring the World Economy: 1820–1992*, Paris: OECD.

Modiano, P. (1984) 'La collocazione internazionale dell'industria italiana: un tentativo di interpretazione di alcune tendenze recenti', *Economia italiana*, 3, 425–57.

Mutoh, H. (1988) 'The Automotive Industry', in R. Komiya, M. Okuno and K. Suzumura (eds), *Industrial Policy of Japan*, Tokyo: Academic Press Japan.

Nakakita, T. (1993) 'Trade and Capital Liberalization Policies in Postwar Japan', in J.Teranishi and Y.Kosai (eds), *The Japanese Experience of Economic Reforms*, New York, NY: St.Martin's Press.

NIESR (1963) 'Fast and Slow Growing Products in World Trade', *NIESR Review*, 25, 22–39.

Nogués, J.J., A. Olechowski and L.A. Winters (1986) 'The Extent of Nontariff Barriers to Industrial Countries' Imports', *World Bank Economic Review*, 1, 1, 181–99.

Noland, M. (1991) 'Comments' to Lawrence (1991), in P. Krugman (ed.), *Trade with Japan: Has the Door Opened Wider?*, Chicago, IL: University of Chicago Press.

Noland, M. (1993) 'The Impact of Industrial Policy on Japan's Trade Specialization', *Review of Economics and Statistics*, 75, 2, 241–48.

Noland, M. (1997) 'Public Policy, Private Preferences, and the Japanese Trade Pattern', *Review of Economics and Statistics*, 79, 2, 159–66.

Onida, F. (1998) 'L'industria italiana in un contesto aperto', *L'industria*, 19, 2, 279–86.

OECD (1997) *Globalisation and Small and Medium Enterprises (SMEs)*, Paris.

Ozawa, T. (1980) 'Government Control over Technology Acquisition and Firms' Entry into New Sectors: The Experience of Japan's Synthetic-fibre Industry', *Cambridge Journal of Economics*, 4, 2, 133–46.

Peck, M.J. (1976) 'Technology', in H. Patrick and H. Rosovsky (eds), *Asia's New Giant: How the Japanese Economy Works*, Washington, DC: Brookings Institution.

Prodi, R. and D. De Giovanni (1990) 'Quarantacinque anni di politica industriale in Italia: protagonisti, obiettivi e strumenti', *Rivista di politica economica*, 80, 5, 35–62.

Rapp, W.V. (1976) 'Firm Size and Japan's Export Structure: A Microview of Japan's Changing Export Competitiveness since Meiji', in H. Patrick (ed.), *Japanese Industrialization and its Social Consequences*, Berkeley, CA: University of California Press.

Saucier, P. (1987) *Spécialisation internationale et compétitivité de l'économie japonaise*, Paris: Economica.

Saxonhouse, G.R. (1983) 'What is All This about "Industrial Targeting" in Japan?', *The World Economy*, 6, 3, 253–73.

Saxonhouse, G.R. (1993) 'What does Japanese Trade Structure Tell Us about Japanese Trade Policy', *Journal of Economic Perspectives*, 7, 3, 21–43.

Stone, J.A. and H.-H. Lee (1995) 'Determinants of Intra-industry Trade: A Longitudinal, Cross-country Analysis', *Weltwirtschaftliches Archiv*, 131, 1, 67–85.

Vestal, J.E. (1993) *Planning for Change: Industrial Policy and Japanese Economic Development, 1945–1990*, Oxford, Clarendon Press.

Yoshikawa, H. (1990) 'On Equilibrium Yen-Dollar Rate', *American Economic Review*, 80, 3, 576–83.

Yoshitomi, M. (1996) 'On the Changing International Competitiveness of Japanese Manufacturing since 1985', *Oxford Review of Economic Policy*, 12, 3, 61–73.

7
Labour Market Performance and Job Creation

Yuji Genda, Maria Grazia Pazienza and Marcello Signorelli

1 Introduction

The aim of this chapter is to examine differences in labour market performance between Italy and Japan. The two countries have long shared a number of common economic features – the weight of the agricultural labour force has been very high for many years, the employment composition across major sectors is today quite similar (Pazienza and Signorelli, 1998), the importance of small and medium-sized firms has traditionally been, and still is, pronounced, and so on. Yet, there are also remarkable differences in labour market outcomes and in the job creation process between the two countries. As will be made clear from what follows, Japan exhibits a much higher (regular) employment rate than Italy, while the Italian labour market is characterized by a much higher degree of 'churning' (or job creation and destruction) than is the Japanese one.

To analyse these various differences in employment performance, this chapter uses two comparative approaches. Section 2 adopts a macro framework to examine developments over the period 1970–95 in employment, unemployment and participation rates. Section 3, on the other hand, applies the job creation and job destruction approach, that has been recently studied in several OECD countries, to micro data of employment changes at the firm or establishment level in the first half of the 1990s. Combining both sets of findings, Section 4 attempts to interpret the large differences in employment performance between Italy and Japan, focusing, in particular, on institutional divergences and firm behaviour in the two countries. Section 5 concludes with some speculation on possible future labour market developments.

%

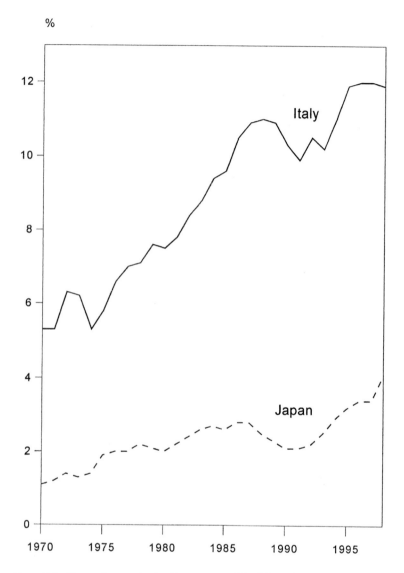

Figure 7.1   Unemployment rates (in per cent of the labour force)
Source: OECD, *Labour Force Statistics* (various issues).

2   Labour market structures and performance

The unemployment rate is often used as a summary measure of a country's labour market performance. Figure 7.1 illustrates how, in this area, Italy and Japan have shown large and persistent differences. While in Japan unemployment has been exceptionally low by international standards throughout the last three decades, Italy's unemployment rate (already relatively high in the early 1970s) has stood at double-digit levels since the late 1980s. The gap between the two countries' rates, which stood at 4 percentage points in 1970, has increased to about 9 percentage points in the 1990s.

The unemployment rate is, however, an imperfect indicator of labour market performance in view of the interactions that occur between changes in employment and participation rates.[1] Looking at the joint evolution of these two indicators allows a better comparison of an economy's ability to create jobs. Italy's inadequate longer-run performance is confirmed by the remarkable difference in its employment rate when compared to Japan (Figure 7.2). Between 1970 and 1990, Italian participation rates rose, but the employment rate remained almost

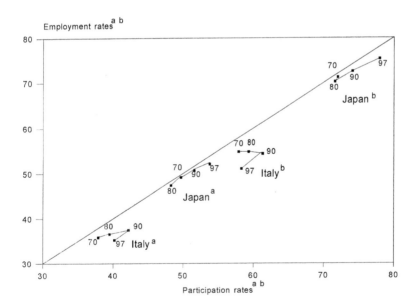

Figure 7.2 Employment and participation rates
a. Participation rate = share of civilian labour force in total population; employment rate = share of civilian employment in total population.
b. Participation rate = share of civilian labour force in working age population (aged 14–64 in Italy; 15–64 in Japan); employment rate: share of civilian employment in working age population.
Source: OECD, *Labour Force Statistics* (various issues).

constant (hence unemployment, equal to the distance between the employment line and the 45 degree line, increased sharply). In the 1990s, though output growth decelerated, unemployment increased little, but this masked a steep decline in employment as falling participation rates bore the brunt of the adjustment. Something similar, if in much milder form, took place in Japan in the 1970s, a time at which GDP growth had slowed down sharply. Since then, however, both participation and employment rates have risen regularly, despite the near stagnation that has affected the economy since the stock market crash of 1991.

Even more than unemployment rates, it is the comparison between the employment rates which shows Italy's structural weakness in creating (regular) jobs. In 1970, 55 per cent of the Italian working age population was employed, compared to 71 per cent in Japan. By 1996, Italy's employment rate had decreased to 51 per cent, while Japan's had risen to 75 per cent. If one takes the 1996 employment rates in percentage of the total populations (35 per cent in Italy, 51 per cent in Japan), one obtains

Table 7.1 Comparative labour market indicators, 1995

| | Unemployment Rate[a] | |
	Italy	Japan
Total	12.0	3.1
Centre-North/Chubu	7.8	3.3[b]
South/Kansai	21.0	5.3[b]
Female	16.2	3.3
Youth	32.8	6.1
Long-term unemployment[c]	63.6	18.2

| | Employment Rate[d] | |
	Italy	Japan
Total	51.2	74.1
Female	36.0	60.3
Youth	26.1	44.7
Older workers[e]	27.0	63.7

a. In per cent of the respective labour forces.
b. Japan's regional unemployment data are not based on the same definitions as the national ones; for the country as a whole they give an unemployment rate of 4.3 per cent in 1995, as against the 3.1 per cent shown in this table.
c. In per cent of total unemployment.
d. In per cent of the respective working age populations (aged 14–64 in Italy, 15–64 in Japan).
e. Workers aged 55 to 64 years.
Sources: ISTAT, *Introducing Italy, 1997* and *Indagine sulle forze di lavoro* (various issues); OECD, *Employment Outlook, 1997* and *Labour Force Statistics, 1973–1996; Japan Statistical Yearbook, 1998.*

the result that for every Italian employed worker there are almost two 'dependents', compared with only one for a Japanese worker. Thus, among the old, just over one-quarter of Italians aged 55 to 64 is in employment, compared with nearly two-thirds in Japan.[2]

The Italian labour market is also characterized by significant segmentation (such as by sex and age) and by pronounced regional dualism (Table 7.1).[3] Thus, the country's employment performance is particularly inadequate as regards the female, young and southern populations. This is true in absolute terms, in the sense that the unemployment rates of these groups are from almost two to more than three times higher than those of the male, adult or Centre-North labour forces. It is even truer vis-à-vis Japan where the corresponding unemployment rates reach barely 20 to 30 per cent of the Italian levels. A further unfortunate Italian characteristic is the very high incidence of long-term unemployed – those who have been without a job for more than one year. While in Japan the share of the long-term unemployed in the total number of jobless was, in the mid- or late 1990s, one of the lowest in the OECD area, in Italy it was the highest.

Some of these very unfavourable indicators need, however, to be put in perspective. Thus, a further characteristic of Italian dualism is the distinction between 'regular' and 'irregular' jobs,[4] with the latter not incorporated in the official definition of the employment rate. Available estimates suggest that the 'underground economy' may account for between 20 and 25 per cent of total Italian employment (Fondazione G. Brodolini, 1997), and for as much as 30 per cent in the *Mezzogiorno* (Dallago, 1990). In Japan, by contrast, this phenomenon is virtually unknown.

Overall, in the quarter-century from 1970, Italian employment rose at an annual average rate of 0.4 per cent (for a GDP growth rate, over the same period, of 2.6 per cent per annum). In Japan, both employment and output growth were more rapid (1.0 and 3.9 per cent respectively). In other words, most of Italy's GDP growth was achieved through productivity increases. In Japan, by contrast, both productivity and employment were able to rise. It is also interesting to look at changes in the importance of the three major sectors in the two countries and at their net job creation over the period (Table 7.2). In 1970, the two economies were quite different, with Italy both more agricultural and industrial than Japan (at least in so far as the allocation of the labour force was concerned). By 1995, the two countries had come much closer together – the shares of service sector employment were virtually identical and the differences in the weights of the primary and secondary sectors were very small.

Table 7.2 Changes in labour market structures (percentages)

	Italy	Japan
Employment shares, 1970		
Agriculture	20.2	17.4
Industry	39.5	35.7
Services	40.3	46.9
Employment shares, 1995		
Agriculture	7.5	5.7
Industry	32.2	33.6
Services	60.3	60.7
Employment changes, 1970 to 1995 (percentages)		
Agriculture	−61.6	−58.6
Industry	−15.3	20.7
Services	55.1	64.2

Source: OECD, *Labour Force Statistics* (various issues).

Italy's relative 'de-industrialization' is at the root of this process of convergence of sectoral employment shares. Between 1970 and 1995, the declines in the two countries' agricultural labour forces were of similar orders of magnitude, as were the increases in employment levels in services. What was very different, however, was the performance of the industrial sector. Despite a sharp real exchange rate appreciation, employment in Japanese industry rose through most of the period under examination. In Italy, by contrast, although there were net job gains in the secondary sector in the 1970s, there were losses throughout the 1980s and in the first half of the 1990s.

3 Job creation and job destruction

This section compares the process of job creation and destruction in Italy and Japan. As already mentioned in the introduction to this chapter, these two economies share an important labour market similarity in the sense that a relatively high proportion of employees works in small companies. Thus, at the turn of the 1980s for instance, some 70 to 75 per cent of the two countries' workforce was active in firms with less than 100 employees, as against figures of the order of only 40 to 50 per cent in other major economies.[5] However, this similarity does not tell us whether the process of job creation is also similar. Nor do we know what kind of economic fluctuations affect the creation and destruction of jobs in Italy and Japan. Knowledge of such processes is important for economists and for policy-makers wishing to reduce unemployment and create new job opportunities. Recent research in this area (see, for example, OECD, 1994; Davis et al., 1996) suggests that in a number of countries, even when employment growth is only modest, there can still be substantial labour turnover resulting from the creation and destruction of jobs.

3.1 Differences in gross job creation and destruction rates

Table 7.3 shows gross job creation and destruction rates for Italy and Japan from 1991 to 1995 (for a definition of the concepts used and for a discussion of the data problems encountered, see the Appendix to this chapter). It also contains results by firm/establishment size. The data suggest that both job creation and job destruction rates have been higher in Italy than in Japan over this period (the more so as the Italian data are likely to be biased downwards compared to the Japanese ones – see the Appendix for details). The difference is particularly marked for job destruction where Italy's average rate is some 50 per cent above Japan's (and 30 per cent above its own job creation rate). It is clear that the persistence of such a gap between job creation and job destruction can make a huge difference to the stocks of employment and unemployment in the longer run, as was illustrated in Section 2 above.

Looking at job flow rates by firm size, significant differences between the two countries appear for small firms (differences that are unlikely to reflect statistical problems of non-comparability given that such firms consist overwhelmingly of single-unit establishments). In this section of the labour market, therefore, job reallocation rates are really much higher in Italy than they are in Japan. While the data in Table 7.3 suggest that the opposite is the case for large-scale companies, this finding must be qualified given that the Japanese data cover establishments rather than just firms. Genda (1988a) has shown that significant labour turnover occurs in large Japanese enterprises because of employee transfers across establishments. If fully comparable data were available, Italy's figures could well rise to, or even lie above, those of Japan.

Trends in Japan, while not as unfavourable as in Italy, can also give some cause for anxiety. Gross job creation in the economy as a whole declined in every year of the period, while job destruction continued to rise. This tendency was particularly marked in large firms: the job creation rate fell from 4.5 per cent in 1991 to only 1.9 per cent in 1995 while the job destruction rate doubled from 2.1 to 4.2 per cent. Even in small firms which, as in Italy, had accounted for most of the employment growth until then, net job creation turned negative in 1995 and may well have remained negative in the closing years of the 1990s, given the near stagnation of the economy.

Table 7.3   Job creation and job destruction rates[a]

	1991	1992	1993	1994	1995	Mean
Italy						
Total						
Employment share	100.0	100.0	100.0	100.0	100.0	100.0
Job creation rate	4.6	3.9	3.6	4.8	5.2	4.4
Job destruction rate	5.4	6.3	6.4	5.6	5.1	5.8
6–99 employees						
Employment share	53.1	53.7	53.9	53.7	53.6	53.6
Job creation rate	6.5	5.6	5.2	6.7	7.1	6.2
Job destruction rate	7.4	8.2	8.5	7.2	6.7	7.6
100–999 employees						
Employment share	25.3	25.1	25.1	25.3	25.2	25.2
Job creation rate	3.5	2.6	2.5	3.6	4.3	3.3
Job destruction rate	3.7	4.9	4.6	4.3	3.4	4.2
1000 or more employees						
Employment share	21.5	21.2	21.0	21.0	21.2	21.2
Job creation rate	1.4	1.2	0.8	1.2	1.4	1.2
Job destruction rate	2.5	3.1	3.2	3.3	3.0	3.0
Japan						
Total						
Employment share	100.0	100.0	100.0	100.0	100.0	100.0
Job creation rate	4.9	4.6	4.0	3.9	3.6	4.2
Job destruction rate	3.4	3.4	4.0	4.5	4.3	3.9
5–99 employees						
Employment share	47.2	45.6	48.5	48.5	49.4	47.8
Job creation rate	5.6	5.5	4.7	4.7	4.2	4.9
Job destruction rate	4.4	3.9	4.1	4.6	4.7	4.3
100–999 employees						
Employment share	30.9	31.9	29.0	27.6	27.6	29.4
Job creation rate	4.1	3.7	3.1	3.4	4.0	3.7
Job destruction rate	2.7	3.1	4.3	4.0	3.6	3.5
1000 or more employees						
Employment share	21.9	22.4	22.5	23.9	23.0	22.7
Job creation rate	4.5	3.8	3.4	2.7	1.9	3.3
Job destruction rate	2.1	2.8	3.4	4.6	4.2	3.4

a. In per cent of total employees at the beginning of the year.
Source: Authors' elaboration of ETS and INPS data (see the Appendix for details).

3.2 The driving forces of gross job flows (I): persistent and temporary shocks

What main forces have driven job creation and destruction in the two countries? This sub-section looks at the persistence[6] of the various (demand and supply) shocks that can generate employment or unemployment. Results for the two countries, distinguished by firm size, are shown in Table 7.4. In Italy, the persistence of both job creation and destruction increases with firm size. In Italian firms with less than 20 employees, only half of newly created jobs survive after two years. And the persistence rate of job destruction at these firms is about 60 per cent, so that almost 40 per cent of jobs that are destroyed reappear within two years. This implies that a large proportion of the jobs created and destroyed in small Italian firms are due to temporary shocks.

Japan's results are rather different. First, no clear relationship can be observed between the persistence of job creation and firm size. The data suggest that the relatively high percentage of job creation in small and medium-sized firms (close to 60 per cent for two-year persistence) is brought about by persistent shocks. Second, most jobs destroyed in Japan do not reappear within a two-year time span and the persistence of job destruction increases with firm size. Jobs in larger firms are less likely to be destroyed but, once destroyed, very few are re-established. While the persistence rate of job destruction over two years is 72 per cent at Italian

Table 7.4 Persistence of job creation and job destruction rates[a]

	Persistence of job creation		Persistence of job destruction	
	1 year	*2 years*	*1 year*	*2 years*
Italy (1984–93)				
Firm size				
1–5 employees	63	48	70	60
10–19 employees	64	49	73	63
100–199 employees	72	58	77	68
500 or more employees	75	61	79	72
Japan (1993–95)				
Establishment size				
30–99 employees	67	57	82	72
100–299 employees	70	61	85	79
300–999 employees	74	66	82	78
1000 or more employees	58	49	88	85

a. Percentage of newly created or destroyed jobs at time *t* that remain filled/destroyed at time *t* + 1 or *t* + 2.

Sources: Contini and Filippi (1995) for Italy; Genda (1998b) for Japan.

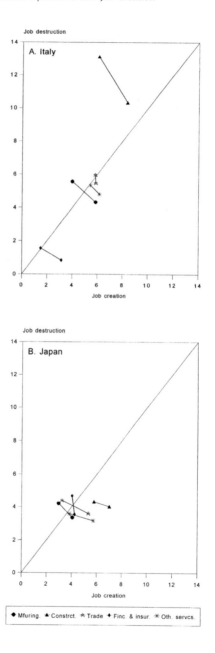

Figure 7.3   Job creation and destruction rates[a] by major industry group
a. In per cent of total employees at the beginning of the period.
Source: Authors' elaboration of ETS and INPS data (see the Appendix for details).

firms with 500 or more employees, it is 78 per cent at Japanese establishments with 300 to 999 employees. Even at small Japanese units with 30 to 99 employees, the two-year persistence rate of job destruction is 72 per cent, which is comparable to the persistence rates of medium and large Italian firms. In other words, temporary shocks have less impact on job destruction in Japan than in Italy. Conversely, persistent shocks play a more important role in creating and destroying jobs in small firms in Japan.

3.3 The driving forces of gross job flows (II): aggregate and sectoral shocks

A further refinement that can be made when analysing the driving forces of gross job flows is to distinguish between the role of aggregate and sectoral shocks. An aggregate shock can be defined as one that has a common effect on job flows across all industries, either generating or destroying jobs more or less uniformly, irrespective of sector. By contrast, sectoral shocks have a specific impact on employment changes in one particular industry. Thus, if sectoral shocks were dominant in the economy, job creation might occur in one sector, but job destruction in another.

Figure 7.3 shows changes in gross job flows at existing firms or establishments between 1991 and 1995, by main industry. The results suggest that aggregate shocks played a dominant role in changing employment in Japan since the movements in all five sectors between 1991 and 1995 are in a north-easterly direction. That is, the job creation rate decreased and the job destruction rate increased in each industry (a result that is, in some ways, similar to the one presented in Table 7.3 above which showed that, over the same period, job creation fell and job destruction rose in each size category of firms). In Italy, by contrast, it was sectoral shocks that seem to have had a greater effect on employment reallocation in the labour market. Thus, the directions in which gross job flows have changed differ by industry. While the job creation rate decreased in construction, finance and other services, it increased in manufacturing and moved little in trade (with opposite developments for the job destruction rate).

These findings have an important bearing on the nature of the unemployment problem faced by the two countries. The relative importance of sectoral shocks in changing employment in Italy is consistent with the economy's dual and segmented labour market. These shocks have specific effects on various sub-sectors classified by industry, firm size, region, and so on. In this sense, much of Italy's unemployment may be structural and caused by sectoral differences in labour demand and supply. On the other hand, the fact that aggregate shocks played an important part in employment changes in Japan in the first half of the 1990s suggests that a lack of aggregate demand may have been a significant component of rising unemployment in this period.

3.4   Stability of gross job flows

A further difference between the two countries concerns the relative stability/instability of the gross job flows recorded over the period. Such flows appear to be more stable in Japan than in Italy. Japan's increases in job destruction, in particular, were relatively modest in most industries. On the other hand, job creation and destruction in Italy showed large movements, especially so in manufacturing and construction. In order to confirm the existence of such differences, one needs to trace job flows over a longer time-period and use more precise statistical measures, such as the ratio of the variance of job destruction to the variance of job creation, or the coefficient of variation of gross job creation and

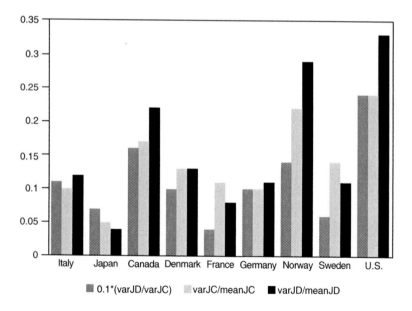

Figure 7.4   Variance of gross job flows
Notes: the time coverage of the data varies according to country; broadly, observations go from the early or mid-1970s to the late 1980s or early 1990s.
JD = Job destruction; JC = Job creation.
Sources: Garibaldi (1998) and Genda (1998c).

destruction. Such computations are available for Japan for the years 1986–96 from Genda (1998c), and for Italy for the period 1984–93 from Garibaldi (1998). The latter source also provides comparable estimates for several other industrialized countries.

This evidence is plotted in Figure 7.4. It is striking to note that in North America, but nowhere else (with the partial exception of Norway), job destruction is a good deal more variable than job creation (this is indicated in the chart by the ratio of the variances being above 0.1).[7] The results for both Italy and Japan are very different from those for Canada and the United States. Italy is a country in which the variance of job creation is almost equal to that of job destruction (as is also the case in Denmark and Germany). Japan, on the other hand, is one of the few countries in which job creation is more volatile than job destruction. In addition, Japan is an outlier in so far as its coefficients of variation for both job creation and destruction are the smallest in the sample. Overall, these findings suggest that Japan's low unemployment rate may be related to a relatively low and very stable pattern of job destruction when compared to that of other OECD countries.

3.5 Firms' demography

The results provided so far suffer from one major shortcoming – they do not take into account the influence of births and deaths of firms on job creation and destruction, because the Japanese data source does not provide such information. If changes in the demography of firms were frequent in Japan, job flows in the economy might be much greater than what has been observed so far (for instance, in Table 7.3). Since the Italian data provide the necessary information, an attempt was made to generate equivalent figures for Japan (for details, see the Appendix).

The main results of this exercise are shown in Table 7.5. Over the 1991–94 period both the birth and death rates of Italian firms were more than twice as high as their equivalents in Japan, and this was also broadly true for each one of the five major sectors that are separately shown. Job creation in new firms was, however, higher in aggregate in Japan. New Italian firms in the manufacturing, construction and trade sectors generated more jobs than their Japanese equivalents over this period, but this was more than offset by the much more rapid creation of jobs in Japan's miscellaneous service sector and, especially, in the country's financial industry (even at a time of retrenchment in view of the bursting of the 'bubble' economy). On the other hand, job destruction caused by the closing of firms was clearly lower in Japan than in Italy and this was true in every industry.

Table 7.5 Births and deaths of firms and job flows, 1991–1994

	Italy	Japan
Total		
Firms birth rate	9.6	4.0
Job creation in new firms	3.4	4.0
Firms death rate	10.8	4.4
Job destruction in closed firms	4.4	3.6
Manufacturing		
Firms birth rate	7.3	2.7
Job creation in new firms	2.8	2.4
Firms death rate	9.4	4.6
Job destruction in closed firms	4.3	2.9
Construction		
Firms birth rate	13.1	4.5
Job creation in new firms	5.3	4.8
Firms death rate	15.0	3.9
Job destruction in closed firms	6.5	3.8
Wholesale and retail trade		
Firms birth rate	9.9	3.8
Job creation in new firms	4.6	4.4
Firms death rate	11.2	4.8
Job destruction in closed firms	5.2	3.9
Finance and insurance		
Firms birth rate	9.9	6.3
Job creation in new firms	2.1	4.3
Firms death rate	9.9	6.3
Job destruction in closed firms	3.6	3.4
Other services		
Firms birth rate	10.3	4.4
Job creation in new firms	4.4	4.8
Firms death rate	9.3	3.8
Job destruction in closed firms	4.2	3.6

a. Job creation in new firms is equal to the number of employees at end period in firms that were created during the period; job destruction is equal to the number of jobs at the beginning of the period that have disappeared because of firms closures during the period.
Source: Authors' elaboration of EDMS and INPS data (see the Appendix for details).

3.6 Summary

Over the period here considered there seems to have been significantly more 'movement' on the Italian labour market than on the Japanese one, in so far as gross job creation and destruction tended to occur more frequently in Italy than in Japan. Substantial job flows at small Italian firms were a major contributory factor to the high job creation and destruction rates experienced in Italy. By contrast, job destruction at existing small firms, or caused by the death of firms, was relatively limited in Japan.

Job creation and destruction in Italy appear to have been driven primarily by temporary shocks especially in small firms, while persistent shocks seem to have had a larger impact on job flows in Japan. Moreover, the shocks affecting Japan have tended to be common across industries, while those that have hit the Italian economy have been more differentiated across various sectors. In other words, aggregate shocks have been more important for employment changes in Japan, while sectoral shocks have been more important in Italy. Finally, thanks to the lower incidence of both temporary and sectoral shocks, the volatility of job destruction in Japan has been well below Italy's and may, indeed, be the lowest (or one of the lowest) among industrialized countries.

4 Why has employment performance been so different?

This section looks at some of the reasons for the very different employment and unemployment performances in the two countries illustrated in Section 2 above. The discussion is mainly based on an interpretation of the differences in job creation and destruction, as outlined in Section 3. Some considerations is also given to the existence of structural and institutional factors which can throw light on the longer-run persistence of labour market divergences between the two countries.

As is well known, the theoretical and applied literature on what causes differences in employment and unemployment performance is vast (see, for instance, Solow, 1990; Malinvaud, 1994; OECD, 1994; Sen, 1997), and the conclusions reached are seldom in agreement. The present text will not survey this literature, but simply use a (partial) comparative approach which highlights a feature of the two countries' labour markets that does not appear in the many separate studies that have been conducted on Italy and Japan (see, for instance, Hamada and Kurosaka, 1986; Modigliani et al., 1986; Ito, 1992; Yoshikawa, 1995).

An important finding in Section 3 was that, in the first half of the 1990s, job losses were much more frequent (and more volatile) in Italy than in Japan, and especially so in small Italian firms compared with small Japanese firms. A possible explanation for Italy's relatively poor performance in this period might be provided by macroeconomic developments. The early 1990s were years of great turmoil in the country. Political instability was high as a consequence of frequent changes in government and the discovery by the judiciary of widespread administrative corruption and illegal party financing (the so-called *Tangentopoli* scandal). Uncertainty was also amplified by exchange rate instability (the currency was ejected from the EMS in September 1992, and nose-dived further in 1995) and by the deep recession of 1992–94. It was further strengthened by the difficulties encountered in reducing the public debt/GDP ratio and the ensuing widespread doubts about the likelihood of Italy's participation in EMU. Uncertainty, however, must have also increased in Japan. The yen's gyrations on the currency markets were even more pronounced than those of the lira (Figure 8.2), the bursting of the 'bubble' economy severely affected business and consumer confidence, and the political stability of earlier periods gave way to more frequent changes in what turned out to be much less effective governments. Partly as a consequence, the deceleration in growth was more pronounced than it was in Italy.[8] Yet, the job creation/destruction patterns, as well as the unemployment performances of the two economies, were very different.

More structural reasons are almost certainly behind these contrasts and suggest that similar contrasting developments were probably also present in earlier periods. One possible explanation might come from employment protection legislation – the stricter this is, the more likely, ceteris paribus, that firms will try to avoid redundancies. Yet, Italian firms were less inhibited in firing their employees than their Japanese counterparts, even though the available evidence suggests that Italy's regulations in this area are a good deal more binding than their equivalents in Japan (OECD, 1994). A much more plausible reason for the wide divergence in job destruction rates can be found instead in the long-standing differences that exist between the two countries in the training systems which firms apply to their work forces.

Taking Japan first, it is well known that a key aspect of the behaviour of Japanese firms is on-the-job training (OJT). Numerous studies have shown the importance given to firm-specific skill accumulation, even in small enterprises (see, for example, Odaka, 1984; Koike, 1988; Mincer and Higuchi, 1988; Koshiro, 1989; Ono, 1989). These studies emphasize that the shortage of skilled workers during the high economic growth period of the1950s and 1960s, was a very important reason for the development of internal labour markets in Japan. Rapid technology transfers from abroad during these years required a large supply of skilled labour, but the supply of such labour in the external labour market was insufficient. This made it necessary for employers to train their employees by increasing human capital investment within the firm. The development of internal labour markets made such investment worthwhile since it made it costly for workers with firm-specific skills to leave the enterprise.

Given these sunk costs of firm-specific investment in the form of OJT, Japanese firms, when faced with temporary negative shocks, tend to avoid destroying jobs. Similarly, when upturns occur, it would be expensive for firms to create jobs and hire new employees because of the need to provide for substantial additional training. The presence of such higher hiring and firing costs will tend to reduce both job creation and destruction in response to temporary economic fluctuations. The outcome is a more stable employment pattern in Japanese enterprises.

The Italian system is different. Though no comparative data on the extent of OJT are available, it is almost certain that the quantity and quality of Italian firms' investment in the human capital of their employees is much more limited. The reasons for this are, no doubt, numerous. In the 1950s and 1960s, when Italian industry faced conditions not dissimilar to those in Japan, OJT was relatively neglected – employers seemed more interested in short-run results and employees felt less 'identified' with the firms they worked for than they did in Japan. Since the 1970s, reluctance to undertake OJT must, in addition, have reflected the high degree of conflict and tension which pervaded the labour market (Signorelli, 1997). The degree of industrial strife, in particular, has been much higher in Italy, when compared to the more stable and more co-ordinated Japanese system of industrial relations (Soskice, 1990). The high uncertainty created by endemic conflicts on the factory or office floor is bound to have negatively affected firms' longer-run decisions to invest in the training of strike-prone workers. The relative lack of OJT, in turn, has meant that employees were less valuable to the enterprise. Hence, Italian firms have tended to destroy jobs more frequently than their Japanese counterparts, unencumbered, as they were, by considerations of sunk costs.

Pervasive uncertainty was felt much more among large-scale enterprises than it was among smaller ones. Large firms were saddled not only with persistent industrial conflicts, but also with organizational rigidities imposed on them by trade-union-backed legislation. Small firms, on the other hand, particularly in the so-called 'industrial districts' were (and are) characterized by a much higher degree of flexibility of their labour force, thanks, in part, to a much lower presence of unions (Signorelli and Vercelli, 1994). These differences can partly explain why in the 1970s and 1980s there was net job creation in small firms, but net job destruction in larger ones.

The differences between the Italian and Japanese labour markets go beyond these various considerations. A number of institutional features can also throw light on the large gap in employment and unemployment performances. Thus, the organizational rigidities that have just been mentioned and that severely limit the freedom large firms have to flexibly manage their workforce are one of the reasons for the existence of a large 'underground' economy. This provides widespread 'irregular' employment, particularly in small firms and in the Southern part of the country. In Italy such rigidities were imposed by unions in the late 1960s and were codified in a Workers' Statute approved by Parliament in 1970. In Japan, union behaviour has been much less confrontational and such rigidities are virtually unknown.

A further reason for the diffusion of irregular forms of employment is the presence of a very high fiscal wedge – the total cost of an average production worker to an Italian firm was, in the mid-1990s, twice the net wage paid to that worker (in Japan the corresponding difference is of only 20 per cent) (Table 7.6). This creates a very strong incentive to hire workers without providing a regular contract, while, on the supply side, many individuals accept irregular jobs in view of the lack of regular employment opportunities. Distortions are also introduced by the structure of the social security systems. Italy's much more generous provision for invalidity and old age, together with an early retirement policy (often encouraged by the government), have clearly contributed to the very low employment rates of the population in the 55-to-64-years age bracket, as documented in Table 7.1 above.

Table 7.6   Labour tax wedge[a] for average production workers,[b] 1996 (percentages)

	Single worker		Worker married with two children	
	Italy	Japan	Italy	Japan
Take-home pay/gross earnings	72.0	86.3	82.3	91.0
Gross earnings/total labour cost	68.3	93.4	68.3	93.4
Total tax wedge[c]	50.8	19.4	43.8	15.1

a. Difference between total cost of labour paid by employer and after-tax wage received by employee.
b. Earning the average wage.
c. Equal to 1 minus the product of the first two lines.
Source: OECD, *The Tax/Benefit Position of Employees*, Paris 1997.

5 Conclusions

This chapter has looked at some aspects of the Italian and Japanese labour markets and has stressed, in particular, the two countries' differential employment performances and their job creation and destruction processes. The attempt that was made to interpret the remarkable differences that exist shows that labour market structures and evolutions are very complex phenomena and confirms Solow's view (1990) that it is impossible to consider labour as just another good.

A key term that was used to explain differences between the two countries is the degree of 'uncertainty' faced by firms when making employment decisions, and, in particular, the uncertainty generated by the system of industrial relations (Signorelli, 1999). The relative presence or absence of such uncertainty has an important bearing on the intensity of investment in human capital within firms. And lower human capital investment, in turn, results in a higher rate of job destruction. Japan's superior performance in terms of overall net employment growth and lower overall unemployment owes a lot to a rate of job destruction (particularly in small firms) that is well below Italy's thanks to its widespread system of OJT.

It is not certain, however, that the differences in employment performance between the two countries that have been highlighted so far will persist over the longer-run. The evidence presented in Table 7.3 shows, for instance, that job destruction has increased and job creation has decreased in Japan in the course of the 1990s. Such notable Japanese labour practices as lifetime employment and seniority wages have gradually been weakened since the 1980s in response to changing economic conditions (Genda, 1998d). Moreover, the share of part-time employment in Japan (which is already higher than that in Italy) has been growing steadily. While the average job destruction rate for full-time workers was 3.9 per cent in the period 1991–95, that for part-time workers was 7.4 per cent (Genda, 1998a). And the average job creation rate, which was 4.0 per cent for full-time workers' was as high as 9.1 per cent for part-timers. Given these trends, it is likely that job reallocation rates in Japan will tend to increase.

Further increases in job turnover can also be expected in Italy given the growing importance of atypical forms of employment which are characterized by a high frequency of job creation and job destruction. In the 1990s such forms of employment accounted for a large share of new recruits and they are set to increase further thanks to new labour legislation and changing fiscal incentives. Achieving overall reductions in job destruction rates will be difficult. The late 1990s have seen a much less volatile macroeconomic picture thanks to greater political stability and the achievement of EMU membership. This is unlikely, however, to change the long-term employment decisions and strategies of firms in the absence of other changes. Particularly important would be a decrease in what could be called the 'structural uncertainty' faced by the *Mezzogiorno* and which takes a variety of forms (for example, a lack of infrastructure but also a high rate of criminal activity). Similarly important would be a reform of the social security system that diminished the size of the fiscal wedge, thereby favouring the transformation of irregular into regular employment. Finally, a crucial component of any strategy designed to increase job creation and reduce job destruction would seem to be, in the light of Japan's experience, a strengthening of investment in human capital, combining elements of public good provision with greater private-sector involvement in OJT. Italy's very low employment rate among young workers is, no doubt, partly due to an inadequate link between the educational and vocational training systems on the one hand and the skills required in the labour market on the other. Any reform in this area could greatly benefit from an understanding of the Japanese experience.

Appendix: concepts and data used

The literature on gross job flows distinguishes these into job creation and destruction. 'Gross job creation' is defined as the overall gains of employment in the economy resulting from establishments either opening or expanding. 'Gross job destruction' is defined as the overall losses of employment stemming from establishment closures or contractions. 'Net employment growth' is then defined as gross creations minus gross destructions, while 'total job reallocation' stands for the sum of the two.

The data used for this study come mainly from the Ministry's of Labour biannual *Employment Trend Survey* (ETS) (*Koyo Doko Chosa*) for Japan and from the INPS records for Italy.

Job creation and destruction in Italy are computed from INPS micro data. The Institute collects the social security contributions of both firms and workers and administers various wage supplements, unemployment and retirement benefits. It covers all private, non-agricultural firms with employees. The data shown in Table 7.4 come from Contini and Filippi (1995) who have transformed the INPS's monthly employment observations into annual job flows.

Annual gains and losses of employment at private establishments in Japan can be similarly obtained from the ETS's micro data. The ETS records changes in employment at establishments in all industries except agriculture, forestry and fisheries. However, the ETS covers only existing establishments employing five or more workers, and does not examine the job creation and destruction that result from the birth and deaths of establishments. Hence the ETS data are likely to understate the true magnitude of overall job flows in Japan.

To try and improve the comparability of the INPS and ETS figures, two major adjustments were made. First, the information on job creation and destruction in very small firm – those with five or fewer employees – was omitted from the INPS data. Hence, the job flow rates shown in this chapter cover firms with six or more employees in Italy and five or more employees in Japan (this could impart a very small downward bias to the Italian figures in any comparison with Japan). Second, job creation and destruction by births and deaths of firms was also omitted from the INPS statistics.

However, there still remains a crucial difference between the two sources. The INPS data relate to employment changes at the firm level, while the ETS data cover such changes at the establishment level. Thus, job creations and destructions that result from labour moving between establishments of the same firm are ignored in the Italian statistics, but included in the Japanese ones. As a result, the level of job creation and destruction in Italy is likely to be underestimated when compared to the Japanese figures.

To calculate firms' births and deaths in Japan (as discussed in Section 3.5), use was made of the 1994 *Establishment Directory Maintenance Survey* (EDMS) (*Jigyo-sho Meibo Seibi Chosa*) conducted by the Statistical Bureau of the Management and Co-ordination Agency. This covers all establishments, including those born or closed, during the 1024 days between 1 July 1991 and 20 April 1994. Since only firms are considered, the births and deaths of branch-office establishments were ignored. Jobs created by the births of firms were measured by counting the number of employees on 20 April 1994 at establishments that were opened during the period. Conversely, jobs destroyed were made equal to the number of employees on 1 July 1991 at establishments that were closed during the period.

Notes

1 It is well known, for instance, that when demand for labour (and hence the employment rate) is low, workers are 'discouraged' from looking for jobs. Hence labour supply (that is, the participation rate) tends to decline. As a result, this so-called 'discouraged worker effect' keeps the recorded unemployment rate below the economy's 'real' unemployment rate.

2 Not only do fewer Italians work than is the case in Japan; they also work a good deal less. For dependent employees (in establishments with 30 workers or more), the number of annual hours worked was, in 1994 for instance, 12 per cent below the Japanese level (Source: OECD, *Employment Outlook*, 1999).

3 This is not say that there is no dualism in the Japanese labour market. On the contrary, through the 1950s and 1960s much economic discussion in the country was focused on the economy's 'dual' nature (see, for instance, Minami, 1973). Indeed, estimates using micro data suggest that the dual labour market hypothesis cannot be rejected even for the 1980s or early 1990s (Ishikawa, 1995). Japanese dualism, however, unlike the Italian kind, has no regional dimension of any significance (other than, perhaps, for Okinawa) and reflects mainly the productivity and wage level differences between large-and small-scale manufacturing firms, often coexisting within the same sectors and/or regions.

4 'Irregular' jobs are defined as jobs in legal (as opposed to criminal) activities, but devoid of a regular work contract and undeclared to the authorities.

5 The figures for Italy (1989) and for Japan (1991 – establishments rather than enterprises) were of 69.1 and 75.9 per cent respectively. Elsewhere, they ranged (in 1990) from 38.9 per cent in the United States to 44.6 per cent in Germany, 49.2 per cent in the United Kingdom and 50.0 per cent in France (Sources: Eurostat, *Enterprises in Europe, Third Report* and *Japan Statistical Yearbook, 1995*).

6 The persistence rate of job creation and destruction is computed, according to the definition given by Davis et al. (1996, pp. 191–2): the N-period persistence of job creation is the percentage of newly created jobs at time t that remain filled at each subsequent sampling date through time $t + N$. Likewise the N-period persistence of job destruction is the percentage of newly destroyed jobs at time t that do not reappear through time $t + N$.

7 This issue has generated an abundant literature; see, for instance, Mortensen and Pissarides (1994); Davis et al. (1996); Baldin et al. (1998).

8 Italy's average GDP growth rate fell from 2.5 per cent in 1979–89 to 1.3 per cent in the period 1989–95; the corresponding figures for Japan are 3.9 and 2.0 per cent.

References

Baldin, J., T. Dunne and J. Haltiwanger (1998) 'A Comparison of Job Creation and Job Destruction in Canada and the United States', *Review of Economics and Statistics*, 80, 3, 347–56.

Contini, B. and M. Filippi (1995) 'A Study on Job Creation and Job Destruction in Europe', mimeo, *Ricerche e Progetti*, Turin.

Dallago, B. (1990) *The Irregular Economy: the 'Underground' Economy and the 'Black' Labour Market*, Aldershot: Dartmouth.

Davis, S.J., J.C. Haltiwanger and S. Schuh (1996) *Job Creation and Destruction*, Cambridge, MA: MIT Press.

Fondazione G. Brodolini (1997) *Labour Market Studies: Italy*, Luxembourg: FGB.

Garibaldi, P. (1998) 'Job Flow Dynamics and Firing Restrictions', *European Economic Review*, 42, 2, 245–75.

Genda, Y. (1998a) 'Job Creation and Destruction in Japan, 1991–1995', *Journal of the Japanese and International Economies*, 12, 1, 1–23.

Genda, Y. (1998b) 'Job Gains and Losses in Japan: a Comparison with Italy', *Japan Labor Bulletin*, 37, 1, 4–8.

Genda, Y. (1998c) 'Jugyoinno Koreika to Koyo Kikaino Gentai' ('Hiring Practices, and Labour Demand'), ISER, Osaka University, Discussion Paper, No. 477.

Genda, Y. (1998d) 'Japan: Wage Differentials and Changes since the 1980s', in T. Tachibanaki (ed.), *Wage Differentials: an International Comparison*, London: Macmillan.

Hamada, K. and Y. Kurosaka (1986) 'Trends in Unemployment, Wages and Productivity: The Case of Japan', *Economica*, 53, 210S, S275–S296.

Ishikawa, T. (1995) *The Japanese Economy*, Lectures, Dipartimento di economia politica, University of Siena.

Ito, T. (1992) *The Japanese Economy*, Cambridge, MA: MIT Press.

Koike, K. (1988) *Understanding Industrial Relations in Modern Japan*, New York: St. Martin's Press.

Koshiro, K. (1989) 'Koyo Seido to Jinzai Katsuyo Senryaku' ('The Employment System and Human Resource Management'), in R. Komiya and K. Imai (eds), *Nihonno Kigyo (Business Enterprises in Japan)*, Tokyo: Tokyo University Press.

Malinvaud, E. (1994) *Diagnosing Unemployment*, Cambridge: Cambridge University Press.

Minami, R. (1973) The Turning Point in Economic Development: Japan's *Experience*, Tokyo: Kinokuniya.

Mincer, J. and Y. Higuchi (1988) 'Wage Structure and Labor Turnover in the United States and Japan', *Journal of the Japanese and International Economies*, 2, 2, 97–133.

Modigliani, F., F. Padoa Schioppa and N. Rossi (1986) 'Aggregate Unemployment in Italy: 1960–83', *Economica*, 53, 210S, S245–S273.

Mortensen, D.T. and C.A. Pissarides (1994) 'Job Creation and Job Destruction in the Theory of Unemployment', *Review of Economic Studies*, 61, 3, 397–415.

Odaka, K. (1984) *Rodo Shijo Bunseki (Labour Market Analysis)*, Tokyo: Iwanami Shoten.

OECD (1994) *The OECD Jobs Study: Facts, Analysis and Strategies*, Paris.

Ono, A. (1989) *Nihonteki Koyo Kanko to Rodo Shijo (Japanese Industrial Relations and Labour Markets)*, Tokyo: Toyo Keizai Shimposha.

Pazienza, M.G. and M. Signorelli (1998) 'Occupational Performance, Employment Structure and Demography of Firms in the Japanese and Italian Economies', mimeo.

Sen, A. (1997) 'Inequality, Unemployment and Contemporary Europe', *International Labour Review*, 136, 2, 155–72.

Signorelli, M. (1997) 'Uncertainty, Flexibility Gap and Labour Demand in the Italian Economy', *Labour*, 11, 1, 141–75.

Signorelli, M. (1999) 'Industrial Relations Systems and National Employment Performances: a Comparative Approach', AISSEC Research Paper, No. 77.

Signorelli, M. and A.Vercelli (1994) 'Structural Changes in the Post-war Italian Economy', in B. Boehm and L.F. Punzo (eds), *Economic Performance: a Look at Austria and Italy*, Heidelberg: Physica-Verlag.

Solow, R.M. (1990) *The Labor Market as a Social Institution*, Oxford: Blackwell.

Soskice, D. (1990) 'Wage Determination: the Changing Role of Institutions in Advanced Industrialized Countries', *Oxford Review of Economic Policy*, 6, 4, 36–61.

Yoshikawa, H. (1995) *Macroeconomics and the Japanese Economy*, Oxford: Oxford University Press.

8
Small Firms and Manufacturing Employment

Paolo Carnazza, Alessandro Innocenti and Alessandro Vercelli

1 Introduction

Italy and Japan have the highest share of manufacturing employment in small firms (hereafter, SFs) among the major industrialized countries. In the early 1990s the percentage of workers active in small manufacturing establishments or firms was of the order of 60 per cent in these two countries, as against figures ranging from only 20 to 40 per cent in economies such as Germany, the United Kingdom, the United States or France (OECD, 1996). In both Italy and Japan, the occupational weight of manufacturing SFs, after declining in the 'Golden Age' period of the 1950s and 1960s, increased in the 1970s, as it did in most other advanced countries. While this upward trend continued in Italy and elsewhere over the subsequent decade and a half (Storey, 1994), there was a reversal in Japan, where the SF share has shown a moderate but almost continuous decline (Figure 8.1). This chapter aims to provide an explanation for this divergent behaviour, by comparing some structural features of the two countries' manufacturing sectors, as well as the evolution of their international trade performance.

Section 2 sets the scene, by looking at the development of the occupational weight of SFs over the longer run. Section 3 examines a structural feature that differentiates the two economies (the nature of the prevailing subcontracting arrangements), while Section 4 looks at the different responses of Italian and Japanese industry to changes in their exchange rates. As briefly summarized in the conclusions, the interaction between these two factors provides a major explanation for the reduction of the occupational weight of SFs in Japan and its increase in Italy in recent years.

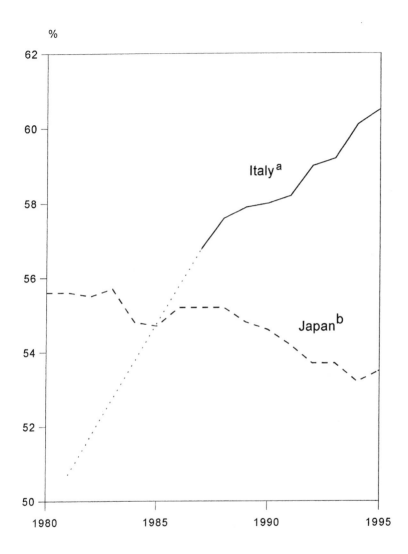

Figure 8.1 Employment in small units in manufacturing (in per cent of the manufacturing labour force)
a. Firms with between 1 and 99 employees.
b. Establishments with between 4 and 99 employees.
Sources: INPS, *Serie storiche* for Italy; *Japan Statistical Yearbook* (various issues) for
  Japan.

2   Longer-run trends

In the 1950s and 1960s it was common opinion amongst most economists that the economic importance of small firms[1] in industrialized countries was in an inevitable decline. In particular, it was expected that their share of aggregate employment would fall inexorably, as had happened in the primary sector. The sizeable role still played by SFs in economies like Italy and Japan was interpreted as a sign of these countries' economic backwardness, which would be wiped out in the process of development. For a number of years, the available evidence seemed, on the whole, to confirm this picture. Thus, the average size of manufacturing firms, measured in terms of employment, increased in the 1950s and 1960s in the OECD countries (Sengenberger et al., 1990). In Italy and Japan, the available data suggest that the occupational weight of small firms declined – or, at best, remained constant – during that period (Table 8.1).

Various factors contributed to reduce the share of employment in SFs in both economies. Among these was the rapid creation of a national market and of national tastes, particularly in many of the traditional sectors – such as food products, textiles, clothing and furniture. This process (which was importantly helped by the spread of television) led to a sharp reduction in the number of small handicraft firms operating in very limited geographical areas. In addition, the adoption of US technologies

Table 8.1   Manufacturing employment by establishment size class (percentage shares)

	1951	1961	1971	1981	1991
Number of employees					
		Italy			
1–99	54.5	57.0	52.8	59.1	67.8
100–499	20.4	21.5	23.2	21.2	19.2
> 500	25.1	21.5	24.0	19.7	13.0
		Japan			
1–99	57.8	52.7	51.8	58.2	56.6
100–499	18.0[a]	21.8	22.6	21.2	23.1
> 500	22.1[a]	25.5	25.6	20.6	20.3

a. 1954.

Sources: Brusco and Paba (1997) for Italy; Statistical Bureau, Management and Co-ordination Agency, *Historical Statistics of Japan* (Vol. 2), Tokyo, 1987 and *Japan Statistical Yearbook* (various issues) for Japan.

put a premium on economies of scale and this effect was reinforced by the two countries' process of internationalization: European integration, in the case of Italy, MITI's industrial policies in the case of Japan, forced or encouraged increases in the average size of firms, designed to raise external competitiveness.

However, and quite surprisingly, the almost unanimous prediction that such trends would continue unabated, was not confirmed by the experience of the 1970s and 1980s. The employment share of SFs, after mildly declining in the 1950s and 1960s, began to increase in most industrial countries in the 1970s, and this upward trend has not yet been interrupted, at least in manufacturing (in many service activities, on the other hand, average firm size has continued to fall). Changing tastes and changing technologies are, in this instance too, likely to be among the more important reasons for this inversion in trend. Thus, consumers' tastes have tended to become more personalized and differentiated, and this process has been helped on the supply side by new technologies (in particular, numerically controlled machine tools) that have made small-scale production more economical. A further factor, specific to Italy, has been the imposition by legislation in the 1970s of labour market rigidities that affected primarily large-scale firms. This, together with a sharply rising tax burden in the 1980s, encouraged the growth of SFs, since these were less constrained by legislation and often operated in the 'under-ground' economy.

Yet, while the weight of SF manufacturing employment since the war seems to have followed a broad U-shape in most countries, this has not been the case in Japan. After declining in the 1950s and 1960s and rising again in the 1970s (as happened elsewhere), the occupational weight of small-scale establishments began to fall again from the early or mid-1980s (Figure 8.1). The decline has been modest, but it stands in sharp contrast to the continuing and rapid increases recorded in, for instance, Italy.[2] Understanding the reasons for this contrasting behaviour may help to better assess the role of SFs in sustaining employment in manufacturing. This role is clearly dependent on an economy's industrial structure as well as on its performance in foreign markets.[3]

3   The nature of subcontracting

Subcontracting relationships exist in all countries and SFs are, obviously, deeply involved in them. Italy and Japan are no exception, even if the importance of subcontracting and its role in economic growth have been mainly emphasized by Japanese rather than by Italian economists. It has been argued that this lack of balance in the literature might be explained not only by the different sizes of the phenomenon, but also by the rather different nature of the two countries' subcontracting arrangements – in Japan, SFs are very dependent on, and often exploited by, larger firms, while in Italy they are much more likely to maintain an independent status. When Piore and Sabel (1984) originally applied their 'flexible specialization model' both to Italy and Japan, they pointed out that, while Italian SFs operated primarily in so-called 'industrial districts' in which flexible networks of relationships improved small plant productivity, the bulk of Japanese SFs belonged to a hierarchical system in which mass production prevailed and in which subcontractors had little autonomy and were technologically and commercially dependent on their contractors.

As is well known, from the 1950s the Japanese productive system was based on the domination of the large *keiretsu* – these organized vertical chains of suppliers and created a dual industrial structure, characterized by significant wage differentials between small and large firms (Watanabe, 1970; Friedman, 1988; Koshiro, 1990) and by the dependence of subcontractors on contractors.[4] A notable feature of this system was the dominance of 'capacity' over 'specialized' subcontracting. By 'capacity' (or overflow) subcontracting is meant a system in which the contractor hands over to the subcontractor responsibility for the supply of a product, or part of a product, only when the contractor himself has insufficient capacity to deal with a temporarily high volume of orders. 'Specialized' (or expert) subcontracting, on the other hand, denotes a relationship in which the contractor relies on the subcontractor for the supply of a specific input for which there is no in-house supply. Clearly, a much higher degree of control is exercised over the subcontractor in the first system – as, indeed, captured by the Japanese expression *shita-uke kankei*.[5]

Although much of the debate on subcontracting might be subject to a wide gap between reality and image (Miwa, 1995), it has been argued that, especially in the 1950s and 1960s, large firms exercised their monopsonistic power by using SFs as a buffer in the course of the business cycle. To some extent, this pattern was an inheritance of the *zaibatsu* domination that re-emerged little changed after 1945 with the *keiretsu* system, in view of the American occupation's failure to dismantle the old corporate structure.[6] But it was also a consequence of the pattern of development pursued after the war. This was characterized by a strong emphasis on rapid industrial recovery in a situation of labour surplus and capital shortage. Such a policy imposed a concentration of financial and R & D resources in a relatively limited number of main companies, those that were at the apex of vertical groups of subcontractors. Public support to small firms was, inevitably, delayed to the 1970s.

A 1970 MITI White Paper (MITI, 1970) on small and medium-sized enterprises may be considered the starting point of a radical change in the direction of policy. It also opened a wide debate on whether the dual economy was gradually disappearing. One particular issue that received much attention was the question of whether the earlier hierarchical arrangements between contractors and subcontractors had remained broadly unchanged in what MITI called a 'new dual structure', or whether the traditional pattern of inter-firm relations had been abandoned in favour of mutually beneficial and longer-term relationships between 'parent' and 'supplier' firms.[7]

The same problem has been analysed by Italian economists in connection with the restructuring of the chain of suppliers to large firms, especially in the car industry, that took place in the 1980s. It is not, however, an issue that would seem very relevant to a discussion of the subcontracting relationships that exist in Italy's industrial districts. These, as mentioned earlier, have always been characterized by a certain degree of independence of subcontractors from their contractors. According to Brusco (1982, 1989), this relative independence was achieved in the industrial districts by the existence of a large number of subcontractors constituting horizontal networks without any leading companies. While this interpretation may not provide a full picture,[8] it does point to a fundamental difference between the Italian and Japanese systems that may well have increased in importance in the 1980s, a period in which the volume of subcontracting in the Italian economy appears to have grown.

The aim of the next two sub-sections is to look in greater detail at these two (quantitative and qualitative) differences in the two countries' subcontracting relationships and to see to what extent they have been changing over the last decade.

3.1 Changes in the extent of subcontracting

Quantifying the extent of subcontracting is no easy task even within one economy, let alone when comparisons are attempted with another,[9] and the shortcomings of the underlying statistical base must be borne in mind in what follows. The main source of information on the evolution of subcontracting in Italian manufacturing is provided by sample data regularly collected by Mediocredito Centrale over the period 1968–94. Unfortunately, the series is not homogeneous because both the number of firms and the selection criteria have changed through time. To give an idea of the non-comparability of some of the data, it is sufficient to note that the number of firms considered in the 1984 survey was more than double that considered in other years. On the other hand, the last two sets of observations, covering 1991 and 1994, examined a broadly similar panel of firms, thereby offering better evidence on more recent patterns. For Japan, the data provided by the *White Paper on Small and Medium Enterprises in Japan*, edited by the Small and Medium Enterprises Agency (SMEA) and published annually by MITI, are more reliable because they cover a homogenous sample.

A comparison of these sources for the 1980s (Table 8.2) shows that first, and as might have been expected, the weight of subcontracting in the Japanese economy is significantly higher than it is in the Italian one – the figures, as argued earlier, are far from comparable, but the differences between the two countries are so large that they are bound to reflect some genuine diversity. Second, it is interesting to note that, over the period, the changes that have occurred in the importance of subcontracting moved into opposite directions.

In Italy, there was a sharp rise in the proportion of firms that were involved as subcontractors,[10] especially in branches such as textiles, clothing, leather products and general machinery, which are character-ized by the presence of industrial districts; conversely, there was almost no

Table 8.2 The importance of subcontracting in selected sectors (percentage shares)

| | Share of small firms/establishments[a] engaged in subcontracting | | | |
| | Italy | | Japan | |
	1978	*1984*	*1981*	*1987*
Foodstuffs	4.5	14.8	17.5	8.6
Textiles	18.3	54.9	84.9	80.1
Clothing	18.7	43.2	86.5	79.3
Wood and furniture	4.5	16.2	49.6	28.8
Leather products	8.1	30.7	68.8	65.7
Metal products	12.0	54.4	78.6	71.1
General machinery	12.1	34.1	84.2	75.0
Electric machinery	11.2	23.3	85.3	80.5
Transport equipment	12.6	16.6	87.7	81.2
Precision machinery	17.5	28.7	80.9	71.1
Total manufacturing	9.5	30.1	65.5	55.9

a. SFs are defined as firms with less than 250 employees in Italy and as establishments with less than 300 employees in Japan.

Sources: Mediocredito Centrale, *Indagine sulle imprese manifatturiere, 1978* and *1984* for Italy; SMEA (1996a) for Japan.

increase in the transport equipment sector, a sector that is well known everywhere for its heavy reliance on subcontracting arrangements. In Japan, on the other hand, the importance of subcontracting seems to have modestly declined, and this in every sector of activity. The declines were well below average in two sets of industries, both highly dependent on subcontracting – the traditional textiles, clothing and leather product branches and the two engines of Japan's industrial strength (electric machinery and transport equipment).

More recent evidence confirms that the aggregate trends in evidence between the turn of the 1970s and the mid- or late-1980s have continued over the subsequent decade in both countries. In Italy, for instance, the share of subcontracting firms in the total number of enterprises rose by some 6 percentage points between 1991 and 1994. The intensity of subcontracting also increased, with the share of firms in which subcontracting accounted for less than 10 per cent of total sales falling by about 12 percentage points. For Japan, the continuing decline in the extent of subcontracting activity was confirmed for more recent years by various issues of the *White Paper on Small and Medium Enterprises in Japan*. The survey for 1995, for instance, showed a significant fall in orders for subcontractors, mainly due to two features – poor sales by the main contractor (cited by nearly two-thirds of the respondents) and the main contractor's expansion overseas (cited by some 40 per cent) (SMEA, 1996a, p. 78). In particular, the sharp increase in FDI by Japanese firms (including a significant number of SFs), a phenomenon particularly pronounced in the automobile industry, transformed erstwhile suppliers of standardized components from net exporters to net importers. More generally, the domestic production of less sophisticated components declined considerably in the 1990s and reduced employment in subcontracting SFs.

3.2   Changes in the characteristics of subcontracting

The above evidence, however imperfectly comparable across both time and space, suggests, nonetheless, that over the last decade or so subcontracting activity has risen in importance, if from a small base, in Italy and has declined in importance, if from a much larger base, in Japan. An explanation for these changes requires an examination of changes in the character of the subcontracting relationships in the two countries, changes which may well have gone in the direction of a greater convergence in this area between Italy and Japan.

For Italy (and for other European economies), information on the characteristics of subcontracting has been made available by the European Network for SME Research (ENSR, 1996), which has examined the evolution of subcontracting in the country on the basis of a number of case studies. The main points highlighted by this report deserve being quoted extensively:

> Subcontracting is developing in every country, although it is subject to the influence of growth cycles. In most European countries, it is notable that while speciality subcontracting is increasing, capacity subcontracting is decreasing.
>
> ... The increase of speciality subcontracting supports the generally accepted assumption that subcontracting relationships tended to move from 'supplier/customer' relationships in which the subcontractor is heavily dependent on the principal to strategic partnerships in which there is a greater interdependency and a more equal relationship.
>
> ... There has been a clear tendency by principals to get back to their core activity, to reduce their number of subcontractors and to 'delegate' a greater part of the development phase to their first tier subcontractors. (ibid., pp. 149–50)

Fieldwork carried out in Italy confirms this picture and in addition suggests that the growth in specialized subcontracting prevalent since the 1980s has followed two distinct patterns. First, in many industrial districts firms have increasingly allocated part of the production process to outsiders, either by providing the finance needed to acquire machinery by their own previous workers, or by moving specific elements of the production process out of the district. Second, in those industrial sectors dominated by large-scale firms, since the 1970s there has been considerable outsourcing of production towards small subcontractors (and this was a major reason for the sharp decline in employment in such firms). These two trends have gradually raised the specialization of subcontractors for both technological and commercial reasons.

At the technological level, it is increasingly the case that many new techniques involve activities requiring different capabilities at various stages of the production process (see, for instance, Håkansson, 1987; and von Hippel, 1988). Therefore, subcontracting firms can find technological niches that the main firm cannot easily fill itself. This trend increases the degree of interaction between SFs and larger firms, giving rise to vertical structures characterized by many tiers of subcontracting, stable relationships and a lower number of subcontractors for each contractor. Interestingly, it also increases interactions between SFs themselves, particularly in the industrial districts. Turning to commercial causes, these are related to interactions with final demand. A feature of the early growth of industrial districts in the 1970s was their fragmentation and the ensuing inefficiency of their distributive organization. At the time, this was eased by specialized middlemen – the buyers – who provided some co-ordination between dispersed and anonymous SFs and the market. More recently, however, competition for market share has been increasingly based on factors other than price, such as product quality, flexibility in meeting volatile consumer demand, and services to customers. To comply with these changes and to become more visible in the customer's eye, some firms have specialized in interacting with final markets, thereby further developing their subcontracting production networks.

It is very difficult to document any of these trends with hard data. The Mediocredito Centrale surveys point, however, to structural features of Italian subcontracting that indirectly support some of the statements just made. In particular, Table 8.3 shows a rather uniform distribution of subcontractors by firm size and by importance of turnover. If anything, smaller companies were less involved than larger ones. Even more interestingly, SFs outsourced more work than did larger firms, supporting the idea that a significant part of the increase of subcontracting in the country concerned SFs on both sides and probably involved extensive co-operation between partners of similar size. Though no figures on the same basis seem to be available for Japan, all that one knows about the Japanese system suggests a very different pattern.

According to SMEA reports, it is only recently that the structure of Japanese subcontracting has begun to change in the direction of greater partnership between the various participants. Thus, subcontractors have attempted to raise their profiles by improving product quality, by raising sales capacity and, in particular, by trying to diversify themselves away from one main contractor. The changes reported in this area have been

Table 8.3 Selected data on Italian subcontracting, 1994

	Share of firms providing subcontracting	Share of sub-contracting activity in turnover	Share of firms using sub-contractors for > 30% of turnover[a]
Size classes			
11–50	28.9	22.9	12.1
51–250	35.2	23.1	9.6
> 250	29.5	21.1	8.2

a. 1991.
Source: Mediocredito Centrale, *Indagine sulle imprese manifatturiere, 1991* and *1994*.

striking (Table 8.4). In as short a time-span as three years, the percentage of subcontractors engaged in exclusive contracts with only one parent company was halved, while the perceived importance of establishing contracts with a larger number of buyers increased by more than 20 percentage points.

This evolution is clearly linked to a technological up-scaling of smaller firms, as also confirmed by SMEA (1996b). In particular, significant changes have occurred in the importance placed by main firms on the various criteria used in selecting their subcontractors. Thus, demands for 'thorough cost reduction', 'greater quality and precision', or 'quality assurance' double their importance when compared with the early 1980s and now rank first. Conversely, the more traditional preoccupations with 'stable quantities of parts and finished products', 'fixing delivery time' and 'volume production' drop sharply in significance. Similarly, main firms increasingly take into consideration the availability among subcontractors of 'specialist technologies' or the 'ability to perform technical development', while the proportion of contractors expected to choose their partners on the basis of an 'existing business relationship' declines considerably. This changing nature of subcontracting is clearly leading to a more horizontal network of inter-firm relationships that goes beyond the vertical *keiretsu* structure and to a rearrangement of the traditionally rigid Japanese supply chain (Lakshmanan and Okumura, 1995).

In both countries, therefore, the nature of subcontracting relationships has been changing. In Italy, the substitution of specialized for capacity

Table 8.4   Changes in the nature of Japanese subcontracting (small and medium-sized establishments[a])

	Share of subcontractor	
	1987	*1990*
Type of contract		
Exclusive contract[b]	34.5	15.8
Semi-exclusive contract[c]	38.6	36.8
Semi-dispersed contract[d]	24.5	38.0
Dispersed contract[e]	2.4	9.4

a. Establishments with 1 to 300 employees.
b. One contractor only with more than 90 per cent of subcontracting turnover.
c. 2 to 5 contractors with more than 90 per cent of subcontracting turnover, or one contractor only with less than 90 per cent of subcontracting turnover.
d. 2 to 5 contractors with less than 90 per cent of subcontracting turnover, or more than 5 contractors with more than 70 per cent of subcontracting turnover.
e. More than 5 contractors and less than 70 per cent of subcontracting turnover.
Source: SMEA (1996a).

subcontracting is a process that goes back to the 1980s and was continued in the 1990s. In Japan, capacity subcontracting, traditionally a good deal more extensive than in Italy, continued to dominate for longer. Yet, by the early 1990s, Japan had also begun to experience a shift to new forms of partnership between large and small firms and towards a greater role for specialized subcontractors.

4 The impact of exchange rate changes

Both Italy and Japan experienced significant real exchange rate changes in the 1980s and early 1990s (Figure 8.2). Italy went, first, through a long-drawn-out phase of currency appreciation between 1980 and 1992, as periodic downward realignments within the EMS were not sufficient to offset a continuing inflation differential with its major trading partners. The September 1992 EMS crisis then led to a steep depreciation which was further reinforced in 1994–95 by political uncertainties. All in all, the real value of the lira rose by some 11 per cent between 1980 and 1991 and then depreciated by 20 per cent in the five years to 1996. Japan, on the other hand, went through two phases of very sharp appreciation. The first one (after the 1985 Plaza agreements) lifted the yen's real value by 41 per cent between 1985 and 1988. Following a few years of relative stability, the yen then rose again, by a further 35 per cent from 1992 to 1995, before falling back to somewhat lower levels in the recent past.[11] Inevitably, these sharp exchange rate gyrations have had a significant impact on the activity and employment of SFs in both countries.[12] For Japan, in particular, it has been estimated that the negative effects of the yen's rise between 1991 and 1995 were much more pronounced for SFs than they were for larger enterprises (EPA, 1996).

The appreciation of the yen triggered off a process of structural change in Japanese manufacturing which is bound to have reduced the occupational weight of SFs or, at least, to have contributed to its stabilization. More specifically, the car and home electronic industries – which had been the stars of Japanese industrial efficiency and competitiveness in the 1970s and 1980s – lost much of their comparative advantage after 1985 (Yoshitomi, 1996). There was, as a consequence, a drastic reduction in the volume of exports and a concomitant increase in Japanese foreign direct investment into countries with lower labour costs, particularly in Asia (Nakamura and Matsuzaki, 1997). As a result, local labour was substituted for Japanese labour and the importance of foreign production soared.[13]

The effect of this on subcontractors differed depending on the latters' specialization. In the car industry, for instance, domestic suppliers of

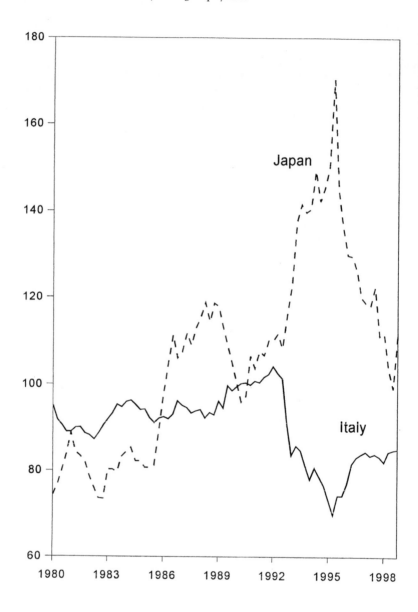

Figure 8.2   Real exchange rates (indices; 1990 = 100; based on relative, normalized, unit labour costs in manufacturing)
Source: IMF, 'International Financial Statistics Data Bank'.

technologically more sophisticated components (such as engines and brakes) were now able to maintain their subcontracting links by exporting their products to the newly established foreign operations of the main company or, at times, even shifting their operations abroad; on the other hand, suppliers of more standardized components (such as tyres, lead batteries or seatbelts) were not only unable to supply Japanese plants abroad (where small local subcontractors were substituted for Japanese ones), but also found themselves having to compete with imported products at home. The increasing difficulties suffered by SFs and their declining occupational weight in the first half of the 1990s can, at least in part, be linked to these developments (SMEA, 1996a).

These shifts were accompanied by two further important structural changes. First, Japan's export composition shifted towards higher value products, including sophisticated capital goods (such as industrial robots) and components (such as liquid crystal displays and other devices for computers and telecommunication equipment). This shift mitigated the decline in net exports: the share of high-tech products in Japan's total exports in the period 1985–95 rose sharply, at the expense of capital-intensive but medium-technology goods (such as cars, steel and home electronics) (Yoshitomi, 1996). Second, this switch towards more sophisticated products was, at least in part, responsible for the sort of changes in subcontracting that were discussed in Section 3 above. More specifically,

> the demands made by main contractors on their subcontractors are becoming increasingly sophisticated. In other words, subcontractors are being called on to provide products of higher quality and greater precision. Moreover, ... there has today been a very clearly discernible decline in the use of traditional and technical development strengths. (SMEA, 1996a, p. 85)

While yen appreciation almost certainly contributed to the fall in the employment share of Japan's SFs in this period, the lira's (relatively modest) appreciation in the 1980s may, paradoxically, have had almost opposite effects on the occupational weight of SFs in Italy. This appreciation was perceived by many entrepreneurs as a structural phenomenon, likely to persist in the longer run. As a result, numerous SFs, operating within the industrial districts, launched a vigorous reaction by upgrading their production and by devoting resources to a better understanding of consumer needs. Such strategies, mainly carried out in the so-called 'sophisticated traditional goods' sectors,[14] have led to significant export successes, despite lira appreciation (between 1984 and 1993, for instance, the share in total exports of the furniture and mechanical sectors increased from just over 20 to 30 per cent) (Fortis, 1996).[15]

The lira's sharp and unexpected depreciation in September 1992 was probably perceived by the majority of SFs belonging to the 'sophisticated traditional goods' sectors as a temporary phenomenon. They thus continued to search for lasting improvements in efficiency, while maintaining or even increasing their shares in the 'specialized' markets they serve – markets that are, in any case, relatively inelastic to exchange rate variations. On the other hand, the devaluation had a strong favourable impact on SFs producing simple traditional goods and on large firms producing standardized ones.

To summarize, exchange rate changes have had important effects on the occupational structure of SFs in both economies in the 1980s and in the first half of the 1990s.[16] The clearest and best documented impact has been on Japan, where the strong appreciation of the yen clearly contributed to the reduction in the share of employment in SFs. It also caused a general increase in industrial efficiency through a significant change in subcontracting relationships (towards a greater stress on technological factors and a significant reduction in capacity subcontracting), and a further shift in Japan's export composition towards higher-value and higher-technology products.

In Italy, by contrast, there has been little change in the nature of comparative advantage as a result of the lira's appreciation in the 1980s – if anything, the 'traditional' sectors reinforced their international competitiveness (though it should be borne in mind that the technological sophistication of many of the firms operating in these sectors defies any simple categorization between high- and low-tech products). Depreciation from 1992, on the other hand, was particularly beneficial to SFs in less competitive industries. Throughout the period, therefore, exchange rate changes may well have contributed to raise the share of employment in small Italian enterprises, while doing the opposite in Japan.

5   Conclusions

The contrasting behaviour of the occupational weight of SFs in Italy and Japan in the period 1985–95 may be partly explained by the different structures of subcontracting and by the different reactions of the manufacturing sectors to the evolution of the terms of trade in the two countries. There is, of course, a close link between these two factors. Japan's large firms have traditionally relied on 'capacity' subcontracting. This has been a key factor in their successful export sectors, characterized, on the one hand, by fairly standardized medium-technology products and, on the other, by a number of high-tech goods. The prevalence of 'specialized' subcontracting in Italy, on the other hand, arises from the importance of the 'sophisticated traditional goods' which have been the backbone of the country's exports in this period.

The reaction of both countries' manufacturing sectors to currency appreciation in the period here considered has been that of developing or strengthening sectors characterized by non-price competitive advantages in international markets – high-tech goods in Japan and sophisticated traditional goods in Italy. The success of this strategy relied on a continuing important role for capacity subcontracting in Japan and for specialized subcontracting in Italy. In Japan, however, given the magnitude of the currency's appreciation, foreign capacity subcontractors were substituted for domestic ones. In Italy, on the other hand, this process of substitution was much weaker, partly because the lira's revaluation was more modest and partly because specialized subcontracting in the production of sophisticated traditional goods could not easily be transferred abroad. The stagnation of the Japanese economy in the period since 1992 has further depressed the activity of domestic capacity subcontractors, while Italian SFs, particularly those working as specialized subcontractors, were able to weather the 1992–94 recession better than large firms.

These various changes in subcontracting systems were a contributing factor to the divergent behaviour of the occupational weight of SFs in the two countries. In Japan, the external shock represented by the yen's appreciation led to a process of substitution away from domestic capacity subcontractors and towards outward direct investment. At the same time specialized subcontracting, needed to cope with the shift of many firms' production towards higher-technology lines of activity, increased. This, however, was insufficient to preserve the former levels of employment in SFs, because the reduction in the large population of capacity subcontractors was only partially compensated by the growth of specialized ones. In Italy, on the other hand, the growth of industrial districts led, throughout these years, to a growth in subcontracting relationships characterized not only by an increasing reliance on specialized suppliers, but also on the creation of horizontal networks of SFs. Combined with the efforts made by many of these SFs in upgrading their technology and competitiveness, this allowed the aggregate employment share of SFs to rise, a phenomenon that was then further reinforced by the lira's depreciation after 1992.

Notes

1. The concept of a small firm is by no means crystal clear and no accepted definition, from either an economic or a statistical point of view is available. The size of firms can be measured in different ways, focusing on output (such as turnover or value added) or on production factors (labour or capital). The choice depends on the aims of the analysis – since this chapter's main purpose is that of studying the evolution of the employment share accounted for by SFs, the size of firms will be measured by the number of their employees. Where exactly to set the thresholds between small, medium, and large firms is far from obvious, and any such threshold may require periodic downward revisions given the continuous growth of labour productivity. Japanese accounts, designed in the 1950s, define SFs as having less than 300 employees; most of the Italian data used here, set the threshold at 250 employees. A further important difference between the two countries is that Italy's data usually cover firms, while Japan's data cover establishments. This is likely to overestimate the level of employment in small units in Japan compared to Italy. On the other hand, most of the available Japanese data omit information on very small establishments with less than four workers, a factor which works in the opposite direction. It is impossible to say in which direction the net bias operates.
2. Absolute employment in SFs rose in both economies between the mid-1980s and the mid-1990s, but the increase was much more pronounced in Italy than in Japan.
3. The share of tradable production in value added is, of course, particularly large in an economy's manufacturing sector; in the early 1990s this share was of the order of 63 per cent in Italy and 34 per cent in Japan.
4. Such a dualistic view of the Japanese economy has been the focus of debate among researchers for a long period. For a contrasting view on this, see Miwa (1996).
5. This term

   is usually used for the case where an ordering firm has some degree of control over a supplying firm in the production relations between them. This gives 'subcontracting' a meaning beyond the simple commissioning by one firm of work from another, instead of producing in its own factory. (Thoburn and Takashima, 1992, p. 103)

6. See Chapter 2 by Barca et al. in this volume for an account of this story.
7. Thus, in the 1970s, the weight of subcontracting changed cyclically, even in Italy's industrial districts. During periods of expansion, contractors usually subcontracted additional demand, but they resumed in-house production in phases of recession. In other words, subcontracting SFs were dependent on the capacity decisions of their contractors (Innocenti, 1998).
8. Arguably, this was not the case for 'just-in-time' forms of subcontracting.

Though such methods greatly improved the performance of the manufacturing sector, they were imposed by large firms on SFs. They are thus not discussed in this chapter whose aim is to highlight the specific contribution of small firms to subcontracting relationships.

9. There are at least two major reasons for this. First, international statistics employ a variety of definitions of the phenomenon. Second, different schools of industrial economics tend to devise different terminologies to describe what are basically similar facts – see, among others, the 'flexible firm' or the 'boundaryless firm' (Atkinson and Meager, 1986), 'flexible specialization' (Piore and Sabel, 1984), 'the independent subcontractor opposed to dependent subcontracting' (Brusco, 1989), 'the shift from hierarchy to contract' (Colling, 1995) or the implications of the Japanese word *shita-uke kankei* discussed in note 5 above.

10. Some of the increase shown in the table may, however, reflect the much larger coverage of the 1984 survey data mentioned above.

11. Its trend rate of appreciation over the decade was of the order of $4\frac{1}{2}$ per cent per annum.

12. In Japan exports accounted for perhaps 20 per cent of SFs' value added in the early 1990s (OECD, 1997); in Italy for some 25 per cent of their turnover in 1994.

13. Thus, between 1980 and 1995 the share of overseas production (expressed as a percentage of domestic plus overseas output) of the automobile sector, for example, rose from 4 to as much as 37 per cent (OECD, 1996).

14. This sector includes fashion goods, furniture and 'Mediterranean diet' products, as well as the manufacture of machinery for the textile, food and leather industries. Many of these goods can be considered quite sophisticated in view of the various technological improvements and product innovation processes that have been adopted by Italian firms.

15. It is, of course, true that not all such exports come from industrial districts, particularly so in the case of mechanical products.

16. There are, of course, further factors which may explain the different behaviour of the occupational weight of small manufacturing firms in Italy and in Japan over the period examined here. To name just one, the significant increase in unemployment experienced in Italy since the early 1980s has clearly provided a strong incentive to self-employment, including the start up of new businesses. There has been nothing comparable in Japan, where the rate of unemployment has remained exceptionally low throughout these years (see Chapter 7 by Genda et al. in this volume).

References

Atkinson, J. and N. Meager (1986) *Changing Working Patterns: How Companies Achieve Flexibility to Meet New Needs*, London, National Economic Development Office.

Brusco, S. (1982) 'The Emilian Model: Productive Decentralisation and Social Integration', *Cambridge Journal of Economics*, 6, 2, 167–84.

Brusco, S. (1989) *Piccole imprese e distretti industriali*, Turin: Rosenberg & Sellier.

Brusco, S. and S. Paba (1997) 'Per una storia dei distretti industriali italiani dal secondo dopoguerra agli anni noranta', in F. Barca (ed.), *Storia del capitalismo italiano dal dopoguerra a oggi*. Rome: Donzetti.

Colling, T. (1995) 'From Hierarchy to Contract? Subcontracting and Employment in the Service Economy', Warwick Papers in Industrial Relations, No. 52.

EPA (1996) *Economic Survey of Japan, 1995–1996*, Tokyo.

ENSR (1996) *The European Observatory for SMEs. Fourth Annual Report 1996*, Brussels.

Fortis, M. (1996) *Crescita economica e specializzazioni produttive*, Milan: Vita e Pensiero.

Friedman, D. (1998) *The Misunderstood Miracle: Industrial Development and Political Change in Japan*, Ithaca, NY: Cornell University Press.

Håkansson, H. (1987) *Industrial Technological Development: a Network Approach*, London: Croom Helm.

Innocenti, A. (1998) 'Gerarchia e contratti. Il ruolo dei rapporti di subfornitura tra piccole imprese nell'evoluzione dei distretti industriali', *L'industria*, 19, 2, 391–415.

Koshiro, K. (1990) 'The Re-emergence of Small Enterprises: Japan', in W. Sengenberger, G. Loveman and M.J. Piore (eds.) *The Re-emergence of Small Enterprises: Industrial Restructuring in Industrialised Countries*, Geneva: International Institute for Labour Studies.

Lakshmanan, T.R. and M. Okumura (1995) 'The Nature and Evolution of Knowledge Networks in Japanese Manufacturing', *Papers in Regional Science*, 74, 1, 63–86.

MITI (1970) *The Transformation of the Dual Structure and the Increasing Variety of SME Problems*, Tokyo.

Miwa, Y. (1995) 'Five Misconceptions about the Japanese Economy', *Economic Notes*, 24, 1, 1–13.

Miwa, Y. (1996) *Firms and Industrial Organization in Japan*, New York, NY: New York University Press.

Nakamura, Y. and I. Matsuzaki (1997) 'Economic Interdependence: Japan, Asia, and the World', *Journal of Asian Economics*, 8, 2, 199–224.

OECD (1996) 'Size Distribution of Output and Employment: a Data Set for Manufacturing Industries in Five OECD Countries', Economics Department Working Paper, No. 166.

OECD (1997) *Globalisation and Small and Medium Enterprises (SMEs)*, Paris.

Piore, M.J. and C.F. Sabel (1984) *The Second Industrial Divide: Possibilities for Prosperity*, New York, NY: Basic Books.

Sengenberger, W., G. Loveman and M.J. Piore, (eds) (1990) *The Re-emergence of Small Enterprises: Industrial Restructuring in Industrialised Countries*, Geneva: International Institute for Labour Studies.

SMEA (1996a) *White Paper on Small and Medium Enterprises in Japan*, Tokyo: MITI.

SMEA (1996b) *Survey of the Structure of Subcontract Work*, Tokyo: MITI.

Storey, D.J. (1994) *Understanding the Small Business Sector*, London: Routledge.

Thoburn, J.T., and M. Takashima (1992) *Industrial Subcontracting in the UK and Japan*, Aldershot: Avebury.

von Hippel, E. (1988) *The Sources of Innovation*, Oxford: Oxford University Press.

Watanabe, S. (1970) 'Entrepreneurship in Small Enterprises in Japanese Manufacturing', *International Labour Review*, 102, 6, 531–76.

Yoshitomi, M. (1996) 'On the Changing International Competitiveness of Japanese Manufacturing since 1985', *Oxford Review of Economic Policy*, 12, 3, 61–73.

9
The Distribution Structure: An Evolutionary Analysis*

Kiyohiko G. Nishimura and Lionello F. Punzo

1 Introduction

The distribution sector is of significant economic importance.[1] Thus, retail and wholesale trade alone accounted for between one-fifth and one-quarter of total employment and 14 to 17 per cent of value added in Italy, Japan and the United States in 1990 (Table 9.1). In spite of its importance, however, there has been little research on the role of distribution in long-run economic growth and international competitiveness. This may be due to the fact that the sector is very heterogeneous: the distribution of agricultural products, for example, is very different from that of machinery. Such heterogeneity requires careful disaggregate analysis, but detailed and internationally comparable disaggregated data are not easily available in most countries.

* This is a modified version of a paper originally published by Physica-Verlag in *Economic Systems* (Kiyohiko G. Nishimura, and Lionello F. Punzo, 'The Distribution Structure in Three Continents: An Evolutionary Analysis of Italy, Japan and the United States', 23, 1, 85–106, 1999). That article, in turn, was partly based on Nishimura and Punzo (1998) which is available from the authors upon request. We are indebted to Andrea Boltho for very detailed suggestions on an earlier version of the chapter, which have considerably improved both its content and exposition. We also thank Drs Savio and Tommasi of ISTAT for kindly providing us with the Italian data, and Mr Tsubouchi of the EPA, for helping us to understand the Japanese data. Yuji Nakayama provided us with extremely able research assistance. The work of Nishimura was partly supported by a Ministry of Education Grant-in-Aid; Punzo's work was supported by a grant from the Italian Ministry of Higher Education and Scientific Research.

Table 9.1   The importance of the distribution sector in Italy, Japan and the United States, 1990

	Share in economy (per cent)		Productivity ($000s)	
	Employment	Value added	Net output per employed (at market exch. rat.)	(at PPP exch. rat.)
Italy	21.0	16.7	42.2	35.8
Japan	19.4	13.8	34.4	29.7
United States	25.3	17.0	41.4	51.4

Source: OECD, *Economic Survey of Japan, 1995.*

Moreover, the study of the distribution sector may also have been hampered by a conceptual problem. Mainstream macroeconomics often considers the distribution sector as mimicking its manufacturing counterpart. It is assumed, in other words, to produce 'distribution services' that have no connection with the goods it sells, and these services are provided to consumers independently of the goods themselves. Once this assumption is accepted, there is no special need for a separate examination of distribution channels.

Following this line of reasoning, macroeconomists find that there is a vast 'productivity' difference between Japan and Italy on the one hand, and the United States on the other. Table 9.1 shows, for instance, that labour productivity in distribution is substantially lower in Japan than in the United States and this difference is even more pronounced if the value added data are converted at PPP rather than at market exchange rates. Although the market-exchange rate productivity figure is similar in Italy to that of the United States, it is at least one third lower if one uses the more appropriate PPP conversion. Moreover, the differences become even greater, at least between Japan and the United States (data for Italy are not available), if one takes output per man-hour instead of per person or considers total factor productivity rather than labour productivity alone (McKinsey Global Institute, 1992). Using such information, it has often been argued that Italy's and Japan's distribution sectors are highly inefficient and at least in part responsible for the high prices faced by consumers, when compared to the situation in the United States.

In the following, we argue that this conventional wisdom is inadequate in understanding the dynamic evolution of distribution in a growing economy, and propose a new way of looking at the sector, based on its role in connecting producers and consumers. Although we do not deny the existence of inefficiencies due to government regulations and other factors, the difference between Japan and Italy on the one hand and the United States on the other is more likely to reflect the efficient adaptation of the distribution sector to local conditions. These, in turn, are strongly dependent on the evolution of a country's industrial structure. In the present context we distinguish two types of distribution structures: a manufacturer-controlled and a retailer-controlled one. These two modes cope differently with the inefficiency that inevitably arises in an atomistic distribution system that faces product complexity and uncertainty. We examine the validity of our claim using internationally comparable input–output tables over 20 years. We argue that the aggregate dynamic behaviour of Italian and Japanese distribution can be considered as a transition from a manufacturer-oriented to a retailer-oriented system, while the history of the United States can be interpreted as an evolution within a retailer-oriented distribution set-up. We also provide an explanation for the industrial differences between Japan and Italy, taking into account the type of competition present in the relevant mode of distribution of each country.

The chapter's plan is as follows: Section 2 develops the basic framework of manufacturer-oriented and retailer-oriented distribution and discusses its implications. Section 3 defines and clarifies the concept of the 'distribution margin ratio' and looks for evidence on its evolution in the input–output tables of the three countries. Section 4 presents an interpretation of the main results, while Section 5 sets out some concluding remarks.

2 Theory

2.1 The old dichotomy and its problems

The conventional view about how the distribution sector is organized in most economies is based on the following dichotomy: the sector is either a modern, large-scale system, as in the United States and the United Kingdom, or an old-fashioned 'mom and pop' store system characteristic of less mature economies, such as Japan and Italy. Table 9.2 illustrates the point, showing that many Japanese and Italian retail stores are very small and that their productivity, measured by sales per worker, is very low compared to that of the larger shops. In contrast, large stores dominate distribution in the United States and the differences in sales per worker between small and large establishments are relatively limited.

Thus, the conventional characterization is that Japan and Italy have too many inefficient small outlets, while efficient large-scale shops pervade the US market. Consequently, the argument goes, consumers have to pay

Table 9.2   Establishment size and worker 'productivity' in the retail sector of Italy, Japan and the United States

	Sales share (per cent)	Sales per worker (>100 employees = 100)
Italy (1994)		
1–9	49.4	25
50–99	5.2	89
>100	19.1	100
Japan (1994)		
1–9	43.5	43
50–99	7.0	56
>100	16.2	100
United States [a] *(1992)*		
0–9	8.6	70
50–99	16.6	84
>100	16.6	100

a. Excluding owner-appropriators.

Sources: ISTAT, *I conti economici delle imprese con 20 addetti ed oltre, 1994* and *I conti economici delle imprese con addetti da 1 a 19, 1994* for Italy; MITI, *Census of Commerce, 1994* for Japan; Department of Commerce, *Census of Retail Trade, 1992* for the United States.

higher prices to cover the high costs of such an inefficient system. It is also pointed out that inefficiencies have been encouraged in both countries by widespread restrictions on the opening of large retail shops (via detailed government regulation in Italy and the operation of the Large-scale Retail Store Law in Japan).

This rather simple characterization poses, however, at least two major questions. First, how can such 'inefficiency' persist over long time-periods? When inefficiencies are present, this always means that new business opportunities also present themselves. And if the inefficiencies are really as large as the conventional view suggests, this means that such opportunities are also large. Second, why are consumers content with such high prices? If the so-called 'inefficiencies' really hurt them, they would presumably try to change the system through the political process.

In fact, it will be argued that, in reality, these so-called 'immature' structures can be considered as 'efficient' adaptations of the distribution system to the particular local conditions of each economy. First, the existence of a large number of retail outlets can be seen as the consequence of consumer tastes. Consumers in these economies show a strong preference for handiness, freshness in the case of food, and personal attention. These are services typical of small shops, and are very different from large stores' services such as low price and wide range of products. Second, the low labour productivity of small shops may simply reflect an efficient use of the low-productivity labour of 'grandpa's and grandma's' who would otherwise be unemployed. In addition, not all small shops have low productivity. The success of Japan's 'convenience stores' (or ubiquitous, mini self-service outlets open for long hours) is a case in point. Thus, in order to be 'efficient', retail shops do not need to be large.

Of course, we do not argue that the small-store-dominated distribution system is always efficient. In fact, one of the present authors has examined the issue in detail and has shown that, even when a framework is used which takes proper account of the efficiency argument, the Japanese distribution system shows signs of inefficiency (Nishimura and Tachibana, 1996) because of government regulations of large stores and tax distortions favouring small ones. However, we argue that a variant of the efficient adaptation approach, which will be explained in the remainder of this section, provides us with a framework for analysing both institutional changes through time and differences across countries in distribution systems. This, it seems to us, cannot be done by the conventional approach in which the distribution sector is treated as a sector producing distribution services independently of the products that are sold.

2.2 A new dichotomy: manufacturer-controlled versus retailer-controlled distribution

The starting point of our analysis is an *atomistic distribution* system in which manufacturers and retailers are independent of each other and there are active wholesale markets. Both wholesale and retail markets are assumed to be imperfectly competitive. It is well known that in such an industrial structure a problem of 'successive monopoly' can arise (that is, monopoly inefficiencies are accumulated at both the retail and wholesale stages). Thus, vertical integration would improve efficiency. However, vertical integration between manufacturing and retailing is rather rare in reality for reasons that have been extensively discussed in the literature (see, for instance, Tirole, 1988).

Moreover, products are becoming increasingly complex so that their quality is no longer apparent and various services must be provided to make full use of them (cars and sophisticated consumer electronics are cases in point). In such circumstances, the producer is dependent on the retailer providing an adequate service to the customer, while the retailer is dependent on the manufacturer supplying him with a product of good quality.

Here we encounter a problem of bilateral (or two-way) moral hazard. When product quality is high, consumers will go on buying a particular product, even if the retailer (in order to reduce his costs and raise his profits) were to lower the standard of the services he provides. Similarly, when the quality of the services provided by the retailer is high, consumers will go on purchasing various products even if the manufacturer were to reduce these products' quality (so as to cut costs and increase his profits). Clearly, in such circumstances, both the manufacturer and the retailer have an incentive to reduce the quality of the good or service they provide, as long as the other party maintains its commitment to quality. Theoretically, a combination of so-called non-linear pricing contracts can eliminate this kind of moral hazard (see Tirole, 1988). In practice, however, given that we live in a world of uncertainty and imperfect information, this is virtually impossible. Hence, the market will tend to end up with both low quality and low service.

Moreover, as an economy grows and demand expands, manufacturing shifts from made-to-order production to mass production with inventory build-ups. This creates an additional problem of risk-taking. Production now takes place in anticipation of demand, not after actual orders are placed. Such a mode of production, though it enables cost-cutting, introduces considerable risk for both manufacturers and retailers. To cope with these various problems, two distinctive types of industrial organization seem to have evolved in the world economy. The main difference between them lies in who of the manufacturer or the retailer has the upper hand in the distribution channel and bears the major risk.

Retailer-controlled channel. The first type is the distribution channel in which the retailer has the upper hand over the manufacturer. In the United States and the United Kingdom, for instance, large retail companies operate various chains with many private brands. The retailer determines the specification of the products he wishes to sell, and procures them from the lowest bidder among the manufacturers. He also determines the various after-sales services that accompany their products.

However, the retailer cannot directly control the quality of the products he purchases. If there is no such control, quality will eventually deteriorate and this will hurt him. In order to check for quality, the retailer has to institute costly inspection mechanisms. He may also be able to persuade his suppliers to invest in expensive machines, which produce more reliable products, by incurring part of the investment cost. Such additional expenses incurred to maintain quality are not present in the case of vertical integration.

In this mode of distribution, the major risks are borne by the retailer. Well-diversified large retail companies, often equipped with a better standing in financial markets than their manufacturers, are capable of absorbing the risk of occasional over- or under-production. It is this capacity to absorb risk that allows the retailer to buy his supplies at lower prices than otherwise, since he virtually provides insurance for the manufacturer.

Manufacturer-controlled channel. The second type is the distribution channel in which the manufacturer has the upper hand over the retailer. A typical example is found in Japan, whose system is often called the *keiretsu*, or exclusive distribution, system. In this instance, the manufacturer virtually determines the final sales price (that is, de facto imposes resale price maintenance). However, the manufacturer cannot directly control the service provided by the retailer. Hence, he himself often supplies the same, or a similar kind of, service by setting up his own after-sales service centre and by providing product information through various channels that by-pass the retail store.

In this mode of distribution, it is the manufacturer who bears most of the risk by allowing the return of unsold merchandise by the retailer with no or only token fees (a so-called 'liberal returns' policy). Typically, the manufacturer is a large and well-diversified firm while retailers are small, so that there are considerable differences in risk-bearing capacity. By using this capacity, the manufacturer collects a virtual insurance premium from the retailer, by squeezing retail margins.

An historical digression may help the reader understand the development of the *keiretsu* system as an attempt by manufacturers to cope with inefficient atomistic distribution channels (Miwa and Nishimura, 1991). Just after the devastation of the Second World War, the Japanese retail market was very underdeveloped. The low skills of the retailers caused serious difficulties for the manufacturers and the quality of service they provided was considered inadequate. In order to overcome these various marketing problems, the manufacturers established distribution channels in which only a single retailer was given the right to deal with one type of product in a particular area. Intra-brand competition was, de facto, abolished. The *keiretsu* distribution channel was characterized by the active commitment of the manufacturer to support his retailers. There was no franchise fee. On the contrary, manufacturers usually incurred substantial training and financial costs on behalf of their retailers.

Although Italian manufacturers do not have the same degree of dominance over retailers, the Italian system seems, on the whole, to be closer to the manufacturer-oriented than to the retailer-oriented model (Pellegrini, 1996). Italy does not have large retail outlets that dominate the market (the only exceptions to this can be found in the groceries and in some Northern areas, partly as a result of a recent inflow of foreign capital and outlet models, such as hypermarkets and discount stores). Basically, therefore, manufacturers tend to vertically control the distribution of their products. A typical example is provided by the car industry in which, since the Second World War, Italy has had very much the same arrangements as Japan, with manufacturers controlling the outlets for automobiles. The move in this branch towards a more retailer-oriented market has, so far, been slow. It has been basically led by the parallel market for imported cars which has started to impinge upon the market for domestically produced ones.

Benetton's success is also in accordance with our view of the Italian system as being primarily a manufacturer-oriented one. Benetton can be considered as a 'merchant-producer', organizing a large number of formally independent manufacturers of very small, or family-sized firms. Although it does not produce directly, Benetton controls production and has an upper hand over retailers who are franchisees.

In reality, of course, both types of industrial organizations coexist side by side in the same economy. For example, although most of the US and UK distribution channels are considered as retailer-controlled, the car distribution system, which is controlled by manufacturers in both countries, is a conspicuous exception. Moreover, both types can even exist in the same industry. Thus, in the distribution of TVs, videos, and CD players in Denmark, Bang and Olufsen, the high-end product manufacturer, has a distinctive manufacturer-controlled distribution network, even though the majority of the Danish distribution channels can be characterized as retailer-oriented. Usually, high-quality products tend to have a manufacturer-oriented distribution, while bulk-products are traded through a retailer-oriented one. The recent tendency, noted above in Italy, for the grocery line to develop large outlets fits with this conclusion which can, perhaps, be taken as a stylized fact.

Interactions between the two systems. The distribution system is not static. There are constant changes or switches between the two modes,[2] under the influence of changes in product standardization and in product reliability. Product standardization, for instance, makes quality rather transparent, while more reliable products make both point-of-sale and after-sales service less relevant. Standardization also reduces the cost of quality inspection and the perceived need for service provision by manufacturers since it allows the emergence of an independent service industry to which consumers can turn when they face problems with the products. This evolution, at some point, leads to the emergence of a number of large-scale retailers. In some instances the two distribution systems may coexist, in others the manufacturer-oriented distribution may be completely replaced by the retailer-oriented one.

The Japanese camera industry is one example of this transition. After the Second World War, camera makers tried to develop their own distribution system. But, as camera technology became more standardized and reliable thanks to the advancement of electronics, the need for point-of-sale and after-sales service declined, and the camera makers eventually abandoned their attempt to build their own distribution network.

On the other hand, if an entirely new and complex product is created (such as personal computers) whose quality, at least in the early stages of development, is not readily assessable, a need for point-of-sale and after-sales retail services clearly re-emerges. Thus, a large-scale major product innovation is likely to bring about a switch-back from a retailer-oriented system to a manufacturer-oriented one. It is interesting to note that manufacturers producing high-end products often have, or have tried, to develop manufacturer-oriented distribution channels which, they stress, are the best way to market their high-quality products. The previously mentioned case of Bang and Olufsen is one such example in consumer electronics, while IBM in its global operations and Olivetti in Italy are similar examples in computers.

3 Evidence

In this section, we first introduce the concept of the 'distribution margin ratio', a variable widely used in analysing the behaviour of the distribution system. We then examine the implications of the two modes of distribution presented in the previous section for this ratio and calculate its value for Italy, Japan and the United States.

3.1 The distribution system and the distribution margin ratio

The *distribution margin* is defined as the difference between the manufacturer's factory-gate price and the price paid by the final buyer (or purchaser's price). The distribution margin *ratio* (DMR) is the ratio of this margin to the purchaser's price and can be considered as a measure of the cost of distribution services that buyers incur. Since the services provided are likely to differ among product groups and among types of final goods, aggregate analysis of this ratio may be misleading. Thus, we supplement such aggregate analysis with a more disaggregated breakdown which looks at types of final goods and, within the same type of final goods, at groups of products.

In the analysis of the distribution system, it is often assumed that the DMR measures not only the cost of distribution services but also the efficiency of the system itself.[3] However, it is confusing to use this ratio as an 'efficiency' measure, because efficiency is traditionally associated in economics with production efficiency and the absence of allocational distortions. A distribution system which is technologically inefficient in producing distribution services may still show a low cost of producing such services (a low DMR) if operating costs are low (for example, due to low wages). Thus, we stick to the 'cost-of-distribution-service' interpretation of the DMR.

The definition of the DMR used here assumes an economy with no indirect tax. The possible complications due to the existence of indirect taxes are discussed in Nishimura and Punzo (1998) where it is shown that the definition is still generally valid even in the presence of such taxes. If there is no indirect tax, then the market price that users of the manufactured goods pay is the sum of the manufacturer's factory-gate price and various distribution margins added on at the wholesale, retail and transportation stages (for more detail, see the Appendix to this chapter).

Let us now consider the effect on the DMR of the difference between the two modes of distribution.[4] The basic difference, discussed above, is whether the manufacturer or the retailer incurs the cost of reducing inefficiency due to bilateral moral hazard, and bears the risk of over- and under-production. In the retailer-oriented distribution, the retailer incurs costs in the form of, for example, quality inspection, and bears the risk of buying products outright from the manufacturer. In contrast, in the manufacturer-oriented distribution, the manufacturer incurs costs, such as manufacturer-originated marketing activities to supplement inadequate retailer services, and bears risks by, for example, adopting a liberal returns policy. This suggests that, in order to cover such costs and risks, retail margins (and hence the DMR) should be higher in a retailer-oriented system, while factory-gate prices should be higher in a manufacturer-oriented one.

To examine this hypothesis, we look at the distribution margin for consumption goods and investment goods in Italy, Japan and the United States. To do this, we use the three countries' input–output tables which are the most comprehensive and internationally comparable data set showing information about both factory-gate and retail prices (the Appendix provides a full list of the input–output tables that were used). For consumption goods distribution, we calculate the DMR of household consumption, while the DMR of private fixed investment is taken as representative of investment goods distribution. We do not consider public consumption or public investment, since the definition of these two variables differs considerably among countries (notably so for defence spending).

3.2   Similarities and differences between Italy, Japan and the United States

Table 9.3 shows the evolution over three decades of the aggregate DMR for the two types of final good for each country. It will be seen that the ratio in the consumer goods sector is more than twice as high as that for investment goods, reflecting the extra costs (such as transportation, handling or advertising) involved in the distribution of consumer goods, for which demand is heterogeneous and scattered geographically.

Although the Japanese ratio for both types of final goods is usually higher than the Italian one, the table shows a remarkable similarity in the ratio's longer-run behaviour in these two countries in contrast with the United States. In consumer goods distribution, for instance, both the Italian and Japanese ratios start far below the US level, but increase steadily, with the Japanese ratio now close to the American one. In contrast, the US figure is stable in the period considered. In fact, it has been remarkably stable over the past century, fluctuating around 37–39 per cent except in wartime.[5] In investment goods distribution, the

Table 9.3   Distribution margin ratios by types of final goods (per cent)

Years: Italy	1972	1982	1988
Japan	*1970*	*1980*	*1990*
United States	*1972*	*1977*	*1987*
Consumer goods			
Italy	30.5	30.9	34.6
Japan	28.9	34.9	37.8
United States	38.6	37.5	38.9
Investment goods			
Italy	10.1	13.7	14.8
Japan	15.6	18.2	19.7
United States	12.8	16.0	14.8

Source: Authors' estimates using the input–output tables listed in the Appendix.

Japanese ratio is higher while the Italian one is lower than the US ratio. However, both the Italian and Japanese ratios show a substantial increase of a similar order of magnitude over time. By contrast, the US ratio shows no trend over the period.

4   Interpretation

4.1   Aggregate movements in the three countries

Bearing in mind the evidence from the previous section, we can explain the similarities between Italy and Japan, particularly in the consumer goods sector, as being evidence of a long-run transition from a manufacturer-oriented to a retailer-oriented distribution system. Product innovations in the postwar period (especially in consumer durables and motor vehicles) induced the widespread development of a manufacturer-oriented system in both economies. As a result, DMRs were relatively low in the early years of the period under investigation. However, the subsequent development of more standardized and reliable products made retailer-oriented distribution more viable, leading to the present system in which both modes coexist. Since, as was argued earlier, the DMR is higher in a retailer-oriented system than in a manufacturer-oriented one, the ratio has increased over time in the transition from the latter to the former.

The similarity between the two countries is also founded on the similarity of regulatory laws concerning their distribution sectors and of recent (in some cases still ongoing) attempts at structural reforms. In both countries, distribution was heavily regulated, as has often been the case in so-called 'immature' economies in which 'excess labour' finds employment as the owner-appropriator of small retail and wholesale shops. Governments in such economies frequently restrict the entry and operation of large stores fearing that these may drive small shops out of business and cause serious employment problems and political unrest. Japan has a long history of restrictive regulations centred around the 1937 Department Store Law and its descendant, the 1973 Large-scale Retail Store Law. The latter, in particular, prevents the achievement of scale economies through large-scale retailing. Although the current structure of Japan's retail market can be considered as an efficient adaptation of the distribution system to the country's particular conditions, this does not mean that there is no need for change. In particular, there is now a growing demand for large-scale retailing, allowing what has been called 'one-stop shopping' of a wide range of products at low prices. However, regulation severely restricts experimentation with new forms of large-scale retailing, and inevitably adds to inefficiencies.[6]

In Italy, similar laws have long created similar entry barriers (and, no doubt, similar inefficiencies) by giving local authorities the power to licence the opening of new outlets, and to regulate their allowed sizes and the types of goods that could be sold. In addition, these licences had to comply with predetermined commercial development guidelines, not always designed by the local authorities themselves. Inevitably, these various regulations have stifled competition and the distribution sector has kept its traditional links with the manufacturing sector. This has led to the emergence of a polarized distribution structure that evolved unevenly, with the grocery branch undergoing a process of concentration (and thus becoming more retailer-oriented), while the rest of the sector remained largely centred on the classical family-based, or small-scale outlet.

If such regulations had remained in place, it would have been impossible for the distribution system to gradually move away from the manufacturer-controlled mode of small shops to the retailer-controlled mode of large stores. In order to make the transition possible, regulatory reforms were inevitable, but, as could have been expected, they met with stiff opposition from vested interest groups. Interestingly, in both countries the driving forces of regulatory reform were external. US pressures to open the domestic market to international competition were most important in the case of Japan, while the progress of European integration, and especially the 1992 Single Market Programme, was paramount in the case of Italy. Gradually, if slowly, regulatory reforms resulted in an increase in the number of large stores in both countries and in a continuing shift of control from manufacturers to retailers. Now, in both Japan and Italy, small neighbourhood shops and large suburban commercial outlets coexist. The national DMRs are in fact the average over the two, with their steady increase reflecting the structural shift from small to large stores.

The United States differs from both Italy and Japan in so far as various kinds of retail innovation made large-scale retailers viable and endowed them with an upper hand over manufacturers from as early as the turn of the twentieth century (except for wartime and possibly for automobile distribution). Thus, the US distribution system has been a retailer-oriented one for a long period of time. The country's very stable distribution margin ratio is in fact the result of constant changes and innovations. Thus, new 'no-frill' modes of retailer-oriented distribution channels are usually introduced with substantial price discounts from existing ones. These eventually 'upgrade' themselves into high-cost distribution systems. Then, a new 'no-frill' mode invades the market. It is largely through this continuous process of change[7] that the DMR has remained constant for such a remarkably long period of time.

It is interesting to note that the Japanese ratio reached the level of the US one around 1985–90, a period that experienced a drastic change in the distribution system, often called 'price destruction'. A clear development towards the retailer-oriented mode was seen at the time in various distribution channels. A similar, but less pronounced, change can also be found in Italy in recent years. Thus, we expect that Japan's DMR will stabilize around its current rate, while the increase in the Italian ratio will taper off as it comes closer to the US one.

Although this chapter does not attempt to analyse the distribution system's efficiency directly, the decomposition of the DMR into its commerce (wholesale and retail) and transportation components sheds some light on the issue. Table 9.4 presents this decomposition for Japan and the United States, following the procedure outlined in the Appendix (a lack of relevant data prevented a similar calculation for Italy).

The United States is a large continental economy, and thus one can safely assume that its transportation margin ratio should be substantially above Japan's. This was, indeed, the case in the 1960s when the US ratio was almost twice as high as the Japanese one. However, the US ratio fell substantially in the 1970s and 1980s, thanks to technical progress and government de-regulation. In contrast, the Japanese ratio has remained almost unchanged during the entire period and is now (marginally) higher than the American one despite Japan's smaller size. This suggests that the technical progress that has been forced upon firms in the United States has had little impact on Japan. This disappointing performance is likely to reflect the inefficiency of the transportation sector due, in turn, to government regulation. Transportation is one of the most heavily

Table 9.4 Commerce[a] and transportation margin ratios: consumer goods (per cent)

Years: Japan United States	1965 1963	1970 1967	1975 1972	1980 1977	1985 1982	1990 1987
Commerce[a]						
Japan	24.4	27.4	30.9	33.0	35.1	35.9
United States	35.3	37.5	36.3	35.7	35.5	37.2
Transportation						
Japan	2.0	1.5	1.7	1.9	1.6	1.9
United States	3.9	3.1	2.2	1.8	1.7	1.7

a. Wholesale and retail.
Source: Authors' updating of Nishimura (1993).

Table 9.5   Distribution margin ratios for selected consumer goods (per cent)

	Italy 1988	Japan 1990	United States 1987
Livestock, agricultural and fishery products	56.5	41.0	46.8
Food and products, including tobacco	35.4	31.3	35.0
Fabrics and textile products	30.3	41.7	47.6
Apparel	31.7	53.5	46.2
Footware and leather products	40.5	41.0	50.3
Furniture, fixtures and wood products	29.9	44.6	46.9
Chemicals, including drugs	35.9	42.9	41.7
Petroleum products	13.2	32.8	37.1
Electric equipment, including household appliances	30.2	34.6	45.1
Motor vehicles and other transportation equipment	19.5	40.8	22.8

Source: As for Table 9.3.

regulated industries in Japan, with not only entry but also various business practices screened by the Ministry of Transportation. These regulations suffocate entrepreneurial initiative without which the diffusion of technical advance becomes extremely difficult.

4.2   Industrial differences between Italy and Japan

The aggregate similarities in the DMR between Italy and Japan noted above can, however, be somewhat deceptive since the two countries exhibit large differences in this ratio for specific product groups, as shown in Table 9.5 (which also reports data for the United States, as a standard of reference).[8] It will be seen from the table that the DMR is substantially higher in agricultural and food products in Italy than in Japan. By contrast, the Japanese ratio is far higher than the Italian one in a range of manufactured goods, such as 'fabric and textile products', 'apparel', 'petroleum products', 'electric equipment including household appliances', 'motor vehicle and other transportation equipment', and so on. Despite this, Japan's overall rate is only marginally higher than Italy's because of the large share in total expenditure of low-margin food products.

Japan's low-cost wholesale and retail operations in agricultural products and processed foods (lower even than in the United States) is partly due to public intervention in food distribution, especially in rice and tobacco, which account for a large share of household consumption. Government institutions provide wholesale functions, and their costs are not properly represented in the official statistics.[9] A further reason is linked to the high producer prices of Japanese agricultural products – though the margin ratio may be low, the absolute level of the margin is still high. Finally, there are elements of manufacturer control reducing retail margins in some products (such as, beer) and there has also been some innovation in food distribution.[10] Italy's high margins, on the other hand, simply reflect a costly and atomistic food distribution chain, with many traditional small shops still dominating the industry (the earlier mentioned shift to large grocery stores is too recent to have significantly affected the 1988 Italian figure).

By contrast, Italy's low margin ratios in 'fabric and textile products', 'apparel', and 'furniture, fixture, and wood products' are the result of fierce competition among retailers. Italy's international competitiveness in these industries may well be helped by this, while Japan's high margin ratios in the same sectors may be a manifestation of the country's loss of ground in these product groups. However, high margin ratios do not necessarily indicate a lack of competitiveness. The high margin ratios in Japan for electric equipment and, especially, motor vehicles (two areas in which Japan has traditionally been very competitive) may well reflect the influence of the *keiretsu*-dominated system, in which the distribution channels are virtually controlled by producers.

This may seem to be at odds with our earlier conclusion that manufacturer-oriented distribution systems would normally exhibit low retail margins. Yet, it is not inconsistent if firms compete primarily via the provision of services rather than through prices. In a manufacturer-oriented distribution mode, the retail price or, more precisely, the retail margin becomes a device for controlling the level of services provided by the retailer. Price-cutting in such circumstances could cause a reduction in the provision of such services that would be harmful to the manufacturers. In the Japanese context, in which consumers seem to be sensitive to services more than to price, it makes sense to compete by providing better services. Intense competition (for which these industries are well known) would thus imply higher retail margin ratios in Japan than in Italy and would also constitute a significant barrier to entry. Automobiles are a case in point. Although car distribution is largely manufacturer-oriented in all three countries, Japan's distribution margin is almost double the Italian and American margins *and* has doubled between 1970 and 1990. This, however, comes as no great surprise if it is borne in mind that service competition in Japan takes the very labour-intensive form of in-house calls (with salesmen making frequent visits to current and potential customers and providing personalized services). Not only is this very costly, but it also drives up the margin through time given the rising trend in wages.

Finally, the extremely low DMR in 'petroleum products' in Italy is the joint outcome of: (i) a retail price administrated by a set of government agencies; (ii) the high operating costs of the producers of oil and other related products; and (iii) the direct control over retailing exercised by these producers. Together, these have resulted in a squeeze on distribution margins as producers have attempted to maintain their profits. The licensing system for the equipment of petrol stations has virtually transformed the retail sellers of oil and related products into the status of mere 'representatives' or 'employees' of the petroleum companies.

Table 9.6 extends the analysis through time and looks at the changes that have occurred in Italy and Japan over the last two decades. Unfortunately, the Italian input-output tables of the 1970s do not provide sufficiently detailed information for all the sectors considered above. Thus, we concentrate on only four 'key' and somewhat more aggregated industries. Qualitatively the results are similar to those already shown for the aggregate DMR in Table 9.3 above: the ratio shows a steady increase in all the four sectors and in both countries, with motor vehicles

Table 9.6 Longer-run changes in distribution margin ratios for selected consumer goods (per cent)

Years: Italy Japan	1972 1970	1982 1980	1988 1990
Food and kindred products, including tobacco:			
Italy	30.3	31.4	35.4
Japan	24.4	27.0	31.3
Fabric, textile products and apparel			
Italy	27.9	28.5	31.5
Japan	32.9	47.9	49.9
Machinery, scientific and electric equipment			
Italy	25.9	29.1	31.0
Japan	32.7	40.3	36.8
Motor vehicles and other transportation equipment			
Italy	28.3	18.4	19.5
Japan	19.4	33.9	40.8

Source: As for Table 9.3.

in Italy as the single exception. Thus, the increase in the overall ratio discussed in the previous sub-section is not due to shifts in the structure of demand from low-margin to high-margin industries; rather, it is a virtually universal feature in both countries.

5   Conclusions

Relying on detailed and internationally comparable input–output tables, we have investigated how much final buyers pay for the service provided by the distribution sector in Italy, Japan and the United States. The DMR, or the distribution sector's share in the final product price, has been taken to be the cost of distribution services. This has been calculated for various years between 1970 and 1990, for different kinds of buyers and for different product groups. The results are striking. Although Japan and Italy are far apart from each other geographically, they are similar in the behaviour over time of the aggregate DMR: both exhibit a substantial increase in this ratio, be this for the distribution of consumer or investment goods. By contrast, these two ratios in the United States have been stable, at a higher level, for almost a century.

However, aggregate similarity is somewhat deceptive, since disaggregated rates for product groups reveal substantial differences between the two countries. In general, agricultural and food products have higher retail margins in Italy than in Japan, while most other manufactured products show the opposite pattern. The major reason for these differences lies in the differing structures and degrees of competition of the various industries – themselves, at least in part, a reflection of the varying presence or absence of government regulation.

We have explained these empirical results by appealing to a new framework that analyses the evolving industrial structure of the distribution sector. We have proposed a dichotomy between a manufacturer-controlled and a retailer-controlled distribution system. The Italian and Japanese movements in the DMRs have been shown to reflect a gradual evolution from a manufacturer-controlled to a retailer-controlled mode, while US developments have taken place within a retailer-controlled one. In addition, some of the major industry differences found between Italy and Japan have also been explained in terms of the forms of competition that exist within a basically manufacturer-controlled distribution system.

Italy and Japan are now experiencing major changes in their distribution systems. Large-scale retailing, of the type found in the United States and the United Kingdom (and in other European countries such as France), seems to be spreading. From our standpoint, this is simply the manifestation of a gradual change from a manufacturer-controlled distribution to a retailer-controlled one, a change that has been ongoing since the 1960s, with consumer demand for large-scale retailing as its main driving force.

As explained in Section 2, two conflicting forces are operating to bring about changes in distribution: standardization, which gives cost advantages to retailer-controlled systems; and product innovation, which ensures the continuing superiority of manufacturers. At present, standardization seems to prevail over product innovation. However, manufacturers are attempting to counter this movement by introducing new products and strengthening their existing distribution channels. The future of Italian and Japanese distribution will depend, at least in part, on the result of these attempts.

Appendix: construction of distribution margin ratios and data sources

This appendix provides a more precise definition of the distribution margin ratio (DMR) and briefly explains how the ratios' values, reported in Tables 9.3 to 9.6, were constructed from the base-year input–output tables of Italy, Japan and the United States.

As already mentioned in Section 3.1 above, the DMR is defined as follows:

$$\text{Market Price} = \text{Manufacturer's Factory-gate Price} + \text{Distribution Margins} \tag{3.1}$$

where:

$$\text{Distribution Margins} = \text{Wholesale and Retail Margins} + \text{Transportation Margins} \tag{3.2}$$

Then, the DMR and its components are defined as follows:

$$\text{Distribution Margin Ratio} = \text{Distribution Margins/Retail Price} \tag{3.3}$$

$$\text{Commerce Margin Ratio} = \text{Wholesale and Retail Margins/Retail Price} \tag{3.4}$$

$$\text{Transportation Margin Ratio} = \text{Transportation Margins/Retail Price} \tag{3.5}$$

The data needed to compute the ratio were obtained in the base-year input-output tables which contain information about producers' prices and purchasers' prices for all transactions between sectors, as well as wholesale and retail margins, and transportation margins in the case of Japan and the United States. The DMRs are constructed from this information, on the assumption that the purchasers' price for buyers of final goods is the final retail price, and that the producers' price is the manufacturers' factory-gate price.

Two types of final-goods buyers are considered: buyers of consumer goods and of investment goods. For consumer goods, transactions are further disaggregated into 19 product groups. Detailed explanations of the choice of data and the classification of the various products are reported in Nishimura and Punzo (1998), which is available from the authors upon request

The base-year input–output tables used are: ISTAT, *Tavola intersettoriale dell'economia italiana* for Italy, EPA, *Sangyo-Renkan Hyou: Torihiki Kihon Hyou (Input–Output Tables: Transaction Tables (Basic Sector))* for Japan, and Department of Commerce, *Benchmark Input–Output Accounts for the U.S. Economy* for the United States. The base-years are 1970, 1972, 1980, 1982, 1985 and 1988 for Italy, 1970, 1975, 1980, 1985 and 1990 for Japan, and 1972, 1977, 1982 and 1987 for the United States.

In the base-year tables, there are two different tables: the *Producer Price Table* (or *Tavola a prezzi ex-fabbrica* for Italy), and the *Purchaser Price Table* (*Tavola a prezzi di mercato*). The Producer Price Table shows the value of products evaluated at the factory-gate prices that manufacturers charge, while the Purchaser Price Table exhibits the value of products at the retail prices that buyers pay. The differences between the two sets of prices are commerce and transportation margins as well as indirect taxes.

Notes

1. It is important to define the distribution system at the outset of our study, because the term is often used rather vaguely. We are concerned here with the distribution system of final goods; and we define this system as the system of distributing manufactured goods from producers to final users. Thus, the distribution system consists of the wholesale trade, retail trade and transportation sectors. Intermediate-goods transactions are ignored. This does not imply that such transactions are unimportant, but lack of data and theoretical difficulties in distinguishing inter-firm from intra-firm transactions simply prevent us from including them in our study.
2. We are not suggesting that these are the only possible modes of distribution that can exist. There may well be others, but these two are by far the most important.

3. See, for example, Ito (1992).
4. For a theoretical investigation of the two modes of distribution, and for an analysis of their macroeconomic consequences, see Nishimura and Nakayama (1998).
5. This long-run constancy is theoretically puzzling and we lack, at present, a good interpretation for such a 'stylized fact'.
6. Thus, Nishimura and Tachibana (1996) find that the Large-scale Retail Store Law results in large shops charging higher prices than if there were no such law.
7. This process is often called the 'wheel of retailing' in the marketing literature.
8. More detailed information can be found in Nishimura and Punzo (1998).
9. See Nishimura and Tsubouchi (1990) for details.
10. Thus, the distribution of bread, for instance, seems to be more efficient than in the United States since the final price to consumers is similar, despite higher producer prices in Japan. The main reason for this lies in the streamlined distribution channels set up by the breadmakers.

References

Ito, T. (1992) *The Japanese Economy*, Cambridge, MA: MIT Press.
McKinsey Global Institute (1992) *Service Sector Productivity*, Washington, DC.
Miwa, Y. and K.G. Nishimura (1991) *Nihonno Ryutu (The Distribution System in Japan)*, Tokyo: University of Tokyo Press.
Nishimura, K.G. (1993) 'The Distribution System of Japan and the United States: a Comparative Study from the Viewpoint of Final-goods Buyers', *Japan and the World Economy*, 6, 3, 265–88.
Nishimura, K.G. and Y. Nakayama (1998) 'Competition in Distribution Channels and its Implications on Macroeconomic Fluctuations', paper presented at the New York University Japan–US Center Shimoda Conference.
Nishimura, K.G. and L.F. Punzo (1998) 'The Evolution of the Distribution Sector in Three Continents: Movement of Distribution Margins and its Evolutionary Explanation', mimeo, University of Tokyo and University of Siena.
Nishimura, K.G. and T. Tachibana (1996) 'Entry Regulations, Tax Distortion, and the Bipolarized Market: the Case of the Japanese Retail Sector', in R. Sato, H. Hori and R.V. Ramachandran (eds), *Organization, Performance and Equity: Perspectives on the Japanese Economy*, Norwell, MA: Kluwer Academic Publishers.
Nishimura, K.G. and H. Tsubouchi (1990) 'Gyoushu-betsu, Hinmoku-betsu Ryutu Maagin Suikei: Nichi-Bei Hikaku' ('Commerce Margin Ratios Among Product Groups and Industry Groups: New Estimates for Japan and the United States'), *Keizagaku Ronshu (Journal of Economics)* 56, 3, 111–38.
Pellegrini, L. (1996) *La distribuzione commerciale in Italia*, Bologna: Il Mulino.
Tirole, J. (1988) *The Theory of Industrial Organization*, Cambridge, MA: MIT Press.

10
Education, Training and Labour Market Structure*

Giorgio Brunello and Tsuneo Ishikawa

1 Introduction

Education and human capital accumulation are often viewed as key to economic performance and growth. The presence of adequate skills is considered to be a critical factor in the development of new ideas and designs. When applied to industry, a higher ability to innovate yields both higher competitiveness and higher growth (Rebelo, 1992; Bertola and Coen Pirani, 1995). School enrolment has become a crucial variable in growth accounting exercises (see Barro and Lee, 1994 and the references therein). Active policies to improve the stock of on-the-job and off-the-job human capital are often advocated as an effective way to reduce persistently high unemployment in Europe (OECD, 1994). Finally, the quality of schools is viewed as important for both productivity and real earnings.[1]

This chapter looks at a closely related but often overlooked question: is selectivity and competition at school always *good* for national economic

* This is a modified version of a paper originally published by Physica-Verlag in *Economic Systems* (Giorgio Brunello and Tsuneo Ishikawa, 'Education, Training and Labour Market Structure: Italy and Japan in Comparative Perspective', 23, 1, 61–83, 1999). The authors are grateful to Andrea Boltho, Ronald Dore, Bruno Parigi, Paul Ryan, Toshiaki Tachibanaki, Vittorio Valli, and to audiences in Graz, Naples, Osaka (Kansai Labour Workshop, and ISER), Rotterdam, Siena and Venice for comments, criticisms and suggestions. They also wish to thank Kuramitsu Muramatsu for help in constructing Tables 10.8 and 10.9. Part of the revision of the original draft of this chapter was carried out while the first author visited ISER which provided excellent hospitality. The usual disclaimer applies.

performance? By forcing young individuals to invest heavily in the competition for the best schools, a very selective system increases the stock of basic academic skills (such as reading, mathematics or problem-solving skills). If the accumulation of these skills and training are complements, selective education reduces training costs and increases the relative advantage of adopting complex and highly productive technologies.

When competition is excessive, however, it could hamper the development of *individual* skills – such as self-expression and creative thinking – because of the strong incentives it places on the development of academic ones. If individual skills are also important for industrial performance, too much competition in the schooling system could have negative spillovers for national output and productivity.

We believe that this trade-off between academic and individual skill development in schooling systems is exemplified by the economic performance of Italy and Japan. Broadly speaking, Japan has a very competitive schooling system, which is often criticized because it stifles individual creativity, and an industrial structure that features clusters of export-driven complex technologies. On the other hand, Italy has a less competitive schooling system and an industrial structure characterized by the presence of highly productive so-called 'industrial districts' that specialize in personalized industrial design.

In both countries, the schooling system interacts with the industrial structure and with labour market outcomes. The purpose of this chapter is to clarify these interactions empirically and theoretically. By doing so, we hope to be able to throw some light on the more general question asked above. After describing some of the stylized facts, we discuss a simple model that tries to capture some of these facts and use it to study the relations between competition at school and economic performance.

The material is organized as follows. The next section provides a survey of some of the salient features of education, industrial structure and labour market performance in Italy and Japan. Section 3 uses the differences between the two countries in these various areas to build a model which looks at the interaction between competition at school, the selection of technologies by firms and the relationship between basic academic and individual skills. The presentation is informal, with the emphasis on developing the intuition for the main economic mechanisms at work. We refer the reader who is interested in the technical details to Brunello and Ishikawa (1999). The chapter concludes with a brief discussion of the key implications.

2   The stylized facts

This section illustrates the main features of the Italian and Japanese education systems and examines the relationship between these systems and labour market outcomes. An outline of the institutional aspects is followed by measures of school quality and school performance. We then consider some of the labour market outcomes of, and economic returns to, education. The section's aim is to spell out a few *stylized facts* that emphasize the economic aspects of education in a comparative perspective.

2.1   The school system, school quality and the results of education

The current education systems in Italy and Japan are, formally, quite similar. In both, education is compulsory to the age of 14 or 15, while post-compulsory school education is differentiated into a variety of categories. In Italy, for instance, there are classical, scientific, artistic and technical schools, as well as 'humanistic' schools, which specialize in Italian, Latin and Greek. In Japan, the major differentiation is between occupationally- and academically-oriented high schools, with some 70 per cent of pupils choosing the latter (see OECD, 1995 for further details). An important difference between the two systems arises, however, at the entry stage to tertiary education. In Italy from 1969, a school-leaving certificate obtained on passing a final examination is sufficient to enter any university. In Japan, by contrast, university admission is conditional on passing highly competitive entrance examinations conducted by the various institutions. Indeed, the same is increasingly true for entry into the more prestigious secondary and even primary schools. As a consequence, a significant number of pupils attend cram schools after regular school to prepare themselves for these various exams (Rohlen, 1992).

Economists try to measure school quality by looking at both the inputs and outputs of the schooling system. Commonly used input measures include educational expenditure, pupil/teacher ratios, the intensity of schooling (often proxied by the length of the school term), and teachers' salaries (see, for instance, Hanushek, 1986 and the references therein). Ceteris paribus, a higher level of expenditure, a lower pupil/teacher ratio, a longer term and higher teachers' salaries are expected to improve the average quality of education. In particular, an increase in expenditure or a decrease in the pupil/teacher ratio should improve the quality of instruction and 'lead to higher returns for each year of completed education' (Card and Krueger, 1992, p. 9); an increase in term length

Table 10.1 Pupil/teacher ratios in schools, 1995

	Primary	*Secondary*	*Upper Sec.*
Italy	8.9	9.1	9.0
Japan	19.8	17.0	15.5
OECD average	17.4	15.8	13.5

Source: OECD (1995).

'increase(s) the amount of material covered in a school year and thereby increase(s) the economic value of additional years of schooling' (ibid.); finally, higher teacher salaries should, one hopes, lead to improved classroom instruction by motivating teachers to perform well.

In the early 1990s, public expenditure on education was close to 5 per cent of GDP in both countries. Expenditure per student for primary and secondary education, relative to per capita GDP, is higher than the OECD average in Italy (25.7 per cent) and lower in Japan (19.3 per cent).[2]Largely as a consequence, pupil/teacher ratios are much lower in Italy than in Japan, or in the average OECD country (Table 10.1). Turning to the intensity of schooling, Italian primary and secondary schools are second only to Sweden in the relatively low numbers of hours taught per year (Table 10.2). At the same time, average teachers' starting and maximum salaries as a percentage of GDP per capita are relatively low by European standards. In Japan, while instruction hours for primary school pupils are even lower than in Italy, they are as much as 40 per cent higher in lower-secondary schools. Moreover, the slope of teachers' age–earnings profile is fairly steep, so that the ratio of teachers' maximum pay to starting pay is well above the OECD average.

Table 10.2 Other indicators of schooling quality, 1995

	Italy	*Japan*	*OECD*
Annual teaching hours in primary school	748	723[a]	790[b]
Annual teaching hours in lower sec. school	612	875[a]	717[b]
Starting teachers' salary/GDP per capita	1.0	1.1	1.2
Maximum teachers' salary/GDP per capita	1.6	2.4	2.0

a. Number of instruction hours determined by the Operating Rules of the School Education Act.
b. Data refer to Germany.
Sources: OECD (1995) and Ministry of Education, *Annual Report on the Salaries of Local Public Employees* (for Japanese teachers' pay).

Table 10.3   Educational attainment by age group, 1992 (percentages)

	25–34	35–44	45–54	55–64
Italy	42	35	21	12
Japan	93	84	68	53
OECD average	65	58	50	38

Sources: OECD (1995) for Italy; Bureau of Statistics, *Employment Status Survey, 1992* for Japan.

Turning to the results of the education process, Table 10.3 compares a measure of educational attainment by age group. In both countries, as elsewhere, attainment declines with age. Italian levels, however, are dramatically below those achieved in the OECD as a whole and less than half the Japanese levels for all age groups. The Japanese outcome is the consequence of an extraordinary increase in the high school enrolment ratio during the rapid growth period – from slightly above 50 per cent in 1955 to 95 per cent in 1975. Another useful measure of performance is the share of graduates in the population at the theoretical age of graduation. Strikingly, less than 60 per cent of individuals at this age complete upper-secondary education in Italy, compared to more than 90 per cent in Japan. For tertiary education, these percentages are $10\frac{1}{2}$ in Italy and 25 in Japan. This difference is largely explained by Italy's very high dropout rate. According to a study by Censis (1992), in a cohort of 100 individuals entering the first year of lower secondary education, only 80 enrol in upper-secondary schools. Of these, 49 graduate after five years and 33 enrol in a university course. Of the latter, only 10 graduate.

The importance of dropouts in the Italian system is also highlighted by the very low enrolment rate in schools by pupils aged 16 and 17 (only six out of 10 are still in school at 16 as against more than nine in Japan). Italy's high dropout rate could be interpreted as an indicator of the competitive and selective nature of the system. This, however, is hardly the case. Given the relatively low private cost of education, many teenagers enrol only temporarily in school because of the problems they encounter in finding a satisfactory job. When an acceptable job offer turns up, they simply drop out. Indirect evidence in support of this interpretation is provided by the fact that the dropout rate is highest among vocational and technical schools, unanimously considered to be less competitive and selective than scientific and 'humanistic' ones. Additional evidence is provided by the finding that enrolment in higher education is lowest in the North-East, where employment opportunities are better than in the rest of the country (ISTAT, 1997). It is also frequently the case that the poor use of available resources in the education system interacts with the economic and cultural problems of many parts of the *Mezzogiorno* to produce substantial dropout rates even in the case of compulsory education (see Bernardi and Trivellato, 1995 and the references therein).

The evidence discussed so far suggests that the Italian system uses substantial resources to produce disappointing results in terms both of intensity of education and of graduation rates. According to a recent report by the Italian Employers' Association (Confindustria, 1998), this outcome is partly due to lack of competition among both schools and pupils, to excessive red tape and centralization and to poor personnel management. Compared to the Japanese system, the Italian one offers more flexible curricula and substantial freedom of access in exchange for less intensive education, less keen competition among students and a much lower emphasis on meritocratic achievement, at least to the level of upper-secondary education.

2.2 Firm size, labour turnover and education

Even a very broad evaluation of the performance of the education system in the two countries requires some consideration of the interaction between schooling and labour market performance. In most developed countries, individuals with a lower level of educational attainment are more likely to be unemployed than those with a higher level (Layard et al., 1991; OECD, 1994). This is apparently not the case for Italy. As shown in Table 10.4, the highest rates of unemployment are experienced by the youngest cohorts, quite independently of their level of education. More strikingly, the unemployment rate is highest among individuals with

Table 10.4 Unemployment rates by education and age groups (Italy, 1993; Japan, 1992; percentages)

| | *Italy* | | *Japan* | |
	15–29	30–39	15–24	25–34
Primary	30	14		
			5[a]	2[a]
Lower second.	20	8		
Upper second.	25	6	3	2
Tertiary	26	5	1	1
Total	23	7	3	2

a. Primary and lower-secondary schools together.
Sources: ISTAT, *Indagine trimestrale sulle forze di lavoro* for Italy; Bureau of Statistics, *Special Section of the Labour Force Survey, 1992* and *Employment Status Survey, 1992* for Japan.

primary *and* tertiary education. On the other hand, young cohorts in Japan exhibit a typical pattern in that unemployment rates decline with the level of educational achievement.

By far the major factor reducing youth unemployment in Japan is the willingness, and even preference, that many firms show for hiring untrained school leavers and training them according to their needs. Well over a third of new recruits in firms with more than 1000 employees (those that enjoy the strongest buyers' position in the labour market) were new school graduates, as against only one in eight in small firms with less than 100 employees. Another key factor is the active role played by schools in the placement of their graduates in the labour market.

In Italy, the high level of unemployment among individuals with relatively high education can be explained by a host of factors, a major one being regional and occupational mismatches between labour demand and supply (Brunello et al., 2000). Here, we only stress the lack of systematic links with private industry and the poor signalling role of education. Private industry in Italy has traditionally been characterized by a heavy reliance on internal training rather than on formal education (Jannaccone Pazzi and Ribolzi, 1992).[3] As remarked by Porter in his renowned study of national comparative advantages, the success of Italian industrial clusters has been based more on informal training, often provided by the extended family that operates artisan shops and small and medium-sized firms, than on formal education (Porter, 1989; Trento, 1997). The poor performance of the education system and the lack of emphasis on competition among students and schools has limited the signalling role of schooling as an indicator of worker quality (see Spence, 1973 for a discussion of this signalling role). One consequence is that more than 50 per cent of college graduates are employed by the public sector (ISTAT, 1997), in sharp contrast to Japan, where the equivalent figure is only 20 per cent.

Western observers have often remarked that the Japanese education system, and especially its primary and secondary schools component, is very competitive and has high standards, with a lot of emphasis on learning mathematics and sciences. Porter writes, for instance, that

> even though the Americans often argue (not without reason) that the rigid Japanese educational system stifles individual creativity, the system succeeds in providing the vast majority of students in the whole country with a solid base for further education and training. A graduate of a Japanese high school knows as much mathematics as most American college graduates. (Porter, 1989, p. 465)

Table 10.5   Employment by firm size,[a] 1988 (percentages)

	Italy	Japan	UK	Germany	France	USA[b]
Firm size (no. of employees)						
1–99	71.4	55.6	47.1	45.9	49.4	34.8
100–499	9.7	17.7	17.7	18.0	14.8	15.0
> 500	18.7	26.7	35.2	36.1	35.8	50.2

a. In the industrial and market services sectors.
b. Establishments rather than firms.
Source: Contini and Filippi (1995).

Rohlen also comments on the highly competitive Japanese system and argues that

> in essence, while only the winners benefit directly by recouping their investment, overall the result is a very highly educated population, without undue public investment or coercion, and a clear gain for the collectivity. The national mean level of education has been raised very high and the standard deviation kept comparatively small. (Rohlen, 1992, p. 336)

The relative good performance of the schooling system in Japan must be an important factor in explaining why many Japanese firms are willing to hire straight from school.

In both Italy and Japan, small firms with less than 100 employees dominate the private sector (Table 10.5), yet the age composition of this employment is very different. In Italy, small firms employ some 70 per cent of the country's workforce and close to 80 per cent of workers aged between 15 and 29. At the same time, as many as 55 per cent of workers aged 40 to 49 work in firms with more than 100 employees, which account for only 30 per cent of total employment. The contrast with Japan is stark. Large Japanese firms usually hire young workers and 34 per cent of those aged 15 to 29 work in firms with 500 and more employees (which employ 27 per cent of the Japanese workforce). As workers age, they tend to shift towards small firms.

Table 10.6 illustrates the distribution of employment by firm size and educational level both for the whole working population and for the age group 15–29. Again there is a clear contrast between the two countries. Whereas in Italy firms with less than 100 employees employ a higher than average share of younger workers *for any level of education*, in Japan it is the large firms with 500 or more employees that employ a higher than average

Table 10.6   Distribution of employment by firm size and education (percentages; private non-agricultural sector)

	Italy 1993: All age groups				Italy 1993: Age group 15–29			
	Primar.	*Low.Sec.*	*Upp.Sec.*	*Tert.*	*Primar.*	*Low.Sec.*	*Upp.Sec.*	*Tert.*
Firm size: 1–4	12.5	13.7	10.5	2.0	35.0	21.6	19.6	0
5–19	29.1	28.0	20.6	11.8	45.0	42.2	29.6	15.8
20–49	16.8	15.0	12.3	9.8	12.5	14.2	13.8	10.5
50–99	11.6	9.5	9.1	9.2	2.5	7.8	8.7	21.1
100–499	14.3	14.9	17.9	21.6	5.0	9.2	14.5	21.1
> 500	15.7	18.9	29.7	45.8	0	5.0	13.8	31.6

	Japan 1992: All age groups				Japan 1992: Age group 15–29			
	Low.Sec.	*Upp.Sec.*	*Jr.Coll.*	*Coll.*	*Low.Sec.*	*Upp.Sec.*	*Jr.Coll.*	*Coll.*
Firm size: 5–29	28.4	18.6	16.6	7.9	35.8	15.1	13.9	4.8
30–99	25.7	19.9	15.2	11.1	27.0	18.0	13.1	7.6
100–499	22.5	25.1	29.1	25.7	20.4	28.0	29.5	24.2
> 500	23.4	36.3	39.1	55.4	16.8	38.9	43.4	63.5

Sources: Banca d'Italia, *Indagine sui bilanci delle famiglie italiane, 1993* for Italy; Ministry of Labour, *Census of Wages, 1992* for Japan.

share of younger workers (except for those who have graduated from lower-secondary schools). Thus, in Italy, while firms with less than 100 employees employ some 52 per cent of all workers with upper-secondary education, they employ 72 per cent of workers with upper-secondary education *and* aged between 15 and 29 years. Hence, private-sector labour market entry occurs in Italy mainly through small firms, both because there are many such firms and because these firms employ a higher than average share of younger school graduates. In Japan, on the other hand, more than 60 per cent of young college graduates and about 40 per cent of high school and junior college graduates are employed by large firms that employ respectively 55 and less than 40 per cent of all college and high school graduates.

Small firms in Italy not only hire the majority of school graduates but also experience a job turnover rate that is more than twice as high as that recorded in large firms (Table 10.7). This finding has been used in support of the view that small companies in Italy provide substantial in-firm training to workers, who can then use their acquired skills to move to larger firms, where wages are higher and labour conditions more satisfactory.[4] In Japan, by contrast, job turnover rates are much lower than in Italy, especially in smaller firms.[5]

Table 10.7 Job turnover rates[a] by firm size, 1984–1993 (all industries; annual averages)

	Italy	Japan
Firm size		
< 20	21.5	9.9
20–99	13.6	8.6
100–499	11.0	7.1
500–999	9.3	7.6
> 1000	6.5	6.8

a. Job turnover is defined as the sum of job creation and job destruction (both expressed in percent of the total number of jobs) by existing firms. All data refer only to firms in operation throughout the period and exclude turnover related to business start-ups and closures.

Sources: Contini and Filippi (1995).

2.3 Earnings by firm size and education

The relative importance of small and medium-sized firms in Italy and in Japan raises the question as to whether earnings vary in a significant way by firm size. Evidence based on aggregate data suggests that earnings in firms with less than 100 employees are respectively 65 and 60 per cent of earnings in firms with more than 1000 employees in both countries.[6] Data by major industrial sectors tell a similar story. Table 10.8 shows 1989

Table 10.8 Differentials in labour cost per worker in manufacturing, 1989 (firms with more than 1000 employees = 100)

	Firm size (employees)			
	20–99		100–499	
	Italy	Japan	Italy	Japan
Food, drink and tobacco	81.6	67.4	92.4	73.6
Textiles (incl. synthetics)	85.5	82.6	94.1	92.7
Clothing	66.4	78.9	87.9	85.4
Chemicals	79.9	74.1	94.6	84.8
Metal articles	80.5	90.5	79.5	87.4
General machinery	89.5	72.7	97.7	77.1
Electrical machinery	81.8	54.5	89.5	63.3
Motor vehicles and parts	82.7	61.8	91.4	71.0
Total manufacturing	72.8	61.4	87.0	69.7

Note: the following adjustments were made to ensure comparability between the two countries: for Italy textiles cover NACE 26 and 43, clothing NACE 453–4, total manufacturing NACE 14 and 2–4; for Japan motor vehicles refers to JSIC 311.

Sources: Eurostat, *Structure and Activity of Industry: Data by Size of Enterprise, 1988–90* for Italy; MITI, *Census of Manufactures, 1989* for Japan.

aggregate differentials in total wage costs (for Japan), and in total labour costs per worker (for Italy) for the entire manufacturing sector as well as for eight major sub-sectors. Total labour costs include wage costs, statutory and non-statutory benefits and training costs. Since fringe benefits are known to exhibit greater firm size differentials than wages, the figures for Japan are likely to underestimate the true differentials. The table confirms the fact that firm size differentials are in general greater in Japan than in Italy. This is particularly so for electrical machinery and for motor vehicles and parts, Japan's two leading export industries.

These earnings differentials are partially matched by productivity differentials. Table 10.9 shows Italian and Japanese real gross value added per worker for different manufacturing industries and for different firm sizes. A striking difference that emerges from this table is that, while firm size differentials are quite small in Italy (with the exception of the clothing industry), they are rather large in Japan, and especially so for electrical machinery and motor vehicles, the two key exporting industries. These patterns are likely to reflect, among other things, both the relative importance of highly productive industrial districts in the Italian economy (Brusco, 1992) and the relative abundance of low productivity subcontractors in the Japanese economy.

3   Economic implications

The previous section has shown that the education systems in Italy and Japan differ significantly with respect to curriculum flexibility and

Table 10.9   Gross value added per worker by firm size and manufacturing branch, 1989 (ratios of small and medium-sized firms to large firms[a])

	Italy		Japan	
	Small/large	*Medium/large*	*Small/large*	*Medium/large*
Food, etc.	86.8	82.1	39.8	57.1
Textiles	92.4	97.6	73.6	84.8
Clothing	68.3	103.9	73.0	84.1
Chemicals	87.4	99.3	50.2	63.4
Metal articles	93.6	97.0	47.2	57.7
Gen. machinery	97.3	99.6	58.4	68.2
Electr. machinery	91.9	96.6	29.6	39.1
Motor vehicles	80.9	89.5	39.9	47.5
Total manufact.	72.8	85.5	39.2	51.6

a. Firm size is as follows: small: 20 to 99 employees; medium: 100 to 499; large: 500 and more.
Sources: as for Table 10.8.

competitiveness. At the same time, there are similarities in industrial structure, with both countries having a larger than average share of small and medium-sized firms and significant earnings and productivity differentials by firm size. Yet, there are also important differences in labour turnover, in hiring practices and in relative productivity performance by firm size. To simplify, large firms in Japan tend to hire straight from schools; inter-firm labour mobility is relatively low, especially from small to large firms; small and medium-sized firms are often in a subcontracting relationship with large ones; and there is a significant productivity gap between large and smaller firms. In Italy, by contrast, large firms prefer to hire experienced workers, partly trained by small firms, rather than new school leavers; inter-firm labour turnover is much higher than in Japan and many small firms belong to innovative and creative industrial districts, with little or no relationship with large firms. Moreover, small and medium-sized firms show no great disadvantage in terms of labour productivity vis-à-vis large ones.

In this section, we argue that these stylized features can be related to, and partially explained by, differences in the national education systems. To illustrate the key interactions, we develop a model that, inevitably, makes a number of simplifying assumptions. We feel, however, that these are still sufficiently close to Italian and Japanese reality for the model to provide useful insights on the reasons for the different educational choices and labour market behaviour in the two countries. As already stated in the introduction to this chapter, the presentation of the model is informal – full technical details can be found in Brunello and Ishikawa (1999). It is easiest to start from an abstract economic environment characterized by a single type of skill, called basic academic skill. This will set the stage for the subsequent discussion of the interactions between basic academic and individual skills.

3.1 A model with a single skill

Consider an economy populated by a large number of individuals and firms. Each firm employs a single worker. In each time-period, a fraction of the employed workers quits the labour market and is replaced by an equal inflow of new workers. Single firms can hire either new entrants or workers who quit other firms. For the economy as a whole, however, new recruits must necessarily come from new entrants.

New entrants differ only in the level of education acquired before entering the labour market. While education is provided free of charge by state schools, schooling systems can vary in the degree of selectivity and competitiveness. A very selective system allocates individuals in upper-

and lower-layer schools by adopting tough entry standards. Because of these standards, only a fraction of individuals investing in education can enter upper-layer institutions. Competition for entry into such schools requires costly effort in the development of basic academic skills (such as the ability to solve mathematical problems and language skills). There is a one-to-one relationship between effort spent and accumulated skills. Individuals have the same innate ability and the same disutility of effort spent in the education system. A higher effort is more costly but increases the probability of getting into upper-layer schools.

Firms can choose between two technologies, *C* and *S*. Intuitively, think of the *C*-technology as a complex environment that yields high output and pays high wages but is more difficult to manage. Higher complexity requires adequate skills. These are provided to employees by firms and are more easily acquired by individuals with better (and more) education. Hence, better education reduces the training costs borne by firms adopting this technology (*C*-firms) (Rosen, 1976; Brunello and Medio, 1997). On the other hand, firms adopting the *S* technology (*S*-firms) have a simpler and less productive environment that requires simpler skills. The cost of acquiring these skills, also provided by the hiring firm, depends neither on the quality nor on the quantity of education.

While individuals do not differ in their innate ability, firms differ in their underlying *managerial ability*. More able managers are more likely to attract recruits from upper-layer schools and to properly organize the complexity of the *C* technology, which requires higher training costs. On the other hand, the simpler *S* technology is more likely to be chosen by less able managers. Hence, firms endowed with higher managerial ability face lower training costs. Individuals invest in education and firms select the appropriate technology. Both individuals and firms are too small relative to the size of the market to explicitly take into account the impact of their own choice on the choice of others. Thus, firms ignore the effects of their technology selection on the educational choice of individuals and individuals ignore similar effects on the choice of firms. These features of the game played by each agent imply the presence both of spillovers and of strategic complementarities. As a consequence, there could be multiple steady state equilibria (see the discussion in Cooper and John, 1988).

Given individual investment in education, firms choosing the complex technology can hire either new graduates from upper-layer schools or experienced workers. The former choice is more likely when accumulated academic skills are relatively high, upper-layer schools are of good quality, and previous labour market experience is of little use for training. When firms do not hire experienced workers, who quit other firms, labour market turnover is low. We call this situation the *J*-regime. On the other hand, when accumulated academic skills are relatively low, upper-layer schools are of poor quality, and previous labour market experience matters for training, firms using the complex technology prefer to hire experienced workers from the market. In this case, there are quits, turnover is high and we are in the *I*-regime.

Next, consider the educational investment of individuals in the two regimes. In the *J*-regime new school graduates can be hired either by high wage firms with the complex technology or by low wage firms with the simple technology. Entry in an upper-layer school is attractive because it increases the likelihood of being hired by a high wage firm. When entry into upper-layer schools is restricted by selectivity, individuals must compete with each other to gain access. Individuals who perform at least up to the required standard get into upper-layer schools, while those whose performance is below the standard remain in lower-layer schools. The higher the standard, the higher the effort spent in the development of basic academic skills by all the homogeneous participants.

Since employment in a high-wage firm is more likely when there are more such firms, it can be shown that individual investment in academic skills is higher when the number of high-wage firms is higher and when entry in upper-layer schools is more selective. At the same time, the number of high-wage (and complex technology) firms is increasing in the level of individual investment. The interaction between the individual decision to invest and the managerial selection of technology can generate an equilibrium allocation in the *J*-regime (see Brunello and Ishikawa, 1999 for technical details). In this equilibrium, firms fill their vacant positions by hiring new school graduates. While *C*-firms strictly prefer to hire graduates from upper-layer schools, *S*-firms hire indifferently from either type of school. There is no inter-firm mobility from the *S*- to the *C*-sector and turnover is low. If high managerial ability is the ability to attract and organize not only trainable workers from upper-layer schools but also a large capital stock, we can characterize this equilibrium in terms of firm size, measured by the capital–labour ratio. While large firms typically choose the *C*-technology, small and medium-sized firms choose the *S*-one.

Turning to the *I*-regime, firms choosing the complex technology prefer to hire experienced workers rather than new school graduates and firms choosing the *S*-technology are indifferent to the type of schools new recruits have graduated from. Therefore, the individual incentive to participate in the competition to enter upper-layer schools and to accumulate basic academic skills is zero because access to such schools does not facilitate employment in high wage firms. Hence, the privately optimal level of educational effort in the *I*-regime is equal to its minimum level, quite independently of the distribution of firms among available technologies. With some additional assumptions, it can be shown that the equilibrium share of *C*-firms is smaller in the *I*-regime than in the *J*-regime. If we describe the equilibrium in terms of firm size, with large firms typically choosing the *C*-technology and small and medium-sized firms choosing the *S*-technology, the *I*-regime is characterized by significant labour market flows from small to large firms. Small firms take care of initial training in the labour market, while the schooling system plays only a limited role in the matching of new entrants with private industry since the latter prefers experienced workers to new graduates of relatively low average quality.

To summarize, the economy described in this section can be characterized by: (i) a single *J*-regime equilibrium; (ii) a single *I*-regime equilibrium; (iii) multiple regime equilibria; or (iv) no equilibrium. In the case of multiple regime equilibria, historical accident decides which equilibrium the economy actually settles in. In the *J-equilibrium*, individual investment in education is high because expected returns are high and large firms hire graduates from upper-layer schools. In the *I-equilibrium*, investment in education is low and labour market turnover is relatively high.

A key feature of the model is the assumption that each individual or firm is too small to take into account the effect of his/her own action on the optimal decision of others. This has implications both for the equilibrium level of educational investment and for the optimal number of *C*-firms. To see why, consider the *J*-regime and notice that the equilibrium number of firms is an increasing function of individual investment. While an increase in effort by a single individual has little effect on the number of firms, a co-ordinated and symmetric increase raises the number of firms hiring from upper-layer schools. This in turn makes individual investment more attractive. In a symmetric co-operative equilibrium, positive spillovers and strategic complementarities are internalized and equilibrium individual investment is higher. As shown by Cooper and John (1988), the presence of such positive spillovers and strategic complementarities implies that equilibria can be ranked, with the high investment equilibrium being Pareto-superior to the low investment equilibrium.

Turning to the *I*-regime, individual investment is at its minimum level and the number of firms choosing the complex technology is constant. The absence of a positive relationship between these two variables implies that a co-ordinated increase of individual investment cannot increase individual (expected) utility or net national output and only increases the cost of effort. Thus high investment equilibria in this regime are Pareto-inferior to low investment equilibria.

Going back to the question as to whether more competition at school improves economic welfare, our answer is positive only when the economy is initially located in a *J*-equilibrium. In such an equilibrium, individuals accumulate basic academic skills in the schooling system and firms value these skills because they significantly reduce training costs. In these circumstances, an increase in the competition of the schooling system increases economic welfare. If the economy, however, is initially located in an *I*-equilibrium, the accumulation of basic academic skills is at its minimum and firms prefer experienced workers to new school graduates. In this case, increasing the competition of the schooling system has no effects on the economy, unless this increase can be co-ordinated with a substantial change in the hiring patterns of firms in favour of new school graduates.

3.2 A model with two skills

The model in the previous sub-section is based on the assumption that individuals accumulate a single type of skill, basic academic competencies. This sub-section extends the model to include two skills, basic academic skills and *individual* skills. The former can be exemplified by knowledge of maths and science and the latter by creative thinking. It is reasonable to expect that both skills are useful to firms that face a menu of available technologies. It is also reasonable to imagine a degree of complementarity between them: for instance, creative thinking and innovative skills require common academic skills to be effective. At the same time, however, excessive specialization in one skill could hamper the development of the other. The Japanese case is a good example. According to Rohlen (1992, p. 344):

> the products of Japanese schooling today are deficient in some skills that are given greater emphasis in other nations. The way Japanese are taught emphasizes passive listening and rote memorization. Self-expression, argumentation and creative thinking are not emphasized Large classes, the routines, the emphasis on group social control, and the strenuous pace required for exam preparation all preclude much individualistic activity, the consequence is a degree of overall uniformity and equality of opportunity that is admirable from an egalitarian perspective, but open to criticism for lacking variety, responsiveness to the individual and attention to creativity.

In short, the relationship between individual and academic skills is hump-shaped, with individual skills first increasing and then decreasing in the amount of time and effort spent in the accumulation of basic academic skills. Consider first the case where individual skills increase with basic academic skills. Since the total stock of skills is increasing in the stock of basic academic skills, we expect that introducing individual skills will not affect in a qualitative way the results discussed in the previous sub-section. Things are rather different, however, when we focus on the negative portion of the hump-shaped relationship – that is, when we assume that the two skills are substitutes rather than complements. This could result from excessive competition at school, leading to a substantial accumulation of one skill at the cost of the other.

We analyse this case by introducing the following variations in the model discussed in the previous sub-section. First, we assume that the total stock of skills accumulated by each individual during the schooling period is constant, but allow the composition into basic academic and individual skills to vary. Hence, if an individual accumulates a higher stock of academic skills, he/she accumulates a lower stock of individual ones.[7] Second, we add to the menu of available technologies a third option, the *V*-technology. To help intuition, it is useful to think of the *V*-technology as venture business or as a trial-and-error self-employment sector that relies on the flexibility, the creativity and the specialization provided by individual skills. Output per head in this technology is higher than in the *S*-technology, but lower than in the *C*-technology. Furthermore, and in sharp contrast with the *C*-technology, training costs are lower the higher the level of individual skills held by the hired employee.

Since individual skills reduce training costs in the *V*-technology, the training costs borne by firms adopting it are an increasing function, and profits a negative function, of individual investment in academic skills. Because of this, competition in the schooling system that increases the investment in academic skills negatively affects the selection of this technology. As in the previous sub-section, the economy is also characterized by two regimes – the *J*- and the *I*-regimes. Moreover, it can be shown that the introduction of individual skills and of the *V*-technology does not change the result obtained earlier – there can be a *J*-equilibrium, an *I*-equilibrium, multiple equilibria or no equilibrium at all. As in the model with a single skill, historical accident dictates into which one the economy settles. Finally, the basic properties of the two skills model are similar to the properties discussed for the model with a single skill. Because of this, we shall only stress the differences between the two models.

In the two regimes, individual investment in basic academic skills has both positive and negative spillovers on the selection of technologies. By increasing their investment in academic skills, individuals reduce the training costs faced by firms adopting the complex technology, but increase the costs faced by firms adopting the *V*-technology that uses intensively less abundant individual skills. The share of *C*- and *S*-firms increases but the share of *V*-firms falls. Since *V*-firms are more productive than *S*-firms, we cannot say a priori whether average productivity has increased, nor can we Pareto-rank equilibria with increasing levels of investment in academic skills. As discussed by Cooper and John (1988), this ranking is precluded by the presence of negative spillovers. Thus, when competition at school is already high, so that basic academic and individual skills are substitutes rather than complements, an increase in school selectivity does not necessarily raise national output and economic welfare.

The bottom line of this discussion is that the presence of two skills and of the *V*-technology imply that the *I-equilibrium*, which has both a lower level of investment in academic skills and fewer firms using the complex technology, cannot be generally ranked as Pareto-inferior to the *J-equilibrium* and viceversa. In the *J-equilibrium*, investment in academic skills reduces the training costs in the highly productive large firms sector but increases the costs faced by the venture business sector. While net output is higher in the former sector, it is lower in the latter. The *I-equilibrium* yields minimum investment in academic skills, high investment in individual skills and fewer firms adopting the complex technology. Contrary to the previous case, this leads to higher net output in the venture business sector and to lower net output in the high-tech sector. Whether total output is higher in the former or in the latter equilibrium cannot be established *a priori* and depends on the model's parameters.

4 Conclusions

It is useful to summarize the key differences between Italy's and Japan's education and training systems, illustrated in Section 2, as follows:

(i) Educational attainment in Italy is much lower than in Japan, even though both countries devote a similar amount of financial resources to schooling. Reasons for this difference include the high dropout ratio in Italy and the very steep rise in school enrolment in Japan in the 1955–75 years;

(ii)   While the Japanese schooling system emphasizes competition and the accumulation of basic skills in mathematics and sciences, the Italian system is less competitive and less successful, on average, in providing these skills;

(iii) The relationship between educational level and unemployment is U-shaped in Italy and decreasing in Japan. Italy's high level of unemployment among individuals with relatively high education is partly 'wait' unemployment, as the educated queue for what are perceived as 'good and safe' jobs in the public sector;

(iv)   Italian private industry has relied more on internal and informal training than on formal education. There is a widely perceived mismatch between the supply of educated labour and private-sector demand. In Japan, private firms are willing to hire straight from school or university;

(v)   The two countries' industrial structure is characterized by a significant share of small and medium-sized firms. While these firms in Italy hire the great majority of their young workers independently of their education, Japanese large firms employ a substantial share of young and educated individuals. High job turnover among small Italian firms suggests that these provide substantial training to their workers who then often move to large firms, which prefer to hire experienced workers rather than inexperienced school graduates. In Japan, by contrast, mobility is lower and large firms show a distinctive preference for hiring untrained new school graduates;

(vi)   Earnings and productivity differentials by firm size are significant in both countries but larger in Japan than in Italy;

(vii) Small and medium-sized firms in Italy are often relatively more productive than their Japanese counterparts. On the other hand, large Japanese firms perform much better than Italian ones. These differences could be explained both by the presence of a significant segment of low-productivity subcontracting firms in Japan and by the important role played in the Italian economy by highly productive industrial clusters of small firms.

These differences can be interpreted as features of two distinct locally stable equilibria, similar to those produced by the model discussed in Section 3. In one equilibrium (the *Japanese* or *J-equilibrium*), schooling is very competitive and individuals make a substantial investment in the accumulation of common academic skills. The availability of these skills in the market and the complementarity between education and training facilitates the adoption of complex technologies, which require substantial training costs. Large firms, which use these technologies, pay relatively high wages and attract graduates from the best schools. Small firms, which operate in a secondary labour market and use relatively simple technologies, pay lower wages because they are less productive. The high expected gain from access into a good school stimulates investment in academic skills. Excessive competition at school, however, hampers the development of the individual skills that are important for the venture business technology.

In another equilibrium (the *Italian* or *I-equilibrium*), schooling is not as selective and more time is given to individual development in flexible curricula, both formally at school and informally on the job. Lower accumulation of common academic skills makes the adoption of complex technologies relatively less profitable. At the same time, however, the higher stock of individual skills stimulates the adoption of technologies that are intensive in these skills. Labour turnover is higher and labour market experience matters more than school quality in the reduction of training costs faced by firms. The relative scarcity of large firms that pay higher wages, and the higher turnover rate, further reduce the incentive to accumulate common academic skills, because of the relatively low expected returns.

The chapter's conclusion is that we cannot say a priori whether national output and welfare are always higher in the *I-* or in the *J*-equilibrium. Suppose, for instance, that tastes evolve in the direction of wanting greater variety and that technology allows increasingly small production runs at low costs. In this case the *V*-technology becomes a more productive and attractive option. This would favour the 'Italian model' relative to the 'Japanese model', because of the advantage provided by a schooling system that stresses the development of the individual skills necessary for this technology. Suppose, instead, that international competition increasingly requires that firms master complex technologies. In this case, the less competitive Italian schooling system, by hampering the development of the necessary academic skills, can also hamper the economic performance of the 'Italian model' relative to the 'Japanese model' and Porter (1989, p. 812) might be right when he argues that 'in order to sustain growth and to acquire professional competencies, Italians need to improve their basic knowledge of mathematics, computers and other key disciplines'.

Notes

Note: Tsuneo Ishikawa sadly passed away before the publication of this book.

1. Card and Krueger (1992) give evidence on the relationship between school quality and earnings. Mankiw et al. (1992) relate the growth of real output per head to the rate of human capital accumulation, measured by secondary school enrolment.
2. Public and private expenditure on tertiary education per student was equivalent to 49 per cent of per capita GDP in the OECD area, but to only 37 per cent in Japan and 34 per cent in Italy in the early 1990s.
3. This is confirmed by a number of studies. According to Marsden: 'It is fair to suppose that the main form of training for skilled labour in France and Italy consists of work experience and training organised by individual employers' (quoted by Regalia and Regini, 1995, p. 141) who add: 'more recent research largely confirms that this was indeed the principal way in which skills were formed and developed in much of Italian industry'. According to Blanchflower and Freeman (1996, p. 1): 'In Germany . . . apprenticeships move youths from school to the industry in which they find permanent work . . . in Japan, firms tend to recruit from particular colleges and universities or from specific high schools . . in yet other countries (e.g. Italy), youths rarely work while in school and are often jobless for a long period after leaving school before they obtain their first job'.
4. See Contini and Revelli (1992, especially ch. 11) and Contini and Rapiti (1994, p. 13) who argue that: 'Young workers who have been through on the job training in a small firm make up the large majority of job-to-job changes occurring in the Italian economy'. Substantial turnover from small to large firms has also been promoted by the institutional and legal environment, which has strongly encouraged job-to-job moves; see OECD (1994) and Bertola and Ichino (1995).
5. See also Chapter 7 by Genda et al.
6. The Italian data come from INPS; the Japanese data from Ishikawa and Dejima (1994). Differentials are based on the hourly earnings of regular workers in Japan and on the annual earnings of all workers with a social security account in Italy.
7. Treating individual and basic academic skills as perfect substitutes is clearly a strong assumption that is only used so as to produce more definite conclusions.

References

Barro, R. and J.W. Lee (1994) 'Sources of Economic Growth', *Carnegie Rochester Conferences on Public Policy*, 40, 1–46.

Bernardi, L. and U. Trivellato (1995) 'Scolarità e formazione professionale nel Mezzogiorno: Nuove evidenze da un'analisi dei flussi', *Economia e Lavoro*, 28, 3–4, 1–34.

Bertola, G. and D. Coen Pirani (1995) 'Market Failures, Education and Macro-economics', mimeo, University of Turin.

Bertola, G. and A. Ichino (1995) 'Wage Inequality and Unemployment: United States v. Europe', in B. Bernanke and J. Rotemberg (eds), *NBER Macroeconomics Annual, 1995*, Cambridge, MA: MIT Press.

Blanchflower, D. and R. Freeman (1996) 'Growing into Work', London School of Economics CEP Discussion Paper, No. 296.

Brunello, G. and T. Ishikawa (1999) 'Elite Schools, High-tech jobs and Economic Welfare', *Journal of Public Economics*, 72, 3, 395–419.

Brunello, G., C. Lupi, and P. Ordine (2000) 'Regional Disparities and the Italian NAIRU', *Oxford Economic Papers*, 52, 1, 146–77.

Brunello, G. and A. Medio (1997) 'A Job Competition Model of Workplace Training and Education', Fondazione ENI Enrico Mattei Working Paper, No. 97-4, Milan.

Brusco, S. (1992) 'Small Firms and the Provision of Real Services', in W. Sengenberger and F. Pyke, *Industrial Districts and Local Economic Regeneration*, Geneva: International Institute for Labour Studies.

Card, D. and A.B. Krueger (1992) 'Does School Quality Matter? Returns to Education and the Characteristics of Public Schools in the United States', *Journal of Political Economy*, 100, 1, 1–40.

Censis (1992) *25 Rapporto sulla situazione sociale del paese*, Rome.

Confindustria (1998) *Verso la scuola del 2000*, Rome.

Contini, B. and M. Filippi (1995) 'A Study on Job Creation and Job Destruction in Europe', mimeo, *Ricerche e Progetti*, Turin.

Contini, B. and F. Rapiti (1994) '"Young in, old out": Nuovi pattern di mobilità nell'economia italiana', *Lavoro e Relazioni Industriali*, 1, 3, 51–76.

Contini, B. and R. Revelli (1992) *Imprese, occupazione e retribuzioni al microscopio*, Bologna: Il Mulino.

Cooper, R. and A. John (1988) 'Coordinating Coordination Failures in Keynesian Models', *Quarterly Journal of Economics*, 103, 3, 441–63.

Hanushek, E.A. (1986) 'The Economics of Schooling: Production and Efficiency in The Public Schools', *Journal of Economic Literature*, 24, 3, 1141–77.

Ishikawa, T and K. Dejima (1994) 'Rodo Shijono Niju Kozo' ('The Dual Structure of the Japanese Labour Market'), in T. Ishikawa (ed.), *Nihonno Shotoku to Tomino Bunpai (The Distribution of Japanese Income and Wealth)*, Tokyo: Tokyo; University Press.

ISTAT (1997) *Rapporto sull'Italia*, Bologna: Il Mulino.

Jannaccone Pazzi, R. and L. Ribolzi (1992) *Università flessibile*, Milan: IBM Italia.

Layard, R., S. Nickell, and R. Jackman (1991) *Unemployment: Macroeconomic Performance and the Labour Market*, Oxford: Oxford University Press.

Mankiw, N.G., D. Romer. and D.N. Weil (1992) 'A Contribution to the Empirics of Economic Growth', *Quarterly Journal of Economics*, 107, 2, 407–37.

OECD (1994) *Employment Outlook, 1994*, Paris.

OECD (1995) *Education at a Glance*, Paris.

Porter, M.E. (1989) *The Competitive Advantage of Nations*, Cambridge, MA: Harvard University Press.

Rebelo, S. (1992) 'Growth in Open Economies', CEPR Discussion Paper No. 667.

Regalia, I. and M. Regini (1995) 'Between Voluntarism and Institutionalization: Industrial Relations and Human Resource Practices in Italy', in R. Locke, T.A. Kochan and M.J. Piore, (eds), *Employment Relations in a Changing World Economy*, Cambridge, MA: MIT Press.

Rohlen, T. (1992) 'Learning: The Mobilization of Knowledge in the Japanese Political Economy', in S. Kumon and H. Rosovsky (eds), *The Political Economy of Japan*, vol. 3, Stanford, CA: Stanford University Press.

Rosen, S. (1976) 'A Theory of Life Earnings', *Journal of Political Economy*, 84, 4, S45–S67.

Spence, M. (1973) 'Job Market Signaling', *Quarterly Journal of Economics*, 87, 3, 355–74.

Trento, S. (1997) 'Il grado di scolarizzazione: Un confronto internazionale', in N. Rossi (ed.), *L'istruzione in Italia: solo un pezzo di carta?*, Bologna: Il Mulino.

11
The Silk Industry: A Historical Perspective

Giovanni Federico and Kanji Ishii

1 Introduction

Silk has for centuries been a luxury item, the dress of the rich and powerful. It was only in the later nineteenth century that its consumption spread among the common people under the combined effect of increasing incomes and falling silk prices. From the 1870s to the Great Depression, per capita consumption of raw silk in the four main economies (the United States, the United Kingdom, Germany and France) tripled, from about 50 to more than 150 grams. World trade in silk grew threefold from the 1870s to 1910s and then doubled again in the two decades to 1926–29 (Table 11.1). At the same time, world output expanded by as much as $3\frac{1}{2}$ times – or at a 2.8 per cent annual compound growth rate.[1] The trade/output ratio rose from about 0.5 to about 0.75 – one of the highest among primary products. These buoyant developments were reversed by the combined effects of the Great Depression, of the Second World War and of the invention of nylon (the first real substitute for natural silk). Silk trade plunged, and was to reattain the levels of the late 1920s only in the late 1970s.

The trade/output ratio was comparatively high because the production of silk was unsuited to the climate and/or the factor endowment of the advanced Western countries. Silk production was scattered round the Mediterranean basin and East and South-East Asia. Yet, on the eve of the First World War, three countries, China, Italy and Japan, accounted for 85 per cent of world silk output and for 95 per cent of world exports. Silk (with silk waste, a by-product of processing) was their main staple (Table 11.2) and represented a large and growing business. From the 1870s to 1924, for instance, the production of cocoons increased from 2.2 to

Table 11.1   Silk industry – selected long-run indicators

	World Trade	Production		Relative Price[a]
		Italy	Japan	
	(tons)			*(1913 = 100)*
1873–77	7 906	2 620	1 500	133.1
1878–82	8 479	2 872	1 723	124.8
1883–87	9 709	3 808	2 294	121.3
1888–92	12 851	4 583	3 757	115.2
1893–97	13 850	4 672	5 700	105.0
1898–02	17 116	5 618	6 939	115.2
1903–07	19 103	6 742	7 940	130.1
1908–13	23 963	6 554	12 243	102.3
1914–20	25 730	4 004	19 087	87.4
1921–25	36 565	4 843	26 494	107.8
1926–29	47 602	5 547	38 305	83.0
1930–34	39 852	4 005	43 085	—
1935–38	34 843	2 849	42 772	—

a. Silk unit values deflated with British wholesale prices.
Source: Federico (1997), Tables AII and AVI.

Table 11.2   Shares of silk and silk waste in total exports

	China	Italy	Japan
1860s–1870s[a]	31.2	30.7	39.9
1871–80	29.0	28.9	38.2
1881–90	23.6	28.6	40.9
1891–00	25.0	29.4	33.7
1901–10	25.2	29.0	29.3
1911–20	18.3	16.6	26.1
1921–29	17.5	14.2	38.3

a. China: 1867–70; Italy: 1863–70; Japan: 1868–70.
Source: as for Table 11.1.

14 per cent of Japanese agricultural output (Ishii, 1986). On the eve of the First World War, the silk industry may have accounted for as much as 4 per cent of GDP in Japan and 1.5 per cent in Italy, down from perhaps 2 or 3 per cent around the middle of the nineteenth century.

Thus, the silk industry provides a unique opportunity for a direct comparison of the historical roots of Italian and Japanese growth. What does the case of silk teach us about the long-run features of the two countries? How did the two economies compete on world markets? To what extent did silk exports contribute to two of the most impressive success-stories in the developed world? This brief chapter tries to provide some answers. Interested readers can find more information in Ishii (1972) and Federico (1997).[2] The focus will be on the period going from the 1860s to the late 1920s – in other words, from the opening of Japan to the Great Depression. After a short description of the main characteristics of the industry (Section 2), Section 3 sketches the long-run evolution of the basic variables while Section 4 discusses a number of possible causes for the differing performances of the two countries. The fifth section deals with the role of silk in development and a sixth and final section sums up.

2 Main characteristics of the industry

The term 'silk industry' is somewhat misleading, since the production of silk was largely an agricultural activity. Silk is secreted by an insect (the *Bombyx mori*, or silkworm) to form a protective layer (or cocoon) during its transformation into a butterfly. Silkworms are raised by feeding them on mulberry leaves (sericulture). Cocoons are then unwound (reeled) by plunging them into a hot water basin. The product (raw silk) is a thread, which can be woven, usually after being 'thrown' (a technical term denoting a prior manipulation of the threads).

Sericulture and reeling have tended to be centred in the same location. In principle, nothing prevents different locations since cocoons can be easily transported. However, they are so bulky as to make long-distance shipments uneconomical. The location of sericulture is to some extent constrained by climate. While mulberry trees thrive in all temperate and subtropical climates, Northern Europe is an unsuitable location since silkworms are sensitive to cold. An important difference distinguishes Mediterranean and subtropical countries. In the latter, mulberry trees are in leaf almost continuously, and silkworms can be raised up to six or seven times a year. In Italy, Central China and Japan, on the other hand, trees can be stripped only once, or at most twice, a year. Therefore, sericulture could not be a full-time occupation. These various environmental constraints cannot, however, fully explain the location of sericulture, which was not practised in many climatically suitable areas, such as the South of the United States. Even in China, Italy or Japan, the silk industry was heavily concentrated in a few locations (the areas around Shanghai and Canton in China, the North in Italy, the central provinces of Honshu in Japan).

The key economic factors for the industry's presence in these areas were the availability of land to plant mulberry trees and, above all, of labour. Both reeling and, even more, sericulture were highly labour-intensive activities. On the eve of the First World War, even with Italian technology, which was then the most advanced, the production of one kg of silk required some 17 to 19 days of full-time work. Of these, 14 to 15 were devoted to feeding the silkworms, which require a round-the-clock supply of freshly-cut leaves, and the rest to reel the cocoons (hence agricultural value added accounted for as much as 75 to 80 per cent of silk's final price).

The industry's technology, though relatively simple, was not fully mechanized until the 1950s, and required skilled manpower. The smallest error provoked visible imperfections in the thread. On the other hand, scale and scope economies were almost non-existent, because the reeling equipment was totally specific and almost perfectly divisible. Barriers to entry were thus extremely low: a prominent Italian industrialist complained about 'the great ease for anyone to speculate in cocoons and to play the *filandiere*' (or reeling-plant owner).[3] Turnover among firms was correspondingly high: less than 10 per cent of firms, in both Italy and Japan, managed to survive between 1891 and 1927 (Table 11.3).

The combination of low barriers to entry and lack of scale economies resulted in fierce competition. The Herfindahl measure of concentration regularly exhibited very low values, varying between a minimum of 0.0032 in Italy in 1904 and a maximum of 0.015 in Japan in the late 1920s.[4] In 1911, the top ten firms in both countries accounted for about 10 per cent of the industry's capital stock. Though their share in Japan was growing quite rapidly, it had barely reached a third of total output by 1927.

Table 11.3   Survival and innovation rates for reeling firms (percentages)

		Innovation[a]	Survival[b]
1891–1904[c]	Italy	57.6	29.9
	Japan	63.9	32.2
1904–1917	Italy	49.3	30.7
	Japan	68.8	36.0
1917–1927	Italy	64.7	34.3
	Japan	54.2	50.1
1891–1927[d]	Italy	83.5	7.2
	Japan	92.9	8.0

a. Percent of firms in end-year which were newly established during the period.
b. Percent of firms in initial year which survived during the period.
c. Japan: 1893–1904.
d. Japan: 1893–1927.
Sources: Ministry of Agriculture and Commerce, *Zenkoku Seishikojo Chosahyo* (*National Inspection of Silk Reeling Factories*) (various issues) for Japan; Federico (1997), Table 2.4 for Italy.

Last, but not least, silk reeling was reputed to be very risky. Some risk is unavoidable in any activity that processes throughout the year a raw material harvested once or twice a year. In such cases, the price of the raw material (cocoons) at harvest time depends on the current price of the final product (silk). Any subsequent final product price fluctuation generates gains or losses for stockholders. In the case of silk most of this risk was usually borne by the reelers. Peasants used to sell cocoons to them immediately after the harvest while weavers would only buy at their convenience. Since industrial margins were very small (because of low value added), industrial profits were extremely sensitive to the smallest change in silk prices. Profits oscillated wildly from one year to the next. Thus, the coefficient of variation of profit rates at Gunze, the second largest Japanese silk company, was as high as 2.1 between 1896 and 1921. And profits could vary hugely between firms – a difference of few weeks or even days in sales timing could cause a firm to lose or gain vast amounts of money.

The key asset of a successful company was thus the trading skill of its managers. First, they had to buy cocoons at the lowest possible price (Japan's largest firm, Katakura, for instance, had a wide network of purchasing agents, mostly members of the family, who did not refrain from spreading false information to lower the purchase price of their raw material) (Ishii, 1994). Second, managers had to choose the right moment to sell, on the basis of silk price forecasts. These relied on a wide range of information – ranging from estimates of output in producing countries scattered across the world, to all those factors which could influence demand, including changes in fashion and political news. Traditionally, this information had been conveyed by merchants via personal links and mail. In the new global market of the late nineteenth century, it was transmitted through transatlantic cables and distributed weekly by the specialized press. At least in Italy, all firms were, in principle, on a similar footing and could obtain the same information at a very low cost.

This brief description shows some of the peculiarities of the silk 'industry'. First, it was a vertical industry, with strong links to its agricultural roots. Second, it operated in a very competitive environment, with an unusually high level of risk and a sophisticated process of expectations formation. Third, it was a truly global activity.

3   International competition

The modern history of world trade in silk began in the late eighteenth–early nineteenth century. Previously, Europe, and its offshoots on the eastern shores of the Mediterranean, had been almost entirely self-sufficient. The catalyst for dramatic changes was the outbreak of a silkworm disease, the *pebrine*. First spotted in the 1840s, this spread rapidly in the next two decades, reducing European production by about a half. The gap was first filled by imports from China, and, from the early 1860s, when China was hit by the Tai'ping rebellion, by imports from Japan. Japan thus opened to the world exactly when its silk and disease-free silkworm eggs were most required. Its exports boomed in the 1860s, fell briefly in the early 1870s, when Italian and Chinese production recovered, but rose almost uninterruptedly thereafter, with the country's share of the world market moving from less than 10 per cent to nearly 70 per cent in half a century (Table 11.4).[5] Silk was the first example of the string of export booms which have featured in Japanese economic history since then – cotton cloths in the 1920s and 1930s, steel and ships in the 1950s and 1960s, cars and electronic equipment in more recent times. The silk boom was made possible by a massive increase in domestic production. From the 1870s to the First World War this grew $5\frac{1}{2}$ times – and by a further 5 times from then to the Great Depression.

Though other countries lost market shares, their absolute performances were still remarkable. China's exports more than doubled between the 1870s and the late 1920s, and total output may have increased by 75 per cent (the data are very uncertain). The Italian case is different and can be neatly divided into two periods. From the 1870s to the all-time peak of 1905–7 production grew by about 150 per cent (Fenoaltea, 1988). After that, output began to fall. On the eve of the First World War it was down by 25 per cent and it fell further during the war. In spite of a recovery in the late 1920s, it never regained the level of the early 1900s. Production then halved during the 1930s and continued to fall disappearing in the 1960s. Japan's industry also shrank substantially after the Second World War, and it survives today only by producing for

Table 11.4   World trade in silk – market shares

	Volume			Value		
	China	*Italy*	*Japan*	*China*	*Italy*	*Japan*
1873–75	53.1	30.9	8.3	38.6	46.4	6.4
1905–07	33.9	32.8	27.0	24.6	43.1	26.3
1911–13	35.4	19.2	41.5	27.2	26.5	42.2
1927–29	21.9	10.3	67.2	18.4	13.4	67.6

Sources: Federico (1997), Table 3.4 and Federico (1994a), p. 57.

Table 11.5   Selected relative silk prices (Italy = 100)

	Lyons (market price)			United States (unit import price)	
	Japan[a]	Shanghai[a]		Japan	China
			1890–94	79.4	71.2
1898–01	94.7	100.5	1895–99	74.7	6 0.9
1902–05	94.8	100.8	1900–04	86.9	71.2
1906–09	91.3	97.0	1905–09	93.2	72.0
1910–13	91.3	97.2	1910–14	86.3	63.8
			1915–19	69.9	55.4
			1920–24	96.7	85.6
			1925–29	110.9	92.1

a. Steam-reeled silk.
Sources: Federico (1997), Table AXX for Lyons; Fujino and Ono (1979), Table 65, for the United States.

the domestic market thanks to a high level of protection. Over the long-run China has remained alone among the 'traditional' producers and, in spite of competition from newcomers, such as Thailand and Brazil, still provides three quarters of world silk consumption.

The differences between the market share data expressed in quantity and in value terms (Table 11.4) highlight an important fact – prices differed across countries because silk, as many other primary products, was not a homogeneous commodity. The quality ranking was well defined. Italy was at the top – since the 1840s–1850s its supply consisted almost exclusively of high-quality silk. China's exports, on the other hand, were extremely diversified, ranging from goods produced in the Shanghai filatures – the only ones in Asia able to match Italian and French quality – to some very low-quality products. Most of Japan's exports consisted of standard, medium-quality items, which cost on average 10 to 15 per cent less than Italian silk (Table 11.5). The quality gap began to shrink in the 1910s, as exports of traditional, hand-reeled silk disappeared and Japanese firms accepted almost immediately the request by the American Silk Association to adopt the 'standard American skein', a special way of packaging silk, while Italians were much more reluctant to comply.

It can be argued that growth in output (and a fortiori in exports) is not sufficient by itself to generate development. Productivity in basic commodity production must also grow so as to release labour and capital to the 'modern' sector. There is ample evidence that this was happening. Both the relative price of silk to consumers (measured using the British consumer price index as deflator) and the relative price of cocoons to producers (measured using either domestic wholesale or cereals prices) fell quite steadily (the cocoons/rice price ratio declined in Japan by almost half between 1875 and 1929, for instance). Japan's productivity performance was particularly good. From the 1890s to 1926–29 total factor productivity in sericulture and reeling grew at annual rates of approximately 2.5 to 3 and 2.7 to 3.2 per cent respectively (the range depends on the assumptions made about factor shares, and illustrates the inevitable imprecision of such estimates). Italy's performance seems also to have been respectable. A similar total factor productivity estimate is not possible for sericulture, but the 'rate of shift of supply' (1 per cent per annum between 1870 and 1913) does not compare badly with the 1.6 per cent achieved in Japan over the same period (Federico, 1996a).[6] Total factor productivity in Italian reeling grew at almost 2 per cent annually between 1876 and 1911 and by more than 2 per cent in the next quarter century.[7] The figure is lower than the Japanese one, as befits the industrial leader, but much higher than what is implied in the Italian historical literature, which depicts silk reeling as a backward and stagnant industry (Castronovo, 1980).

4   Reasons for differential performances

The long-run performances of the three major countries' silk industries and the ensuing very sharp changes in market shares could have been brought about by a very wide range of factors. Inevitably, perhaps, these can hardly be sorted out by any simple econometric technique. This section, therefore, simply lists and discusses some of the main forces at work in the two countries, starting with differences in selected features of the industry.

4.1   Product and credit market organization

Market arrangements were quite complex and varied through time. In a nutshell, the difference between Italy and Japan (as well as China) was in the role of intermediaries. In Italy, at least from the 1870s onwards, there were only pure brokers who put buyers in contact with sellers for a small fee. The reeling firms organized both the purchase of cocoons and the sale of silk, and took all the ensuing risks. The funds were provided by banks, which lent on pledge of cocoons or of raw silk, regardless of firm size. By contrast, a substantial part of transactions in the Far East was managed by merchants and trading firms. Local merchants purchased cocoons from peasants and sold them to (smaller) reeling firms; merchants from

Yokohama and Kobe provided capital, borrowing funds from the banks. Exports were organized by big trading firms, at first Western and later increasingly Japanese (some with links to the *zaibatsus*).

The merits of Japanese institutions have received a lot of attention. Though average interest rates were higher in Japan than in Italy, the overall cost of capital was similar because Japan's higher rate was offset by a shorter average loan length. Total transaction costs were higher than in Italy, because of brokerage fees, but the difference was small and is unlikely to have substantially affected farm-gate prices of silk and cocoons, unless the merchants or the trading companies were able to extract monopsony profits. Though this has often been claimed, the supporting evidence is weak.

The system may have had other virtues, though. Some Italian experts have praised it for its alleged capacity to stabilize the Yokohama market, which one of them described as 'wonderfully organized' being managed by the 'disciplined will of a few' (Paini, 1913). Yet, these virtues were not much in evidence, since prices fluctuated in Yokohama as much as in Milan. Chinese experts praised the trading companies for promoting quality improvements by forcing producers to adopt better techniques and a more homogenous supply of cocoons. Again, this claim is dubious (especially if the yardstick is Italy); furthermore, the credit for this must be shared with the producers and with the government. So, all in all, it seems difficult to maintain that differences in trading and financing were the key of Japanese success.

4.2 Firm size

One would expect that an almost perfectly competitive environment, with no economies of scale in production and very low barriers to entry, would have bred very many small firms. This was the case in China and Italy. In 1927 an official report somewhat reproachfully characterized the Italian industry as 'highly divided , with an infinite number of small and medium-sized firms and some larger ones'.[8] Even the large ones were comparatively small – the two biggest owned barely 3 per cent each of the industry's capital stock. Single-mill companies also prevailed in China. In Japan, by contrast, some companies grew from humble origins into veritable giants. The biggest of them all, the already mentioned Katakura, established in 1878 with 32 basins, had as many as 14 706 by 1927, and produced over 3000 tons of silk, or 10.3 per cent of total Japanese output (and an amount which represented as much as 60 per cent of Italian output in that year). There were other firms in the same league – such as Yamaju and Gunze.

Unlike Italian (and Chinese) firms, these giant companies engaged in several related activities, such as the production of specialized machinery and, from the 1910s, the distribution of selected eggs to cocoon-growers, with long-term purchase agreements. These activities may have given the biggest companies some advantage. The proprietary technology embodied in the machines may have been better than that available to lesser firms (but also worse); the control of the supply of eggs improved the homogeneity and the average quality of the raw material, and may have enabled the large firms to obtain some monopsony profits. Last but not least, the big companies had easier access to credit and, since the 1910s, could borrow directly from Japan's main banks, instead of getting funds from regional banks and silk merchants. They saved therefore on intermediation costs, and had some additional guarantees of help in case of distress.

Each of these various advantages may have been small in absolute terms, but as a whole they were substantial enough to explain why big firms grew within Japan. They do not, however, throw much light on the reasons for Japan's greater competitiveness relative to Italy. Indeed, it can be argued that the best Japanese firms grew in order to supplement the shortcomings of domestic institutions, such as the bias against small companies in the credit market and the lack of efficient engineering companies to which the production of machinery could have been outsourced. In other words, large firms may have been rather competitive within Japan, but for the country as a whole this effect was offset by the handicaps suffered by smaller ones.

4.3   Demand characteristics

Supply-side differences were matched by differentiation on the demand side which varied considerably among consumer countries. As might have been expected, the United States needed silk of medium quality, suited to a highly mechanized production process for a mass market. Europe, on the other hand, required a more diversified supply, ranging from very good silk for high-quality cloths to poor-quality silk for cheap goods. From the 1880s, a clear division of labour established itself among the three main producers – Japan specialized in bulk production for the American market, while Italy and China exported more to Europe (mainly to Germany/Switzerland and France respectively). This situation did favour Japan, as demand in the United States grew much more rapidly than in Europe (European consumption of raw silk even fell in the 1920s).

A simple, constant market-share, analysis shows that this country effect accounted for all the growth in Japanese exports between 1894 and 1906 and for about three-quarters of it between 1913 and 1929. Pure increases in competitiveness were only important in accounting for the rise in Japan's share of world silk exports in the years 1906–13. Calculations of this kind are, of course, purely mechanical and throw little light on the underlying causal forces at work. If, for instance, Japanese supply had stagnated, prices would have risen and American consumers would have substituted Japanese silk with some other product. Yet, given Japan's undoubted prowess in increasing its output, being positioned in a fast-growing market was surely helpful.

4.4   The role of government and of exchange rates

In these areas Italian and Japanese experiences diverge. Italy's governments did nothing to promote the silk industry and might even have harmed it through the protection they gave to import-competing activities. Unsurprisingly, the industrialists pleaded for help, especially in bad years (Federico, 1995). They were promised support time and again, but got almost nothing until the 1930s, when the government lavished subsidies in order to prevent the industry's collapse. By contrast, the Japanese government was very active from the Meiji restoration onwards. In a first phase, it engineered the transfer of reeling technology by importing a modern plant from France (the well-known *Tomioka* factory) and tried to improve quality by an elaborate system of silk exports inspection. After the Matsukata deflation (1881–85), it switched to a less intrusive policy, centred on the support of technical progress in sericulture. In the 1890s-early 1900s it set up a large network of research institutes and training schools, and it greatly helped the development of producer associations. Reeling was also given financial support. The state discreetly prodded the major banks to lend to reeling firms and several times in the 1910s and 1920s organized purchasing boards to sustain prices.

Japan's policy enjoyed a very favourable reputation at the time. For instance, the 1929 Zurich World Congress of Sericulture endorsed it as the main cause of the country's success. This conventional wisdom is now being questioned – or at least many scholars stress that the right mix of support policies was found only after a long series of mistakes (McCalliom, 1983). The silk inspection system of the 1870s and the crisis management of the 1920s and 1930s were failures, the latter a really costly one. The *Tomioka* reeling technology was not adopted elsewhere in the country, and the factory served at best as a training ground for a limited number of workers. The most effective (and comparatively inexpensive) measure was the support given to technical progress. In 1914 the main research body, the National Institute of Silkworm Eggs Production, produced a new hybrid, called F1, which was vastly superior to the types then in use (Kiyokawa, 1984). The new hybrid was quickly diffused all over Japan, and the combination of its own intrinsic qualities and the ensuing uniformity of the raw material made the production of high-quality silk a lot easier.

The state undeniably contributed to Japan's productivity growth in sericulture, but the merits have to be shared with the reeling companies which distributed the eggs, and with landlords and, above all, peasants, who used the facilities they were offered. On balance, therefore, state support was helpful, but is unlikely to have been the crucial factor behind Japan's export performance.

Turning to the exchange rate, Nugent (1973) has argued that the depreciation of silver against gold in the late nineteeth century fostered exports from silver-based countries, such as China and Japan. It can be shown that the depreciation of the producers' currencies accounted for about 15 per cent of the world's increase in silk consumption between 1870 and 1913 (Federico, 1996a). Yet, the relevance of devaluation in explaining changes in market shares is dubious. First, it should have been more beneficial to China, which stayed on silver throughout the period, than to Japan, which adhered to the gold standard in 1897.[9] Second, a fluctuating exchange rate increased the risks for silk producers, and was, therefore, only a mixed blessing. The situation changed after 1914, when all three currencies floated. Italian industrialists complained bitterly when the lira re-entered the gold exchange standard in the mid-1920s at a very high rate, but by that time the Italian industry was already in deep trouble.

4.5   Technology

It is difficult to compare the technology of sericulture in Italy and Japan. There is a vast amount of anecdotal evidence on the techniques used, but very few data. The only figures available refer to yields (output of cocoons per unit of eggs). They have often been used as a proxy for technical progress, but this inference is misleading, since yields were positively correlated with labour input. Nor it is possible to assess the quality of cocoons by comparing prices, as Japanese and Italian cocoons were not traded on the same markets. Some evidence suggests that Italian production was 'cleaner' (that is, had a lower proportion of defective cocoons) than Japan's and was at least as homogeneous until the 1910s. Japan was able to forge ahead on both counts with the massive adoption of the F1 hybrid during the First World War. In the 1920s, the quality of Japanese cocoon production was in all likelihood equal if not superior to that of Italy.

The case of reeling is much better documented and clear-cut. Italy enjoyed an undisputed world leadership in industrial processing from the early nineteenth century to the 1920s. The modern technology in silk reeling dates from 1805. However, the very first machines were imperfect, and steam reeling began to spread only in the late 1830s, when the major shortcomings had been overcome (Tolaini, 1994). Diffusion of the new technology was boosted by the shortage of cocoons during the *pebrine*, as steam-reeled silk commanded a 10 per cent price premium over traditional, hand-reeled silk. By 1876 steam-reeled silk accounted for three-quarters of total output, and hand-reeled silk disappeared altogether soon after. At the same time, productivity was raised by a steady flow of innovations developed by specialized suppliers of machinery, and quickly adopted by Italian reeling firms, in a fiercely competitive environment.

The first Western-style reeling factory in the Far East was established in Shanghai in 1861; steam-reeling was imported into Japan about ten years later. As in Italy, the modern techniques displaced the traditional ones, but the process took some time. Thus, production of the (improved) *zaguri* variety accounted for a steady 25 per cent of total output at the beginning of the century. All modern machinery was produced domestically, but with a major difference between China and Japan. In China, the machinery producers simply replicated imported Western equipment, while in Japan new models were developed. Until the 1890s the Japanese reeling technology differed from that employed in Italy mainly because Japanese firms consistently sought the least capital-intensive solutions – such as the use of wood and ceramics instead of bricks and iron. Later, however, the machinery producers elaborated different and original solutions to the same problems.

Despite Japan's rapid productivity growth, the gap with Italy remained substantial. In the 1890s (no data are available for earlier years) output per worker in steam-reeling was approximately double in Italy. The gap was reduced to 60 per cent in 1911 (while China's productivity was still half the Italian level) and to 30 per cent in the early 1930s. The differential for the whole of the silk industry, including hand-reeling, was larger, with overall labour productivity in Japan a mere half that of Italy on the eve of the First World War. Differences in capital intensity explain a sizeable part of this gap, but the tentative estimates for total factor productivity shown in Table 11.6 indicate that the latter too was higher in Italy than in Japan. The most plausible estimates, shown in the table's first column, suggest that, even in the 1930s, Italy maintained a small advantage. It is likely that this persistent gap reflected the better average quality of Italian man-power, which had been exposed to modern techniques and to the factory system for a much longer time-span than Japan's labour force.

Table 11.6   Estimates of total factor productivity in steam reeling (ratio of Italy to Japan)

	Estimate A[a]	Estimate B[a]
circa 1890	1.80	1.76
circa 1910	1.46	1.22
circa 1930	1.09	0.89

a. The two columns are computed using different assumptions about the value of factor shares and about the conversion of the capital stock data into a common currency.
Source: Federico (1997), Table 7.10.

There is no doubt that technological leadership was Italy's main asset. In the words of a French contemporary expert, technical progress: 'has enabled the [Italian] reeling firms to survive and fight on nearly equal terms with their Asian competitors' (Beauquais, 1910, p. 81). Continuing productivity growth more than compensated for wage increases so that unit costs declined (by 1.4 per cent per annum between 1876 and 1911). In Japan, over the same period, unit costs actually rose (admittedly because of higher wage growth). In addition, Italy's better machinery accounted for a sizeable (if unmeasurable) part of the quality gap between the two countries. In fact, the more sophisticated the equipment, the easier it was to produce high-quality silk even with defective cocoons. Italy's technical superiority waned in the 1920s (as shown by Japan's catch-up in terms of both total factor productivity and quality), and this process accelerated the final demise of the country's industry after the Great Depression. The process was to some extent endogenous, as the looming crisis and unfavourable expectations stifled investment and R&D spending. It is nevertheless clear that, given the composition of the final price of silk (and the possibility of technology transfers), no realistic increase in reeling productivity would have saved Italy's industry in the absence of an adequate supply of domestic raw materials.

4.6   Factor endowments and costs

Almost by definition, input endowments in competing countries have to be similar – otherwise they would not specialize in the same product. In comparison with, say, the United States, Italy, Japan and China were all labour-abundant and land-scarce countries – and therefore suited to sericulture. Yet, endowments can still differ, to some extent at least, and above all, they can change in different ways.

Thus, the boom of Japanese sericulture was significantly helped by a favourable factor endowment through a classical 'vent-for-surplus' growth mechanism (Nghiep and Hayami, 1979). There was a large pool of underemployed peasants, who from the 1870s engaged in harvesting summer and autumn crops of silkworms. The implicit rate of return on land was high enough to make the extension of the mulberry acreage rather appealing (this doubled between the 1880s and the 1920s), a process that was essential for the growth of cocoon production. The situation in Italy was altogether different. Some labour surplus may have existed in the eighteenth or in the early nineteenth century, but surely not thereafter. All the available labour in spring was already committed to silkworms, while in the summer and autumn peasants were busy harvesting grapes. Without low-cost labour to tend the worms, there was little incentive to increase the mulberry stock. As a consequence, double cropping never spread in Italy, in spite of the industrialists' requests and of the very many experiments that had shown that it was technically feasible. Increases in cocoon production had to rely exclusively on technical progress.

From the late 1890s onwards, industrialization began to change relative factor scarcities in the sericultural areas of Northern Italy. New cotton plants attracted female labour, raising its opportunity cost. Between 1891 and 1913, cocoon prices fell by about a third relative to industrial wages (Federico, 1994b). In addition, sericulture was handicapped by some of its unpleasant features.[10] As a result of these various forces, the amount of care devoted to silkworms diminished, causing yields to stagnate or fall, and cocoon production growth first slowed down and then stopped. Silk-reeling managed to sustain a 3 per cent annual growth rate between 1895 and 1905 by buying cocoons abroad. By 1913, imports accounted for about one fifth of the total supply. After the war, domestic cocoon production was at least 15 per cent below the prewar peak and many sources of imported cocoons dried up for political reasons. The shortage of raw material made further growth in silk output well nigh impossible.

This brief overview points to some clear-cut conclusions. The comparative performance of the two countries' silk industries was influenced by a number of forces, but in the long run the key factors were technology and the supply of cocoons. Italy's industry was more efficient and technically advanced than Japan's, but it was hopelessly outperformed because Italian agriculture was unable to increase cocoon production. And output could not increase because labour's opportunity cost was rising too rapidly. In the words of a leading Italian expert of the time: 'Sericulture is an industry which can survive only in countries were labour is abundant, and therefore peasants are satisfied with an extremely low wage' (Clerici, 1906). This pattern is familiar and similar crises have affected the silk industry whenever a country has crossed a threshold in industrialization. France was hit in the second half of the nineteenth century, Italy at the beginning of the twentieth, and Japan after the Second World War.

5   Silk and economic development

Any form of production contributes to development, just by creating value added. Silk, however, is often deemed to have been especially helpful, for three major reasons. First, the proceeds of silk exports financed raw material and equipment imports essential for industrialization (Cafagna, 1989; Minami, 1994). In Japan, silk was the only industrial sector with a trade surplus (Miwa, 1973). In a strictly Keynesian framework it could be argued that without silk exports the resulting trade deficit would have jeopardized growth. This, however, is not the only possible balance of payments adjustment mechanism. While this is not the appropriate place for a discussion of alternative models, the most recent literature on the topic, at least in Italy, argues that the Italian balance of payments adjusted to capital flows, so that there was no risk of foreign currency shortage (Federico, 1996b). This may not have been the case in Japan, however, where capital imports were restricted until 1899.

Second, the silk industry is said to have contributed to development by widening the market for manufactures. The revenues of cocoon sales and the wages paid in reeling were a major source of income for many peasant households. In Japan in the 1880s one in four households raised silkworms, and the number soared to one in three in the 1920s. In 1924, the proceeds from sales of cocoons were about three-quarters those of rice.[11] At its peak in 1930, reeling occupied 10 per cent of the manufacturing workforce. In Italy the figures were smaller, but still impressive. Between 0.6 and 0.7 million households raised silkworms and the reeling industry employed some 4.5 per cent of industrial manpower.

Of course, only a fraction of total income was used to purchase manufactures. First, one might want to deduct rents, as presumably landowners had different patterns of consumption. In Japan such rents were not large, but in Italy they were substantial – in the core Lombardy region, the landowner received half of the gross income from cocoons. Second, not all silk income could be spent on manufactures. Third, peasants lost potential incomes from alternative uses of the same inputs. This held true to some extent even for the 'vent for surplus' growth of summer and autumn crops in Japan, which entailed a change of destination in land. A fortiori, it held true where there were no underemployed resources, as in Italy. The additional demand created by the growth of the silk industry was thus equal to the difference between its income and the opportunity cost of the inputs it used. The amounts are extremely difficult to estimate, but must have been substantially smaller than the total income from silk production.

Third, the silk industry is said to have contributed to the development of other industries by purveying capital and managerial skills and by training labour. Actually, a direct transfer of workers from silk to, say, cotton was exceptional, as training in silk reeling was useless in cotton spinning (and vice versa). Cotton and silk were competing for the recruitment of new workers. At the very beginning of each worker's career, parents had to decide whether to send their children as apprentices to the silk mill or to the cotton factory. In the 1900s Italy's silk industrialists bitterly complained about this sort of competition.[12] Similarly, managerial skills for silk were quite specific and hence not easily transferable to other industries.

The evidence on financial links is much less clear-cut. In Japan the links were very close – large *zaibatsus*, such as Mitsui and Mitsubishi, were heavily involved in the silk trade. In 1932 their specialized branches accounted for about half of total silk exports and these, over the 1925–34 period, yielded 6.5 per cent of Mitsui Bussan's profits (Matsumoto, 1978) and 15 per cent of those of Mitsubishi Shoji (Mitsubishi Shoji, 1955). In Italy, the situation seems to have been very different. There is little evidence of a direct transfer of capital from the silk sector to the 'modern' sector of the economy, even if the issue would deserve closer scrutiny. Diversification by silk companies seems to have been very unusual, at least before the 1920s or 1930s, when the impending crisis made it a strongly advisable policy. And, as argued above, the very efficiency of the market for silk prevented the development of big trading companies. The lack of direct transfers of capital does not, however, rule out an indirect contribution. For instance, the profits from silk reeling might have accrued to investments in other industries either via the banking system, or via the informal networks of partnerships, family ties, and so on. Unfortunately there is very little hard evidence on the issue.

6   Conclusions

Silk provides a fascinating case study of the rise and fall of an industry in the process of development. Throughout its history, its market structure has been close to that of perfect competition – large number of firms, relatively easy entry, insignificant scale advantages, very quick transmission of knowledge and information. Yet, despite this and the fact that many areas might have been suitable for sericulture, China, Italy and Japan dominated the global silk market for the better part of a century, accounting for more than 90 per cent of world exports between the early 1870s and the late 1920s. The main reason for this was the presence, more so than elsewhere, of abundant labour at the right time.

Each of the three main producing countries reacted positively to the opportunity that increasing world demand for silk provided, raising both output and productivity – albeit to different degrees. Japan easily outperformed China and Italy, whose output stagnated or declined from the 1900s onwards. This different performance was determined by many causes, but in the long run the crucial factor, as so often, was resource endowment, and above all labour availability. Silk thus moved down the development ladder, first from France to Italy, then from Italy to Japan and, more recently, from Japan to China. The growth of the industry did help Italian and Japanese development, but silk was not, as sometimes argued, a 'super-primary product', which necessarily brought about such development, as shown by China's poor record. Arguably, causation runs in the opposite direction – the overall efficiency of the country and its potential for development affected the performance of the silk industry as much as (or even more than) the latter's performance determined longer-run growth.

Notes

1. The figure is only approximate, as the output data are not fully reliable.
2. Any information cited without specific reference is taken from the latter source.
3. Letter by E. Semenza to L. Luzzati (1 October 1906), in Carte Luzzati, b.106 'Industria serica. Corrispondenza 1878–1906'.
4. The value of the Herfindahl–Hirschman index (which sums the squares of market shares) varies between 0 and 1 (a situation of pure monopoly). As a comparison, America's Anti-trust Commission used to start an enquiry when the coefficient for a particular industry exceeded 0.25. The data in the text have been computed by using the number of reeling-basins as a (reasonable) proxy for output.
5. The distribution of total output was different, as the trade/output ratios diverged between the three countries. Around 1913, for instance, China accounted for some 31 per cent of world production, Italy for 16 per cent and Japan for 36 per cent (the data, however, are not very reliable).
6. The 'rate of shift' is an all-encompassing measure that takes into account the sector's technical progress relative to that in the economy as a whole, changes in the prices of the most intensively used factors and other minor influences. Thus, it cannot be directly compared with total factor productivity. If

anything, it is likely to overestimate Japan's relative performance, which was helped by the availability of underutilized inputs.

7. The latter figure is likely to overstate productivity growth in the 1920s since the crisis of the 1930s almost certainly led to the closure of the least efficient units.

8. Report by the Associazione serica to the Ministero dell'economia nazionale, 9 May 1928, in Ministère des affaires étrangères, RC 1918–40 B, textiles, no. 20.

9. The Italian lira also floated against gold between 1866 and the 1890s, but its depreciation during this time never exceeded 10 per cent.

10. To name but one, during the rearing season, the peasants had to go and sleep in barns or stables, leaving their homes to the silkworms which had to be protected from the open air.

11. This latter figure is obtained by assuming that half of the rice was marketed and that landlords' rents accounted for one-third of total rice proceeds.

12. In 1906, the silk industrialists strongly opposed a law regulating child labour that set a minimum age for factory workers. In particular, they accused the main proponent of the law, Crespi, owner of one of the largest Italian cotton firms, of having argued in favour of raising the minimum age so as to prevent young girls from taking jobs in reeling houses (cotton mills needed older hands).

References

Beauquais, A. (1910) *Histoire économique de la soie*, Grenoble: Imprimerie générale.

Cafagna, L. (1989) *Dualismo e sviluppo nella storia d'Italia*, Padua: Marsilio.

Castronovo, V. (1980) *L'industria italiana dall'Ottocento ad oggi* Milan: Mondadori.

Clerici, F. (1906) 'Se sia conveniente un secondo allevamento estivo-autunnale dei bachi di seta', *Bollettino dell'agricoltura*, No. 21.

Federico, G. (1994a) *Il filo d'oro*, Padua: Marsilio.

Federico, G. (1994b) 'Una crisi annunciata: la gelsibachicoltura', in A. De Bernardi and P.P. D'Attorre (eds), *Il lungo addio: modernizzazione e scomparsa della società rurale*, *Annali Feltrinelli*, 30, 325–51.

Federico, G. (1995) 'Politica industriale, stato e lobbies nello stato liberale: un settore perdente: l'industria serica (1877–1912)', *Società e storia*, 18, 67, 45–73.

Federico, G. (1996a) 'An Econometric Model of World Silk Production, 1870–1914', *Explorations in Economic History*, 33, 2, 250–74.

Federico, G. (1996b) 'Italy 1860–1940: A Little-known Success Story', *Economic History Review*, 49, 4, 764–86.

Federico, G. (1997) *An Economic History of the Silk Industry, 1830–1930*, Cambridge: Cambridge University Press.

Fenoaltea, S. (1988) 'The Output of Italy's Silk Industry 1861–1913: a Statistical Reconstruction', *Rivista di storia economica*, ns 5, 3, 275–318.

Fujino, S. and A. Ono (1979) *Textiles*, Tokyo: Toyo Keizai Shinposha.

Kiyokawa, Y. (1984) 'The Diffusion of the New Technologies in the Japanese Sericulture Industry: The Case of the Hybrid Silkworm', *Hitotsubashi Journal of Economics*, 25, 1, 31–59.

Ishii, K. (1972) *Nihon Sanshigyo-shi Bunseki (An Analysis of the History of the Japanese Silk Industry)*, Tokyo: Tokyo University Press.

Ishii, K. (1986) 'Kokunai Shijono Keisei to Tenkai' ('Formation and Development of the Domestic Market'), in K. Yamaguchi and K. Ishii (eds), *Kindai Nihonno Shohin Ryutsu* (*The Domestic Market of Modern Japan*), Tokyo: Tokyo University Press.

Ishii, K. (1994) *Joho Tsushinno Shakai-shi* (*Social History of Information and Communication*), Tokyo: Yukihaku.

McCalliom, S. (1983) 'Silk Reeling in Modern Japan: The Limits to Change', PhD Thesis, Ohio State University.

Matsumoto, H. (1978) 'Zaibatsu Shihonno Chikusekikozo' ('Capital Accumulation of Zaibatsu') in Tokyodaigaku Shakaikagaku Kenkyusho (ed.), *Showa Kyoko* (*The Showa Economic Crisis*), Tokyo: Tokyo University Press.

Minami, R. (1994) *The Economic Development of Japan: a Quantitative Study*, (2nd ed), London: Macmillan Press.

Mitsubishi Shoji (1955) *Ritsugyo Boeki-Roku* (*History of Foreign Trade*), Tokyo: Mitsubishi Shoji.

Miwa, R. (1973) 'Daiichiji Taisengono Keizaikozo to Kinkaikinseisaku' ('Economic Structure and Policy after the First World War'), in Y. Ando (ed.), *Nihon Keizai Seisakushiron* (*History of Japanese Economic Policy*), vol. 1, Tokyo: Tokyo University Press.

Nghiep, L.T. and Y. Hayami (1979) 'Mobilizing Slack Resources for Economic Development: the Summer–Fall Rearing Technology of Sericulture in Japan', *Explorations in Economic History*, 19, 2, 163–81.

Nugent, J.B. (1973) 'Exchange-rate Movements and Economic Development in the Late Nineteenth Century', *Journal of Political Economy*, 81, 5, 110–35.

Paini, C. (1913) 'Italia e Giappone sul mercato serico americano', *Bollettino di sericoltura*, No. 14.

Tolaini, R. (1994) 'Cambiamenti tecnologici nell'industria serica: la frattura nella prima metà dell'Ottocento', *Società e Storia*, 17, 66, 741–809.

Index of Names

Index of Subjects